FROM HURTING TO HEALING

Our health system is in crisis: defensive medicine, burnt-out care providers abandoning their craft and dissatisfied patients. These are the symptoms of a not-so-mysterious illness that is leaving a trail of broken doctors and nurses as well as suboptimal outcomes. The uneasy truth is: who is caring for the carers?

We urgently need systems that place the well-being of their staff as a key element of best patient care. We require facilities where workers feel heard, appreciated and eager to improve. These should no longer be considered unrealistic goals at the mercy of whatever time and energy is left over after covering costs.

Everyone - patients and professionals - are yearning for wholesome solutions based on understanding and respect of our human nature, kindness and humility. Dr Simon Craig shows a profound knowledge of all the factors that have led us to the current situation and, more importantly, of all possible solutions to get us out of it. His book sheds a bright light in the dark and should be mandatory reading to everyone involved in providing care, from medical students to policymakers.

Dr Tane Luna
MD, FRANZCOG, DDU (O & G).
Head of Obstetrics and Gynaecology, Lismore Base Hospital
Former O&G medical advisor for Medecins sans frontieres (MSF)

Dr Simon Craig offers a unique and refreshing perspective on improving healthcare systems. In my more than three decades of working in healthcare culture change, this is one of the most optimistic takes on a better and kinder future for our medical systems I have ever seen.

Dr Craig is realistic about the complexities and constraints faced by healthcare systems, yet insists we can find better ways to provide care and support healthcare providers. The enquiring way Dr Craig tackles this highly complex topic will inspire reflection and transformation in any healthcare organisation. *From Hurting to Healing* offers a vision of healthcare that is efficient, cost-effective, compassionate, and inclusive. It is a refreshing take on healthcare culture change that deserves a place on every healthcare professional's reading list.

Professor Catherine Crock AM
Physician, The Royal Children's Hospital Melbourne
Deakin University, Faculty of Health
Chair Hush Foundation

from HURTING *to* HEALING

Delivering Love to Medicine and Healthcare

DR SIMON CRAIG

A catalogue record for this book is available from the National Library of Australia

First published in 2023 by Hambone Publishing
Melbourne, Australia

Editing by Mish Phillips, Lexi Wight, Emily Stephenson and John Horan
Typesetting and design by David W. Edelstein

For information about this title, contact:
Dr Simon Craig
simon@simoncraig.com.au
www.simoncraig.com.au

ISBN 978-1-922357-52-6 (paperback)
ISBN 978-1-922357-53-3 (eBook)

For my children

Acknowledgements

I am grateful to the traditional owners of the lands upon which this book was written, the people of the Wiradjuri nation and also the Wurundjeri people of the Kulin nation.

Like any endeavour (even seemingly solitary activities like writing), we require assistance from others. The following people (in no particular order) have guided, supported, encouraged, advised, and helped. Thank you to Pat, Barb, Kae, Nick, Ross, Liz, Georgie, Issy, Anna, Sophie, Ben, Mish, John, Lexi, Emma, and to Catherine without whom this book would not exist.

Contents

Foreword

Just the other day, I was stranded in the city. It was teeming with rain, and I was desperate to get home. I had called an Uber more than 15 minutes ago, but the promised white Camry had not appeared. The little toy car on my phone screen announced that it was 7 minutes away. Then 3 minutes. Then 14 minutes. All the while doing U-turns up and down nameless streets, spinning on the spot, and unfathomably heading in the wrong direction. What had started as gentle fatigue rapidly gave way to exhaustion and despair.

'It's a metaphor', I thought glumly to myself.

All of us in healthcare can see that the well-being of our workforce, and the capacity of our health system, are buckling under an inordinate and unrelenting load. The last few years have widened the chasm between where we are and where we need to be. Yet the solutions offered – more strategic planning, performance measurement, online competencies, working at all hours from home, yoga at lunchtime – find our wheels spinning without traction or careering in the wrong direction. We can find ourselves frustrated, lonely, cynical and burnt out.

My imagination drifts. A limousine pulls up, and I see Simon Craig frantically waving at me through the downpour. I have known Simon since we were Obstetric registrars together. While our career paths have diverged, we have kept in touch. We share both patients and colleagues. He is one of the kindest, wisest, and most skilful doctors I know. So, when he says, 'Need a lift home?', I jump in.

This is a book that brings us home to ourselves. To the healthcare that – as patients, carers and employees – we both recognize and aspire to. A place of trust and care and hope. A place of kindness and belonging. We know this is where health care belongs – in our hearts. We know where we want to go – and why. But the journey to get there needs bold reimagining. In these pages, you will find the 'hope map': the carefully charted trip home.

The journey home has been meticulously signposted. Your kind and knowledgeable driver will shepherd you through the checkpoints of positive communication and authentic leadership. The need for teams armed with courage and a compass. The need to create the requisite space, culture and conditions for innovative solutions to find voice – and then to flourish into transformation. Above all, the humility and kindness needed to bind people and ideas together, to ensure no one is left behind. That all are valued and all belong. If you are looking for a lift home, this book is the bold, generous and honest ride share you have been waiting for.

It is a clarion call to action, and its authentic message resonates with us because it comes from within. It comes from a trusted one of us – a senior and respected clinician, teacher, leader, mentor and friend. It is a joy to read, with countless 'messages in a bottle' for doctors who are fatigued and struggling, a comforting voice in your ear and an expert in your pocket. While pitched at doctors, the themes are universal and the messages generalisable. In this book, you have the VIP backstage pass to creating better health, and healthcare – whatever your role may be.

During a visit to the NASA Space Centre in 1962, it is said that President Kennedy noticed a janitor carrying a broom. He walked over to the man and said: 'Hi, I'm Jack Kennedy, what are you doing?' The janitor replied: 'I'm helping put a man on the moon, Mr

President.' Imagine if each of us in healthcare could answer the same question with, 'I'm making healthcare healthier'. For our colleagues, our patients, our community and ourselves, they – and we – deserve no less.

Enjoy the ride. It's 5 stars all the way.

Professor Sue Walker AO
Sheila Handbury Chair of Maternal Fetal Medicine
Head of Department, Obstetrics and Gynaecology, The University
of Melbourne
Director Perinatal Medicine, Mercy Hospital for Women

{in·tro·duc·ing}

ANY INTRODUCTION IS THE BEGINNING OF A RELATION-
ship. Some relationships may be short-lived. Others can be complex,
difficult, or frustrating. In a few fortunate circumstances, relationships are uplifting and life-long.

We need to reimagine and redesign healthcare in Australia.
Hopefully this book can be a step on that journey. As we begin, perhaps it is wise to keep the words of A. A. Milne's Winnie the Pooh
in mind:

> *"I always get to where I am going*
> *by walking away from where I have been."*

0.1 Health and Healthcare Institutions

Many of humankind's most amazing advances over the last century
have been related to the treatment of disease or injury. Discoveries,
inventions, and breakthroughs have contributed to longer and
healthier lives. We do not succumb as early or as frequently to infections or ailments that once threatened our existence. Major diseases,
such as smallpox, have been eradicated. Modern treatments enable

us to overcome life-threatening trauma, recover from overwhelming sepsis, and sustain life despite massive blood loss.

As we have developed our healthcare professions, we have increasingly helped and cared for people – usually complete strangers. Our societies rightly laud those who devote their lives to the service of others. Community planning has incorporated and prioritised the need for hospitals and many other facilities involved in optimising our health. These systems are now so entrenched that they exist without thought. We unconsciously understand that they are there to help; able to be relied upon in an emergency. Our systems of health, and those who work within them, have become trusted pillars of modern society.

Yet healthcare is struggling – Australian hospitals in particular. The current logistical challenges appear insurmountable. Too many patients, overwhelming demand, growing elective surgical waiting lists, no beds, patients in emergency department corridors. Challenges everywhere, all of them without obvious solutions. On top of this, worsening staff shortages, frequent reports of increasing burnout rates, disillusioned and traumatised clinicians, and streams of highly trained people leaving their professions.

It seems incongruous that institutions devoted to curing disease and caring for patients could adversely affect the well-being of their own staff. However, it raises the question: can a hospital do good but not feel good? The answer to this is, in many cases, in the affirmative. But how have conditions deteriorated to this point, and is there anything that we can do about it?

In many ways, this book is something of a love letter to hospitals. Both to the ones that I have worked in, and to others that I have not. Some of the best moments of my life have taken place at work, especially in hospitals. When I reflect and remember, I realise that I have enjoyed each institution that I have worked in. Some I have loved.

Unfortunately, this love of hospitals doesn't seem to be a universal experience. Not every hospital worker has left with good memories. It is upsetting to recognise that for many, recollections of time spent working in hospitals can trigger negative emotion, and even trauma in some cases. This intolerable situation means that it is time to reimagine our systems. Although the current styles of practice and ways of being have served us well, they now need revision, perhaps even complete overhaul.

The views presented here are not intended as critical commentary on healthcare and hospitals, management and administrators, or medical culture. These people, environments, and areas have faced incredible strain over the last few years and the challenges in medicine are complex and significant. The way forward is unclear and needs discussion. What is certain is that the solution will not come from any one person or one intervention. It will take concerted, stepwise, building of new ways by all of us to resurrect our institutions and systems to the models that we desire.

A system is needed that not only provides optimal care for patients, but also enriches those working within the organisations. A model that understands and values its importance in the lives of each individual and its vital position in the surrounding communities will create the positive change we need. Improving our healthcare systems will not be a rapid process, however it is a pressing and necessary concern that requires attention. Ultimately, if we can achieve the noble aims of improving our system of care – how we look after our sick and vulnerable as well as each other – it will benefit us all.

My opinions and ideas are influenced by 30 years in clinical medicine, hospitals, medical leadership, and a lifetime of interest in teams, both at work and in sports. Of course, sport and healthcare are not the only domains where critical human interaction and high functioning teams can be witnessed. For example, many artistic pursuits are not only beautiful to behold, but also display incredibly supportive interactions between performers to create group success.

The 'team' that is a symphony orchestra cannot create the same sound without near-perfect input from each musician – allowing the collective to achieve success. A theme of this book is the importance and ubiquity of interactions, communication, relationships, and teamwork in all that we do.

A further thread running through the work is the benefit that comes to all of us with attention to these elements. These opinions are informed by my interest in well-being science and positive organisational practices. However, despite my positive slant, I do not think these views are unrealistically frothy. I do not ignore the challenges of the real world. I am, for better or worse, still a conventional, occasionally sceptical middle-aged doctor. A 'grain of salt' informs my exploration and innovation.

Why should positive emotion be considered in a book largely about medical, hospital, and healthcare culture? I believe that we all desire happiness, and emotions give a framework for how we experience the whole of our lives, including our work-life. Wanting a higher level of happiness for ourselves is not a selfish desire. Higher personal levels of well-being influence how we care for others. Happier workers in any field tend to have improved performance, which in health and hospitals translates to better patient outcomes. Collective happiness within a workplace contributes to improved culture with multiple organisational benefits.

There are personal anecdotes throughout the book; some are positive, some are troubling, and others are a combination of a couple of experiences. The negative stories are not intended as a censure of those involved, or to denigrate any particular hospital. The anecdotes are used as an illustration of how an alternative, more generative, way can be produced through a slight alteration of attitudes and perspectives.

The themes presented in the following chapters are those that I believe create flourishing organisations and collectives. These are necessary ingredients to optimise conditions for individuals and teams in healthcare that can lead to the best outcome for all. Of course, there will be common ground in many of these areas and cross-over between the themes. For example, a shared sense of belonging is necessary to build teams, leadership requires an ability to create a vision, organisational culture is constructed around communication, and so on. An inseparable relationship exists between many of these areas; however, it is worth addressing the themes individually to allow for a more thorough investigation and discussion.

We face difficult times in healthcare: never-ending demands, insufficient resources, and concerns about the existing systems being inadequate, if not damaging. Recognition of the problem is the first step. It seems counter-intuitive, when feeling under siege, to imagine new ways of working and more productive and generative styles of interaction. Yet, without an ability to think differently and be curious, nothing will change.

Through my medical career, I have enjoyed many privileges. Accompanying the privilege must come responsibility. These responsibilities obviously relate to patient care and professional practices, yet they also involve a duty to ourselves, colleagues, and team-members. We must strive to improve our systems. The responsibility of attention to well-being and performance of the group, team, unit, department, and institution lies with each of us. I believe that this begins by strengthening the humanistic elements in healthcare cultures. By embracing these principles and acknowledging our own responsibility, it becomes possible to reinvigorate medicine and health.

0.2 Those Within the Institutions

There is a parable about three bricklayers. They are each asked, "What are you doing?" The first answers, "I am laying bricks", the second answers, "I am building a church", the third says, "I am building the house of God". The first has a job. The second a career. The third a calling.

In late 2021, aged 55, I knew that I needed a change. I still enjoyed my work, but it didn't seem to fill me with joy anymore. My standards were fine, and I knew that I was providing a good service. But was this enough? The profession that had been a calling for me had become a career, and at times a job.

Discovering the specialty of obstetrics and gynaecology (O&G) had been the making of me as a young doctor. I loved everything about this area of medicine, from its rich history, through to its cutting-edge developments such as endoscopic gynaecological surgery and intra-uterine fetal treatments. I absorbed and practised everything I could, and through the years I continued this love affair with O&G. Added to the intellectual challenges of providing antenatal care for both mother and baby, and the technical demands of surgery or manipulative obstetrics, was an instinctive aspect to the clinical side of the profession. For example, sometimes I would get a 'gut feeling' about which pregnant women were going to become unwell and therefore needed closer watching. This seemed to me to be related to the art of the specialty, which melded well with the science. All the different aspects made up a wonderful whole, and I felt blessed to be part of this world.

Added to this richness was the advantage that many families whom I had seen throughout pregnancy and birth became friends rather than patients. As well as the fulfilment I took from my work was the pleasure that the support of my team provided. My bonds with colleagues continued to be tight. Going through risky and dangerous situations together with shared experiences created a level of trust, respect, and investment in each other. I recognise that I had a privileged position.

So, when I realised that although I still enjoyed my work, it was just that – work – I was a little confused. I still felt fortunate and knew that I could continue in the role for many years, but in truth, I wasn't in love with the practice of medicine any longer. I wrestled with this for some time, unsure if the passion would return. Getting up in the middle of the night for a difficult birth, helping a patient safely become a mother, or dealing with a dangerous situation such as a massive post-partum haemorrhage still gave me professional affirmation and pride, yet I recognised that I wasn't experiencing the same uplifting sense of meaning that I once had.

Indeed, in my role as the departmental director, I found myself thinking more and more about team building and how to improve the culture of various hospitals including my own, than I ever had before. These activities started to resonate with me more than clinical medicine. I realised that it was time for a change. I hoped that I could find another calling.

At times, I wondered whether I was burnt out. In retrospect, I see that perhaps I was. The practice of obstetrics is certainly intense. With the long hours, interrupted sleep, and occasional very stressful situation, it can be hard physically, emotionally, and psychologically. However, none of this had ever previously been a problem for me. I had actually revelled in the lifestyle and felt lucky to be in the profession. Therefore, I was led to ask myself whether there could there be other issues? Were there institutional factors contributing to my diminished work enjoyment? I questioned whether the daily and weekly grind of dealing with meetings, committees, and bureaucracy had impacted me. I also wondered whether the frustrations and disappointment of hearing stories about poor professional behaviours within the medical culture had caused my response to change from the previous "What the…?" reaction, to wondering whether there was a way to correct these incidents, and improve the workplace so that they didn't happen so frequently.

I also internally debated whether, if I had suffered burnout, it was due to some weakness in my personality, lifestyle, or practices. It seemed to me that if I could have this sense of reduced fulfilment, then others would most likely have it too. And it was clear that if there was an institutional component that had affected me, then it would surely be affecting others within that institution also. I wondered about how different hospitals and institutions cared for their people. Or did they care? I started to think about what could be done to facilitate improvement on an individual basis and at an institutional level, for our doctors and other clinical staff. The subsequent thoughts and further investigation of these areas have led to the ideas and recommendations within this book.

{dam·ag·ing}

DAMAGE IS A POWERFUL WORD. IT IMPLIES THAT TANGIBLE harm to something or someone has occurred. With the understanding that damage has happened, or may be ongoing, comes the question of whether repair can be achieved. Can restoration back to the original condition occur?

Damage can occur to people, reputations, and organisations through acts or events that cause harm. But damage can also happen through inaction, failure to take preventative measures, or refusal to respond to signs of impending problems.

When considering healthcare, damaging behaviours can initially affect standards of conduct and team spirit. As these elements worsen, performance is compromised, and the risk of poor clinical outcomes with adverse effects to patients increases. Unhelpful behaviours and relationships can begin a damaging cycle with deteriorating culture that ultimately impacts the health of employees and leads to an impaired reputation of the organisation.

This cycle of suboptimal events and poor communication can feel impossible to decipher let alone stop. The negative pattern with immediate deleterious effects and later insidious consequences embeds and then is seen more frequently. After it has become established, the persistently damaging environment can be hard to recognise. Negative interactions become normalised and expected. Although there may be fewer overt 'blow ups', the patterns of behaviour have become colder, more silent, less tolerant. The culture of the organisation has been damaged, and the environment damages the workers.

In many ways, this is the point we are at in healthcare. We have poorly functioning systems that are affecting people and causing negative experiences of workplaces. In invisible ways, these unchallenged systems are contributing to the current situation of faltering, understaffed, unhealthy, and unhappy institutions.

1.1 Widespread Suffering

"Check this out! We have really got a problem!"

I had just put my bag down on one of the circular tables. The table also held water jugs, glasses, writing pads, and a multitude of different coloured marking pens. John leaned over to me, holding his mobile phone out. We were both early to arrive at a leadership workshop for our hospital that was designed for a senior group comprising of medical and clinical leaders as well as non-clinical departmental heads. John had recently been appointed Director of 'Support Services' which encompassed kitchen and food, cleaning, and many other areas. I was the medical co-director of women's and children's services. One of the themes to be discussed again today was poor culture in the organisation.

The footage recorded the night before, and now playing on the phone, had been sent that morning. Someone had made a recording of two burly chefs from the kitchen fighting in the hospital carpark, throwing haymakers and beating each other up, over an unknown disagreement.

Yes, we had a problem, and the leadership consultancy advice was definitely timely. However, I also knew that I had taken part in many similar conferences and consultancies in the past, also with stimulating and engaging discussions, the same post-it notes, and butcher's paper presentations to each other. I always enjoyed these sessions and left feeling energised and motivated. So, why didn't these interventions work? Or if they did, why didn't the effect last?

At morning tea, the conversation was around the pressures on staff and what appeared to be increasing burnout rates in the hospital. Later that day, after a stimulating morning of discussion, and writing thoughts on multi-coloured pieces of paper, I was at lunch with two medical colleagues where the topic was three surgeons in our town, all belonging to the same specialty, and currently all individually suing each other after alleged defamatory public comments. A bizarre law triangle. As part of the same specialty, in the same unit, these surgeons were meant to be team-mates in some sense.

Poor behaviour at all levels of the organisation, burnt-out staff, erosion of culture, and team-mates who fought in carparks and courtrooms. Our hospital certainly had many challenges. And we weren't alone – these problems were widespread within the culture of medicine and hospitals. But what lies at the base of all these issues? Why are so many people hurting?

1.2 What Ails Our Doctors?

For a profession focused on optimal health promotion and treatment of sickness and disease, Australian medical practice and doctors are struggling. This may seem an unusual statement given that Australian doctors are among the best trained in the world and our health outcomes also rank highly when compared with the rest of the world. Of course, given our wealthy country and resource rich medical system, we should expect an outstanding level of healthcare. And this excellent standard is delivered. But, at an individual level, our doctors are struggling, just as they are in many other countries.

In the early 2000s, the World Health Organisation (WHO) declared that occupational stress was a worldwide epidemic, and in 2019, burnout was included in the International Classification of Diseases (ICD-11) as a workplace phenomenon. Burnout within our healthcare systems is also now considered of catastrophic proportion in doctors, nurses, and allied health staff. The rate of burnout in doctors in the US was estimated at 40-60% in 2019.[1] In 2020, the Australian Medical Association estimated that some degree of burnout affected 65-75% of doctors.[2] After the emotional and physical exhaustion caused by the Covid-19 pandemic, the situation now feels even worse.

Burnout is described as a combination of (i) emotional exhaustion, with depletion of energy and resources, (ii) depersonalisation, which results in withdrawing and distancing oneself from others, with development of a detached and cynical attitude, and (iii) feelings of diminished personal accomplishment or decreased personal efficacy leading to negative self-evaluation of one's own work.[3]

This worldwide phenomenon with the triad of exhaustion, withdrawal and isolation, and finding less joy and value in your work can be part of a dangerous downward spiral. Burnout has become so prevalent since the mid 1990s that there now exist many scales[4] to simply measure your personal level of burnout. Symptoms of burnout can vary, ranging from physical complaints through to frustration, irritability, anger, insomnia, disengagement, and feelings of hopelessness. These symptoms may be associated with behavioural problems at work such as outbursts and overt unprofessionalism, or the burnt-out health worker might just be the one silently working on their own.

Burnout seems to be partly induced by overwork and fatigue, with coexistent frustration at inefficient practices and systems. Clearly a lack of satisfaction with work and a reduced sense of accomplishment will lead to a lowering of one's mood. And with depersonalisation, one detaches from relationships and becomes withdrawn. Of course, all these changes, including the way one approaches interpersonal interactions, are bound to eventually affect doctor-patient relationships and adversely influence patient outcomes. A further concern for institutions is that burnout can become contagious and spread throughout a team or an organisation.[5] The mechanism of this conductivity is not clearly understood, however, it may have some relation to emotional contagion whereby individuals unconsciously mimic and adopt the emotional experience of others, leading to a shared affective experience.[6] Emotional contagion can occur with either positive or negative emotional states but is obviously of utmost concern to a hospital if it is involved in the propagation of burnout.

While burnout may be a feature of many professions in modern society, medicine seems to be particularly afflicted, with the worrying follow on from personal suffering that translates to poorer clinical results and a lower functioning hospital. In addition to the clinical effects on patients (burnt-out doctors are twice as likely to make major clinical errors),[7] there are significant personal costs to the doctors themselves. Associated with the burnout data are worrying statistics from Australia and other countries of high levels of depression and suicide in doctors.[8] These concerns run in tandem with high rates of alcohol abuse and dependence in doctors of all genders.

With burnout, the withdrawal and tendency towards isolation will affect all areas of the doctor's life: relationships at work, social interactions, and with family at home. All relationships, both at work and elsewhere, will suffer.[9] Without these supportive relationships, which are fundamental to individual well-being, comes additional risk. The doctor will become even more isolated and lonely.

It may surprise some that loneliness is very common in our society. One in four Australians report feeling lonely for at least three or four days each week. In other words: most of the time. Loneliness at work is similarly common, affecting our psychological well-being and work quality. Many people describe having no friends at work. Doctors are not immune. In 2020, a US study found that 43% of physicians reported loneliness and that this was associated with both depression and burnout.[10] Loneliness and depression go together, and the relationships that we have at work are more important than many of us may think. Unsurprisingly, lonely people have increased risk of depression, suicide, and chronic illness.[11]

The increased burden of physical illness that is associated with loneliness may be mediated physiologically through the mechanism of higher inflammation with psychological stress.[12] Ironically, it may be the very relationships we have with work colleagues, a common source of reported frustration in burnout, that can be improved to prevent the problem.[13] Perhaps instead of trying to treat burnout at an individual level, we should be concentrating on collective prevention through optimising relationships in our hospitals.

And what of our future doctors – medical students or doctors-in-training? In this group, the situation is replicated with over 30% of medical students meeting the criteria for alcohol abuse and dependence. Medical students are describing burnout at exceedingly high rates, even before they begin work as doctors, and reporting substantial rates of anxiety, depression, and psychological distress.[14] This situation occurs not only in the US, but also around the world, including Australia and New Zealand.[15,16] A systematic review of studies on medical students in various parts of the English-speaking world excluding North America found unacceptably high rates of anxiety, depression, and psychological distress in all countries reported on.[17] These problems in doctors and doctors-to-be lead to patients being treated with less empathy and compassion, and facing compromised care.[18,19]

The burnout epidemic is causing hospitals to endure reduced

standards and increased costs. In business, it is well known that stress related problems in staff cause decreased productivity[20] and absenteeism, which impact financial performance. In 2010, it was estimated that 20% of a corporate payroll was used on stress related issues.[21] This figure could well be higher in hospitals at the present time.

Aside from the need to optimise patient care, a desire to address the suffering of our co-workers, and a drive to decrease expenses, all Australian hospitals as workplaces have a legislative requirement to attend to workers' physical and mental health. The Federal Work, Health, and Safety Act[22] is adopted by each state, with slight variation. Therefore, we have impetus to address these pressing problems based on clinical, moral, financial, and legislative grounds. This situation requires urgent attention.

1.3 Is It Harder to Deal With Psychological Distress in Doctors than in Other Professions?

Wide scale psychological distress appears to be particularly tricky to deal with in the medical profession. Medicine is a highly conservative, hierarchical area with entrenched attitudes and a culture that seems to adhere to the proverb, 'Physician heal thyself'.

In this environment, doctors who are suffering can feel shame for their imperfection and inability to solve their own problems. In the very industry where these attitudes should have been recognised as unhelpful and shelved long ago, there persists a feeling that any revealed weakness, particularly of a psychological origin, could have negative connotations and an adverse effect on one's career. This can lead to cover-up and secrecy.

Doctors rarely seek out help. Many do not have their own regular family doctor. Associated with this is the pervasive and silently encouraged false veneer of invulnerability and the associated illusion of omniscience.

Medical culture encourages doctors to refuse to admit or acknowledge doubt or weakness. Doctors must be perfect. The quality of compassion that we extend to patients is not then extended to ourselves. Perhaps this is due to a historical overlay from when doctors were in short supply, had to be constantly available and 'on', always ready to work and overwork in the service of the community. Those conditions required an image of superhuman qualities, perfectionism, and an ability to work hours considered unsafe for the rest of the community. The circumstances required doctors to deny any flaws, and always appear strong and impervious.

These once-needed attitudes and work practices are now redundant. However, this style of work continues to be encouraged and propagated by anachronistic practices passed down as the ideal. There can be a sense that one is "soft" or "weak" if affected by self-doubt, tiredness, or expressing a desire to promote self-care.

Of course, our doctors must be confident in their own ability and training, yet an inability to express any weakness will invariably lead to problems. Excessive perfectionism is associated with anxiety, depression, and burnout in many fields, including medicine.[23] In someone with perfectionistic tendencies, thoughts of self-doubt or inadequacy will be even more troubling, and these feelings will be suppressed and hidden, or possibly dealt with by unhelpful behaviours such as alcohol abuse. Also concerning is that doctors who feel a need to appear all-knowing and confident may be performing duties beyond their competency.

It is possible to learn from the United States military when it comes to looking after people. In 2008, the US Army had epidemic rates of post-traumatic stress disorder (PTSD) and rising suicide rates. They wished to introduce measures that would help to build resilience, reduce stress and anxiety, and improve decision making under pressure. They turned to Martin Seligman, described as the father of modern positive psychology, to build a program based on positive psychology principles. The program that was devised was subsequently introduced into the service,[24] and implemented across the entire Army, from the freshest recruit to the most intimidating drill sergeant, and even on to the officers.

Furthermore, the US military has enlisted the help of Brené Brown, pre-eminent researcher on guilt, shame, and vulnerability to help develop their individuals and teams.[25] One may think that Brown's work on vulnerability is the antithesis of a modern-day warrior. On the contrary, it was recognised that being open, honest, and vulnerable allowed strength to develop with subsequent enhancement of team-work and relationship building. The military leaders want the best psychological health and well-being for their people; however, a culture had arisen where weakness was masked, and perfectionism was promoted. The result was diminished individual well-being, isolation, and weaker teams. Brown's research shows that when people allow themselves to face self-doubt and vulnerability, they can connect more fruitfully with their teams in the workplaces and elsewhere.

When we consider the rates of psychological distress affecting the US armed forces, perhaps the problems afflicting Australian doctors are not surprising. Medical culture has similarly encouraged ideals of super-human qualities and attitudes of perfection. However, this way of being has become problematic in recent times. The social expectations, education, and training of doctors to seem all-knowing and invulnerable – still seen as desirable qualities in many quarters – may now be implicated in the creation of adverse outcomes for the clinicians themselves. The culture of invincibility and the need to privately 'heal thyself' could be one of the underlying causes of rampant psychological distress.

1.4 What Is the Current Way That We Produce Doctors?

Given the shocking rates of impaired well-being in doctors, it is time to examine whether there are any identifiable precipitants of this situation. Although working conditions are undoubtedly a component, they cannot be the sole cause, as burnout and psychological struggles are also affecting medical students. The genesis of the problem may relate to something that occurs before students graduate as doctors. Perhaps it has an origin within medical school training, and expectations placed on the students once they graduate. Or could it begin even before that?

High school students must achieve extremely high marks to get into medicine at university, an esteemed and revered course which in some circles is viewed as the pinnacle of high school achievement. Even now, entry to medical school affords significant status and social capital. The competition for places and requirement of top marks can lead to arduous study hours and a predisposition to stress, pressure, and isolation. This commitment to high achievement is commendable but, after entry, the competitive and isolating aspects of the course often continue. There is continued intense jockeying for marks and rankings.

Medical students are driven people who aim for excellence, which is exactly what we want in our doctors. But along the way, is it possible that the competition can become excessive and problematic? Could it be that the competitive nature of the course may impair the establishment of tight relationships and friendships within the cohort?[26]

The final year medical school rankings can influence who is awarded certain residency jobs, and decide the hospital that junior doctors initially work in. Some hospitals carry more prestige than others. Therefore, intense rivalry and focus on final outcomes can over-ride all other concerns, including that of one's own well-being or that of colleagues. The idea that vulnerability or weakness cannot be allowed or acknowledged, even to oneself, permeates.

Being awarded the 'best' residency job is seen as the pathway to success. To gain the most highly sought-after training jobs in the preferred specialties induces a very self-focused attitude in young doctors. They want to be seen and recognised as the cream of the crop. They need to be perfect. So, competition and achievement are prioritised with resulting individualistic attitudes. An understandable tendency towards self-focus and seclusion can ensue.

1.5 How Do We Reward Doctors?

We all want success in life. Unfortunately, within the Australian medical system, and possibly in the wider culture, the definition and understanding of success has become clouded. What is success and what are the markers of success? As in many areas, anything that is hard to define becomes difficult to recognise upon its attainment. In modern culture, many people struggle to feel validation without the acquisition of power, money, or status.

Measuring ourselves by the amount of money we earn, or the level of status and power that we have, could be at the root of some of the subsequent problems individuals face. There is vast disparity of remuneration in the Australian system for doctors working in different areas. By choosing certain areas of medicine to specialise in, such as general practice or paediatrics, the doctor will earn much less through their career than a colleague who moves into a procedural specialty such as surgery. Is this fair? Should caring for one group of people or patients in our community carry, in effect, a financial penalty?

Given the lack of other easily evaluable measures of success in our professional lives, money and accompanying accoutrements are often seen as a de facto measure of ultimate success. Some define themselves by the amount of income generated. Therefore, the most lucrative roles within medicine assume extra attraction. The competitive nature of medicine and medical students will lead to more students wanting to follow those paths because it seems to indicate success. And in other, less well remunerated areas of medicine, there may be an associated sense of frustration that the equally long hours, devotion to patients, and hard work are not rewarded with the same level of recompense.

All young people who enter medicine are talented. They want to care for people, and they are also competitive and driven.[27] If the overriding measures of achievement that society values are money and prestige, does that mean that those doctors with less of these materialistic indicators are not as successful? When material goals are adopted as a de facto measure of ultimate success, some doctors will be left feeling cheated and unfulfilled.[28,29]

Associated with many technological advances in medicine has come the almost constant presence of surgical equipment manufac-turing company representatives in the operating theatre. The compa-nies are motivated to sell more of their expensive products so 'reps' come to the operating sessions and help the surgeons or procedural-ists with the use of the devices, at the same time trying to ingratiate themselves with the surgeon to create sales. This can understandably add to the vanity of those doctors.

With large incomes and being feted by others, it isn't surprising that troubling attitudes can occasionally ensue. Some specialists will be earning massive incomes, multiples of that of a friend from medical school who merely chose a different path. Surely this must create some cognitive dissonance. The disparity in income perhaps leads to a rationalisation that one is somehow deserving of that vastly higher income. To become arrogant and believe in one's own impor-tance. And those who are perceived to have a superiority complex can appear to exhibit rudeness to staff and juniors, and even feelings that patients are commodities. This is fuelled by their belief that the organisation owes them something special because they are, after all, special. Relationships with previous colleagues can become tense or fractured. In the long-term this may lead to less social support and increased isolation for the 'successful' doctor.

On the other side of the income disparity are the areas of medicine such as general practice that are less glamorous and can deal with problems that have less easily assessable outcomes, and where the fees generated for interventions such as counselling for anxiety or eating disorders, have not benefitted from the same rises that many specialists have enjoyed for their procedures. Most general practitioners work diligently and conscientiously for their patients with significant demand on their time. Is it fair that a tense consultation requiring great skill and empathy, such as for a person considering self-harm, will only earn a fraction of that paid for a short simple surgical procedure? Every doctor has a different mix of skills. It is to the detriment of our systems that we seem to value technical procedural ability much more than we value the skills involved in facilitating human centred interactions.

In the end, all people will decide what they value and how they judge themselves. We all desire a good income. But money is only one form of currency. Other currencies are time, trust, and relationships. Once lost, spent, or wasted, only money can be replaced.

1.6 Would an Alternative Method of Judging Success Reduce Suffering?

There is an obvious need to promote excellence, commitment, and best practice in medicine. It is right that a highly skilled practitioner, in whatever field, be lauded and rewarded. However, it seems that in some Australian medical fields, financial considerations have become overly influential, and the relative disparity of medical incomes across the whole profession has become problematic.

Similar to Australia, Scandinavian countries report some of the best health outcomes in the world. However, countries such as Sweden view a successful medical career through a different lens.[30] Scandinavian systems support greater equality of income between different types of doctors. There is also more attention paid to work life balance. This appears to result in better workplace relations, fewer problems with culture, and less depression and burnout.

Research has shown that one's happiness increases as income rises. But only to a certain level, which varies in each country, and after that level of income is exceeded, one's happiness plateaus or even declines with increases in income.[31] After passing a certain level, more money does not bring more happiness. This is the basis of the 'Easterlin Paradox'.[32] In 1974, economist Richard Easterlin found that over the preceding 50 years, despite substantial real income rises in Western countries, there had not been a corresponding rise in reported overall happiness levels.

We all recognise that inequality in any population is damaging to the group's harmony. At the societal level, it has been found that the higher the level of income inequality, the more social discord and unhappiness.[33] It appears that the medical profession in Australia, the 'society' of medicine, is a less happy place due to income disparity and perceived inequity. It is time to rethink our definition of success.

Within my obstetric department, we had always endeavoured to provide excellent obstetric care to all women. Non-privately insured patients were looked after in labour by the team and overseen by the specialist of the day, while privately insured patients were cared for by their doctor of choice, for an extra financial outlay. Other public patients chose a midwife-led model of care. All groups had very good care and outstanding outcomes. As a result, there were choices of different styles of care and the community benefitted.

However, on several occasions I was informed by specialists from other fields that our department looked after public patients "too well", and that this would result in a reduced number of patients going through the private system. This seemed to imply that we should tolerate lower standards of care for public patients to maximise private patient numbers and thereby increase our own personal income. Attitudes that prioritise personal income-generation like this have significant downsides for all. It takes the focus off providing the best care possible for all people in our society, and reinforces the view that success is based around a single measure, with the assumption that personal fulfilment will ensue.

Perpetuating views such as these encourages self-promotion. It can also contribute to professional isolation, and secrecy about negative patient outcomes for fear of adverse effects on one's reputation and practice.

Self-belief, a desire for excellence, and commitment to the task are desirable qualities in our medical professionals. But skewed values may have led to goals becoming harder to define and the achievement of excellence cloudy and unbalanced. Personality traits that are valued by doctors and have enabled single-minded concentration on optimal health outcomes for patients may now be feeding emotions that lead to burnout. A judgement of personal success based on competition, comparison with others, and financial considerations has not been beneficial. Perhaps what we think will bring success and life satisfaction are instead leading us to isolation and unhappiness.

1.7 Do Our Hospitals and Healthcare Institutions Contribute to the Problems With Clinicians?

Administrators and managers of healthcare bodies and hospitals understand the organisational and operational problems associated with reduced staff well-being. Perhaps now more than ever before, as clinicians increasingly struggle, work less effectively, or leave their professions. However, the difficulty for institutions over many years with growing cultural problems in the workplace, and now with ballooning rates of burnout, has been understanding where to direct attention and how to help.

Frequent and well-intended workplace surveys are taken in many hospitals to find an answer to these problems. Often, individual well-being initiatives and programs commence. But things don't improve. Disengagement, burnout, disillusionment, fatigue, and unhappiness become more prevalent by the day. As these conditions become ingrained, they are less easily recognised. A state of malaise and suffering becomes the norm. It becomes invisible to those on the inside. Managers and leaders with good intentions are enveloped in this cloud of poor culture. They stop seeing the problems until they worsen and once more become overt and impossible to ignore.

Initially, when considering fatigue – a contributory factor in burnout – it can be hard for older doctors like me to understand the problem. There are more junior doctors rostered in the hospitals than ever before, they're working fewer hours than in years past, and each junior doctor has fewer patients to look after. The same applies for nurses. The nurse-to-patient ratios have improved, with more nurses per patient than ever before. But both doctors and nurses are overworked, stressed, and burnt out. Why?

The problem does not lie in the make-up of the individual practitioners. They are hard-working and conscientious. They are not intrinsically flawed when compared to their predecessors. This isn't about some generational shift. And the patients have the same ailments and conditions as they always have. So, how can overseeing fewer patients cause more exhaustion that leads to psychological harm?

The answer must lie in the systems that we have designed, created, or allowed to arise within our health organisations. One issue is that the amount of work associated with caring for each patient has increased significantly. Not so much in the work of clinical care, but more the amount of paperwork and data required, together with altered bureaucratic expectations. These days, many clinicians must fill in data on paper as well as computerised records, with the same data entry and information required in multiple areas. Tick-box forms don't take long to complete individually, but when the list of these documents keeps growing, for all sorts of indications, pressures mount.

With recording the clinical data, there are growing requirements for the completion of hospital generated forms, and also information collation required by wider overarching bodies from multiple jurisdictions. Risk assessments must be completed for every patient and every imaginable risk, without allowing nurses to use common sense. For instance, a young fit patient being admitted to hospital for a minor same-day procedure does not need a 'Falls Risk Assessment' form, or an assessment of whether home help will be required upon discharge. But in most hospitals, this paperwork will be completed for every patient. In this way, we exhaust our nurses, disrespect their intelligence, and take away any autonomy.

Within hospital wards, nurses face computer screens for longer than they face their patients. Interactions with peers will take place incidentally as a disjointed chat, with both individuals facing their screens rather than the other person. Less direct human interaction, whether with patients or colleagues, could be a factor in isolation and loneliness.

The patients are, in some sense, forgotten. They become a collection of numbers – observations, intake, output, data points – rather than a whole person to be treated with compassion and care. But it must be this way for the nurses. Analysis of the data and figures are valued by the systems. Other, more humanistic aspects of the patient experience cannot be viewed as data, and therefore lose relevance.

The very reason many students enter nursing is to care for people, yet this aspect is becoming increasingly lost as technology and poor system planning take over. Of course, patients still have satisfactory clinical outcomes, but they are less satisfied with their care. The patient's medical condition gets treated, but they haven't been seen as a whole person in the process or cared for in a traditional, compassionate sense.

Similar problems exist for junior doctors.[34,35] They spend more time on screens looking up investigation results and entering data than treating patients. The treatment style becomes part of the mechanistic way we view hospitals. The patients, in some ways, are also viewed as malfunctioning machines with broken parts to be identified and fixed. They are not treated in a holistic sense and recognised as integrated organic systems where everything is linked.

For example, a patient admitted with an infection will be viewed more through the lens of what their temperature and biochemical markers of inflammation show, rather than viewing the patient history, understanding their background and social situation, and assessing how they are responding in a whole sense. Once the numbers, observations, and investigations are satisfactory, the patient will be discharged... a bit like moving further down the conveyor belt in a factory.

Let's be clear: these systems are not all bad. They were designed for efficiency and reproducible outcomes. And they work – the measurable outcome of patient treatments in Australian hospitals is outstanding. However, the downside is that with less human interaction, there comes a degradation of connections, and potential for staff to lose contact with others.[36] This may be partly to blame for the avalanche of languishing, unhappiness, and loneliness within hospital staff. Loss of the human aspect – facing screens and treating conditions rather than facing and treating people – is not making clinicians more compassionate. The way of work that the systems demand may be contributing to psychological distress within the workers.

Another risk for burnout is how effectively staff can disconnect from work when off duty. Evidence suggests that the ability to fully disconnect from one's job after leaving the hospital is protective against burnout.[37] Those who do disconnect more fully also show more engagement when at work. But in recent times, many health-care institutions are facing extreme shortages of staff with workers absent or unwell, and in this setting, nurses at home are receiving daily text messages asking them to work extra shifts. It is impossible to disconnect fully with this ongoing interaction.

The answer to this problem is unclear. Shifts need to be filled, but constant communication from the work institution will decrease the ability to 'switch off'. Our doctors, with increased technological con-nectivity, are often checking results or making entries into records at all times of the day. Some doctors are constantly responding to work texts or emails while at home and 'off duty'. In this setting, the enthu-siastic, hyper-engaged, committed, even workaholic, young doctor – not an uncommon scenario – is at great risk of becoming exhausted, disengaged, and depersonalised.

1.8 Can Anything Be Done?

It is certainly possible to improve conditions. The initial step is to admit that we have a serious and growing problem in healthcare. Burnout and disengagement are rampant. Bullying, poor behaviour, and toxic cultures are common. For the good of the community, our hospitals must operate at their optimal level. Our hospital staff need to be healthy to work effectively. Therefore, it is mandatory that we address these issues in order to secure the best possible outcomes for patients, the health and happiness of the individuals concerned, and the good of society. To deal with a problem it must first be acknowledged and explored rather than hidden or diminished. From this point, solutions can be considered. From a medical perspective, nothing can be treated until it is recognised and diagnosed. And no patient can be helped unless they have insight into the need for intervention.

When considering burnout in clinicians, it is promising that there is a growing acceptance of the problem, with an understanding that urgent action is required. However, across different institutions thus far, well-intentioned initiatives for treatment or prevention of burnout at an individual level have not been completely successful. The difficult reality is that we need to be open to new methods and prepared to make deeper changes to our systems.[38] Unfortunately, proposals of systemic change often meet resistance.

The systems that exist for the delivery of clinical outcomes for patients continue to function well on the whole for institutions. If a satisfactory rate of successful patient care is our sole objective, then it could be considered that no change is needed. But clearly we cannot tolerate our systems damaging the people working within them, not least because it leads to a critical shortage of staff. Therefore, as well as the best possible patient care, we must embrace other aims. The need for thriving hospital environments to facilitate staff health and well-being will require a re-thinking of the way we work and the systems that we operate in.

These systemic changes may need to be introduced and implemented even before people start working in the hospitals. The most appropriate place may be the educational institutions that supply our nurses and doctors. Nursing education has swung strongly to embrace technology and science, with less focus on the human, caring aspects of the profession. Perhaps it has become overly technical. It is time to re-think nursing training and to once more value the holistic and compassionate side of the profession. Student nurses must spend more time working with and caring for patients in hospitals and less time in classrooms. 'On the job' teaching must be increased and prioritised. Less time facing computer screens to fill in meaningless documents and more time with patients and colleagues would be massively beneficial.

I have discussed the highly competitive nature and single-mindedness of medical students. However, the solution to the problems within medicine does not reside in changing entry to medical school to promote those who are less motivated or driven. We still want the most intelligent and ambitious students to consider a medical career; these are the people who will make advances and breakthroughs. But the inherent competitiveness throughout the course does create stress, and this component of medical training can be challenged. We must become less individualistic. Medical student education, and the profession, should consider a formal relationship-building focus.

It is possible to shift the attention from competing against peers to becoming members of teams that compete together. In collaboration with our colleagues, we can maximise team output for the benefit of patients. At the beginning, within medical school, we can educate the students on the importance of both personal and group well-being, and the role that relationships and connections with others have within that structure.[39,40]

Others with similar concerns have also suggested changes to medical school curricula.[41] Perhaps once entry to medicine has been achieved, the subject grades at university should be pass/fail only for the first two or three years of the course. If the students aren't ranked, competitiveness will decrease and, within that time, team functioning and personal well-being can be promoted. The focus should be on building supportive relationships across the entire cohort. The benefits of team formation and group success versus personal achievement can be emphasised. Prosocial behaviour can be embedded.

These proposed changes may have benefits even beyond the future personal well-being for the doctors involved. Those who have better relationship-forming skills can more quickly integrate into and improve teams. They can immediately become invaluable members of organisations when they graduate as doctors. Better team-mates contribute to better teams, and better teams achieve better patient outcomes.

When their training is completed and new doctors and nurses, indeed all staff, are starting work, the hospitals should consider an extensive and sincere induction process. It must be induction rather than orientation – the words and emotions are important. Orientation implies pointing someone in the right direction to begin a largely solo journey. Induction means being welcomed by the group and being enfolded, embraced, and nurtured as part of the team collective.

This induction helps new members to become aware of the history, traditions, rituals, and present-day workings of the hospital. Newcomers should be welcomed by senior leaders and peers and made aware of the abilities and qualities they possess that will be valued by the organisation. Within the induction process, the expected styles of communication and standards of behaviour should be addressed. The new members should have a sense of the value placed on trusting and supportive relationships and understand that they will be mentored by caring leaders to enable them to thrive in their careers. It is essential that new members of staff are made to feel that they belong.[42]

Once the new inductees settle into the hospital, they must find that the well-being practices they learned in university are still important, respected, and valued by the employer. Whether these practices involve exercise, meditation, mindfulness, or exposure to nature, the organisation and leaders must value and promote these initiatives as part of a modern workplace. Cynical, negative voices must not be allowed to thwart these objectives.

Leadership is key, of course. Caring, wise leaders who set an example of balanced behaviour are those we all want to be associated with. These are the kind of leaders we consider to be mentors – and we still remember them at the end of our own career. These are the people who 'made a difference' to us. Within this framework of striving for excellence while feeling supported and valued, our teams will flourish and provide exemplary care.

1.9 Considering New Attitudes

I have written about what I view as distorted attitudes with an over-emphasis on materialistic values. These factors are often related to an individual need to boost our own self-esteem. If we consider Maslow's Hierarchy of Needs,[43] after the basic physiological and survival needs of food, shelter, and safety are fulfilled, the next psychological need is a sense of belonging. A need for relatedness, or relationships in life. Until this basic psychological need is fulfilled, we cannot satisfy our higher needs of self-esteem and self-actualisation, which lead to the development of purpose or meaning in life.

It may be that in modern medicine and broader society, our work relationships have deteriorated to such a degree that we are unconsciously attempting to bypass the need for relationships. Skipping a level and jumping ahead; trying to boost our self-esteem through materialistic means. We're possibly even believing that we derive meaning in life from this. Seeking to boost self-esteem before our needs for nourishing relationships are satisfied can contribute to isolation, loneliness, and unhappiness.

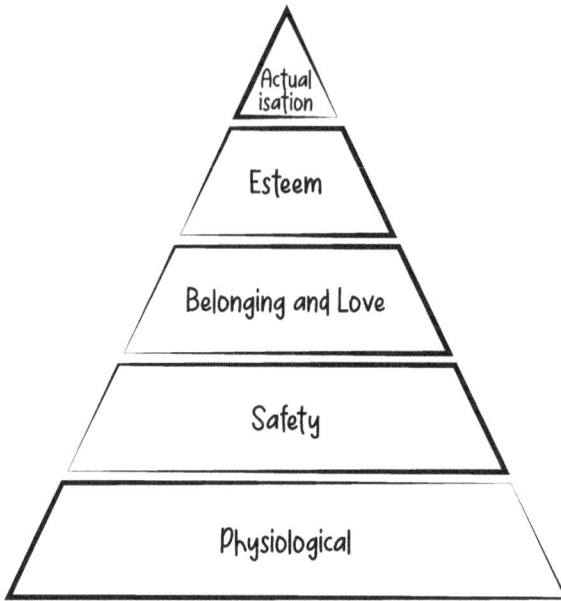

Maslow's Hierarchy of Needs

By no means am I advocating for a decrease in remuneration for any doctors. Highly trained and committed professionals deserve recompense for their dedication, effort, years of training, and expertise. However, there is a profession-wide epidemic of distress and unhappiness. More equity across all areas and specialties will lift the tide of general well-being. This would be to all our advantage.

Of course, we cannot change society overnight. Therefore, we may need to re-think and discuss how to best achieve balance in our lives. It is worth considering how we judge ourselves, and by what measures we judge success. Within this must be a consideration of how the wellness of the group impacts each of us, and how our own well-being is dependent on our interactions with others. Improvements in relationships will improve our lives. A slightly smaller bank balance but higher social capital with more connectedness may lead to individual fulfilment and a greater sense of belonging. It's hard to put a dollar value on having friends at work.

1.10 Systems That Are Damaging Healthcare Workers

The usual system change dialogue within our health organisations revolves around 'efficiencies'. These improvements are prized as they are seen to improve the bottom line through more streamlined and rapid discharge of patients, thereby cutting costs. However, this interest in efficiency never seems to focus on improvements to the working-practices of nurses and doctors, such as deleting unnecessary paperwork or allowing nurses to use common sense.

There are frequent statements from hospital leaders that 'people are our greatest asset' or such-like. But these pronouncements can feel insincere, as the actions do not always match the words. However, with the crisis of mounting burnout and decreasing availability of staff, administrators are now starting to believe their own words. Therefore, this is an opportune time to examine and adjust our systems in ways that help people and enable them to be more productive, engaged, and happy.

The time of every clinician needs to be valued, not wasted. Time that staff spend making bonds with each other must be treasured, rather than treated as frivolous time-wasting. Only now are we starting to realise the value of brief interpersonal interactions.

Of course, every hospital aims for excellence. Within this framework, a more balanced and wise approach is possible. Communication dictates the strength of relationships. Relationship quality influences the performance of teams. Team performance affects patient care, and indeed every other facet of the hospital.

Therefore, communication and human interaction become the currency that dictates the quality and success of any organisation.

Traditional business management theory has come to dominate all organisations, including hospitals, and with this approach our systems have become mechanistic and 'hard'. It's time to change. Hospital systems should be dynamic, organic, adaptive, and emergent. We must embrace the notion of soft-system thinking to improve our failing health services. We need to care for ourselves before we can look after others.

1.11 Can We Recover After Trauma?

There is an ancient art form called *kintsugi* which apparently originated with Ashikaga Yoshimitsu, who was the shogun of Japan during the 14th century. It is told that one day the shogun's favourite tea bowl was accidentally broken, smashing into many pieces. The fragments were sent away for repair but returned having had the broken pieces coarsely re-joined with ugly metal staples. The appearance was not pleasant and distressed Yoshimitsu. He asked his own craftsmen to devise a more aesthetically pleasing solution. What they came up with was kintsugi. *Kint* means golden, and *tsugi* refers to joinery. Literally, the method means *join with gold*. In this tradition, the cracks and breaks in a ceramic piece are joined and sealed with gold powdered lacquer, making the fractures more obvious than before and resulting in an even more beautiful item than before the trauma. There is no attempt to hide the cracks. Instead, the damage and resulting repair are honoured as being part of the history of the piece. In this way, the item has function once more rather than being discarded. The heritage of the piece and repair make it even more visually stunning. The pottery becomes unique and more precious and treasured.

Perhaps the lessons of kintsugi are instructive in our current healthcare crisis. Many institutions will undergo suffering and damage at times. Cracks will appear in our people and systems. The culture of our organisations can undergo trauma. Rather than ignore, suppress, or hide from these issues, we can choose to honour our path, our people, and the difficulties that all have endured. We can be proud of our continued function and the resilience shown.

The cracks, weaknesses, and fractures that have become increasingly evident can be restored to result in better systems. Through this process, we can alter our culture, support each other, and transform into a state that is more beautiful and higher functioning than before. By open acknowledgement of difficulties and commitment to repair, our institutional fractures can heal with gold.

{meas·ur·ing}

AS HUMANS, WE ARE CONSTANTLY EVALUATING OUR CIR-
cumstances. For example, when travelling to an appointment, are we
driving in the right direction? Are there dangers on the road? Will we
arrive in time? Should we go faster? Measuring and evaluating our situation, our interactions, and our wider involvement with the world is
vital as it provides safety and alertness to external risk. Unfortunately,
we also have an associated tendency to overly focus on the negative
aspects of any situation, which can lead us to unhelpful judgements,
unflattering comparisons with others, and rumination over poorer
aspects of a situation, all while seemingly oblivious to positive outcomes. This negativity bias and pessimism can undermine hope
when we desire organisational change.

Within healthcare, we are rightly drawn to measurement as it
facilitates performance assessment and improvement. Of course, any
process of evaluation must be accompanied by consideration of why
we are actually measuring in the first place, as well as what we are
measuring, whom it is for, and what we will do with the information.
Will the process lead us closer to the destination that we are aiming
for? And is there a clear understanding of that end point?

Some information is easier to assess and more objective, while
other data is subjective and more difficult to infer. The subjective

elements often relate to the more humanistic aspects of any organisation. Because they are harder to measure and comprehend should the more elusive elements of life, such as emotion, be ignored? Or should we try harder and aim for a more complete evaluation of ourselves and our organisations?

2.1 How Do We Evaluate Ourselves?

Fifteen years or so ago, the obstetric and gynaecology unit in the organisation where I was working was a functional workplace in terms of achieving very good patient outcomes. All our 'clinical indicators' (similar to 'Key Performance Indicators' in business terms) were satisfactory and favourably comparable to our peers. However, there were some problematic relationships within our unit. Some doctors refused to work together or be rostered on at the same time. Others would not speak to each other, and there were reports of senior specialist doctors denigrating or dismissing the management plans of the previous senior consultant, from whom they had taken over care of the patients.

With some changes in personnel and attention to improvement in communication and styles of interaction, the unit became a more pleasant place to work. The relationships and the mutual respect improved. The unit now consists of colleagues who provide support and speak well of each other even when they may disagree with certain treatments. The capacity and willingness to discuss these differences of opinion is now embraced for the sake of patient care.

Did the objective results change with this shift in attitudes and relationships? Initially, they did not – at least not on paper. There were still excellent patient outcomes and, to an outsider reviewing the numbers, it might have seemed to be the same unit with similar performance. But those on the inside knew that it was different. Better. Happier. The numbers did not yet reflect the change, but the improvement was palpable. Over the next few years, the clinical outcomes did improve constantly, and the change could be tracked from the time when relationships improved. Subjective and hard-to-assess change in interpersonal interaction had led to objective improvements that were then able to be measured. So, in the early days, even before the results had improved, did this purely subjective assessment of change make for a more successful unit? Did the department perform at a higher level even before any change could be defined by objective number-crunching? Absolutely.

This is only one story that demonstrates how difficult it is to measure overall success in a hospital. It is even harder when there isn't a clear picture or understanding of what success looks like, or how to begin to define it. Acknowledging the difficulty in measurement of many of the subjective aspects of how a hospital functions, is it possible to broaden our view of healthcare assessment to include factors other than the conventional measures in considering what constitutes a successful organisation?

Clearly, the reason for existence of any hospital is to treat and care for unwell and injured patients. But this cannot be the only lens through which the degree of success of the overall institution is judged. And does it depend on who is judging? Is it possible to measure a whole hospital, a complex system with many departments and functions, on purely clinical outcomes? Even then, with varied patient groups and the need for subjective assessments of many results, it is difficult to compare any hospital with others. Indeed, even self-assessment within a particular hospital can be complex. Knowing what any institution's optimal set of results looks like can be tricky and is open to debate. Of course, whether for an individual or an organisation, recognising what we are capable of and what our ultimate performance could be requires a rare level of self-awareness.

But it seems that some sort of understanding of what we aim for is a critical initial step in evaluation.

2.2 Evaluating Clinical Care

Each clinical specialty within each hospital will have its own unique set of clinical indicators or outcomes, both positive and negative, that will be counted to try to judge the overall performance of a particular unit. Although a perfect outcome is aimed for with each patient, nothing in life or medicine is ever perfect. Poor outcomes such as complications, infections, or readmissions will always occur. The intention is to reduce these rates to as close to zero as is possible. Unfortunately, complete eradication of sub-optimal outcomes is impossible.

These indicators of care can be compared to those of other hospitals or units to get a relative sense of performance. Some specialties have outcomes and results that are more easily evaluated than others. For example, obstetrics has many outcomes that are easily tabulated such as the percentage of births performed by caesarean, or the numbers of births requiring assistance with forceps. There are many easily measurable variables within this specialty. Indeed, obstetrics is a specialty with a tradition of excellent record-keeping and a history of comparison between units in different institutions. Results can even be compared between countries (for example with stillbirth rates). But other specialties have outcomes and data that is a little more nebulous, and harder to tabulate, such as psychiatry or rehabilitation medicine. How do we measure outcomes of psychological treatments?

In addition, no two hospitals operate under identical conditions. Different geographical areas, and populations with varied demographic characteristics, may have factors which cause patient care to be more difficult. This can include factors such as higher obesity rates, poverty, and incidence of smoking or alcohol abuse. Variables such as these cloud assessment and interpretation of expected outcomes. Further, some hospitals, unfortunately often in areas with lower socio-economic measures, may be less well resourced.

Other challenges include the prevailing attitude towards data collection. This may be an organisation-wide perspective, or may relate to differing sentiments existing between departments within a particular hospital. Some specialties are less enthusiastic about recording clinical indicators that accurately reflect their practice. Other units do not allow results to be widely viewed or discussed. Rather than clinical indicators being seen and used to improve and optimise care, or even to celebrate success, there is a sense amongst many medics that the method and type of data that is collected is not in their best interests. There can occasionally be suspicions voiced that negative outcomes may be 'used against' a particular doctor. These attitudes are not completely illogical and paranoid. For example, a surgeon who operates on older obese patients in difficult socio-economic circumstances will have a higher incidence of infection or wound breakdown rates than surgeons operating on slim healthy young people. Indeed, the performance of the former surgeon may be superior to the latter when the patient characteristics are considered. However, with current data collection, there is no facility for this level of understanding; only the numbers are represented.

The result can be that each unit may have data that is only seen by the practitioners themselves and the hospital executive group. In this setting, data can become secretive and siloed within departments of a particular hospital. This situation has many downsides, one of which is that it prevents a more general idea of how the hospital is performing in its entirety.

Therefore, the measurement of all clinical data within any large hospital is not easy, and can be somewhat unreliable, making comparison between hospitals, and even within hospitals, problematic. Recognising the difficulty of obtaining accurate data representation for all specialties, by what measures can the overall performance of a general or multi-specialty hospital be judged? How do those both within and outside know if a particular hospital is successful?

2.3 Other Measures of Hospital Performance

Are there any other ways of judging the success of a hospital? Is there anything else that we can quantify? There is an old saying in business circles, attributed to business-management thinker Peter Drucker:

"What gets measured gets attention."

Costs and income of all hospitals are certainly monitored. Public hospitals in Australia are overseen by the health department of the relevant state government. The government provides a budget, essentially the income for a hospital, which is dictated by an inscrutable and possibly intentionally opaque recipe of historic data, population, facility size, and nature or 'mix' of the hospital's work – with a healthy dose of current politics added in. There will be income generated by a formula based on the number of treatments and procedures of certain types, which are then 'weighted'. This weighting also means that patients having certain treatments are expected to stay a certain 'average' length of time in hospital.

We can certainly easily measure how long people stay in beds inside the hospital. Indeed, in recent years there has been great focus on how long patients stay in the emergency department with artificial constructs arising around the suggested times that all patients must be discharged or sent elsewhere within. This strategy has not always resulted in improved performance.[44] Most guidelines aim to have patients admitted to an inpatient bed, or treated and discharged by an arbitrary mark, to avoid having patients within the emergency department for more than 24 hours.

The rationale is to produce better flow of patients, more efficient care, and a better service. Honourable aims. However, this construct includes penalties for non-compliance and has led to situations where, when patients are still in the ED at 23 hours, there may be a 'creative solution' in which the patient is 'discharged' without leaving the hospital and then immediately 'readmitted', or admitted to a 'short stay unit' which is often just another room adjacent to the ED. There is often more concern generated around the time-penalty than around thoughtful patient care. This is all because of how the clinical indicators will look and that the hospital may become a 'negative outlier' when compared to other, often very different, emergency departments.

In the rest of the hospital (other than the ED), the average bed stay (length of stay, or LoS) is measured for each patient having a certain procedure, or with a particular condition. The shorter the average LoS, the better the financial outcome for the hospital. The hospital will be remunerated for the generic treatment given. To do it in a shorter time frame with less resource cost will mean greater profit. The hospital will be 'in the black' for that patient.

Obviously, there are benefits with efficiency. But there are risks when a shorter bed stay becomes the focus rather than attention being paid to the overall care of the patient. In this setting, our priorities have become distorted. Consider the patient who may be discharged too early and feel 'pushed out'. What if the nurses and caregivers sense a greater imperative from management to discharge early, rather than providing kind, holistic care? The patient who takes a little longer to recuperate and recover, and therefore stays in hospital a little longer, will go home more mobile, stronger, less likely to fall, unlikely to require readmission, and more satisfied with their treatment. These are good outcomes for our community. However, in the current climate it can seem that what is judged to be optimal hospital functioning is, in fact, more focused on business-efficiencies rather than concerned with each patient or the wider community. It does not seem helpful to have this exaggerated focus on average LoS for each hospital, thereby creating a system where hospitals effectively compete to discharge patients earlier than each other. Does earlier discharge equate to better care? Is this the way our society wants to judge success of any individual hospital?

There is no evidence that having an average LoS that is similar to and consistent with all other hospitals means that any particular institution is performing well. The aim of avoiding being a poor performer or a statistical outlier is not enough. Surely our hospitals can aspire for higher goals. Just trying to be no worse than our comparators is an unsatisfactory way of judging quality. There are many aspects of a patient's care, other than the current clinical indicators and LoS, that can be considered when judging the success of their treatment.

What about the empathy and compassion that the patient was shown in hospital, or the ability to feel listened to, and being in a safe enough space to ask questions? What of the quality of the teamwork and relationships amongst the clinicians, and the observed spirit and happiness of the workers? What of the calibre of junior doctor training and nurse education? Of course, this is all subjective assessment, and hard to measure. But should the associated difficulty with evaluation mean that more subjective and more human-centred measures must be discarded or discounted?

Of course, the counter argument, which carries merit, includes the point that a shorter stay may allow more throughput and therefore facilitate a potential for more patients to be treated. Despite this excellent rejoinder, it still feels as though our priorities with patient care have become hazy and misaligned.

2.4 What of Patient Satisfaction?

In one large regional hospital that I worked in, it came to my attention that the quality of the linen had suddenly changed drastically, and for the worse. Patients and staff were complaining that the previous high-quality towels had become threadbare and scratchy. Patients now needed a couple of towels to dry themselves after a shower. The sheets were so thin, they would often tear when beds were made. It turned out that the seemingly overnight change in quality corresponded with a change of the external linen provider.

One morning, I took a randomly selected towel from the ward linen press to a high-level meeting of clinical leaders and hospital executives. I passed it around, generating widespread consternation about the poor quality. The hospital CEO became agitated and told the group consisting of departmental heads and senior executives – ostensibly some of the leaders of the hospital in a confidential meeting – that this aspect of hospital business was not our concern. Further, we were told that the reason for the change of linen supplier was "commercial in confidence" and that, despite our positions and our direct patient contact, we were not allowed to be privy to the reason behind the decision to change suppliers. We were not allowed any detail about quality control, or any other information.

It later came to light that the new provider was based in a capital city some hours away, and that the company provided linen to many hospitals in that city. Our previous supplier had been a local, family-owned business. Subsequently, without the hospital contract, this local supplier went out of business with loss of around ten jobs from the local economy. I would argue that this was a terrible outcome for all, including the hospital, even if the second supplier was cheaper. It appeared that what was likely to be a saving of a relatively small amount of money was deemed to be more important than the comfort of patients and of greater significance than the effect on local suppliers.

All healthcare facilities are part of a community and have an integral and vital role within that system. The effects go both ways. The hospital influences the community, and the community has an effect on the health service. Just as relationships and human interactions within the hospital are important, so are those with external contractors and suppliers. How we treat people is part of what defines our organisation. Our integrity guides how our institutions are regarded – by both those within and those outside the walls. Our relationships and behaviour simultaneously reveal and create the hospital's principles and culture.

2.5 Does Financial Success Count?

It seems that the over-riding method by which funding authorities measure the success of public hospitals is largely in financial terms. A hospital is considered a success if it comes in on, or under, budget. By avoiding 'blowing' the budget and not having extraordinarily bad clinical outcomes that attract attention, a hospital is seen to be successful – or rather, to be good enough.

Viewing a hospital or health organisation as being essentially a business or corporation can certainly lead to efficiencies in care. Having a known budget that is adhered to allows the government to have a rough idea of what health costs will be for the state. It is certainly part of the equation and must be a consideration in the discussion about how we view quality in health. Costs and balances are essential in any organisation; there is no work done if an organisation goes broke. Budgets are essential. However, the convenience that comes with measuring ourselves only in dollar-terms and the 'bottom line' can create a false reassurance. Not all evaluation of a hospital's worth should revolve around or be measured in dollars; there are other, more humanistic elements that need to be considered.

What other data can we measure that is useful? It is easy to monitor the number of patients treated, the types of admissions, and the procedures performed. This information can be reduced to that consisting only of numbers. Numbers are more efficiently handled. Numbers are straightforward, they give one type of measure, but they also lack detail and flavour. They can tell us what was done, but not give any sense of how it was done. It is likely that the most important aspects of life are the hardest things to assess and measure. Perhaps that is why we prefer cold numbers.

Judging how connected the members of a team are, how well the team interacts, how much support they give to each other – these are factors which are difficult to objectively assess. There are no scales that will accurately reflect these measures. However, these are critical considerations in running a hospital or healthcare institution involved in caring for people and patients. These are the components of care that are currently only able to be 'felt' rather than scored, cognitively assessed, and reported on.

So, where do we go with these critically important features of a hospital? How do we analyse elements and aspects of care that are unable to be easily assessed and quantified? Should we try to measure ourselves in a way that can aid our attempt to improve all that we do? Or do we ignore these 'soft' factors, as is currently the case, because they are so vague and difficult to estimate?

Perhaps we need to consider the words of Albert Einstein:

"Everything that can be counted does not necessarily count; everything that counts cannot necessarily be counted."

2.6 Are There Other Measures of Success?

There are other ways for us to adopt a more holistic approach in healthcare. They relate to taking a different viewpoint. We must incorporate more humanistic considerations into what we regard as organisational success in healthcare, what we measure, and how we see ourselves integrating into our societies. Our systems have become overly influenced by the desire for mechanistic efficiencies and dominated by management practices based on 20th century business principles.

Of course, given the complexity of a healthcare system, it is tempting to simplify things and just consider a hospital as a business corporation. With this perspective, the hospital's production and output refer to the patients who are admitted, treated, and discharged. In this scenario, the financial data assumes even greater significance. Corporate and economic principles become more important. This is certainly the situation in private hospitals and perhaps increasingly so in public hospitals as well. Business strategies in all industries have been largely influenced by Nobel Prize winning economist and business thinker, Milton Friedman who famously said in 1970:

> *"The only responsibility of businesses*
> *is to maximise profits for the shareholders."*

Clearly in the private healthcare system in Australia, these shareholders are the business owners. Financial success is paramount for these investors. Higher profit equals greater success of the hospital or institution. However, even in the public healthcare system, business principles and methods have become dominant. In the public hospital scenario, to extrapolate Friedman's quote, the shareholders, or owners, could be considered the overarching government's department of health. Maximising profits could be taken to mean not running over budget. Therefore, to maximise profits would be to perform the functions of the hospital in a sound financial way with sole concentration on the hospital budget and throughput. An emphasis on staying in the black would be essential.

However, it seems that defining a hospital's success or otherwise by the measure of financial buoyancy, or keeping to budget, is very limited in scope and imagination. Perhaps it is like a nation depending on Gross Domestic Product (GDP) to inform the society how well things are going in that country. GDP is a measure of how many goods and services are produced in a country during a certain period and is often extrapolated to imply the level of a country's success – whether that country is thriving or not. Higher GDP is thought to indicate a more successful country.

Some use the economic data of production and consumption (or GDP) as a means of informing us about other aspects of human life of greater importance. This is a short-sighted outlook. As the United States senator Robert Kennedy said in 1968:

> *"The gross national product does not allow for the health of our children, the quality of their education or the joy of their play. It does not include the beauty of our poetry or the strength of our marriages, the intelligence of our public debate or the integrity of our public officials. It measures neither our wit nor our courage, neither our wisdom nor our learning, neither our compassion nor our devotion to our country. It measures everything, in short, except that which makes life worthwhile."*

If we take the view that operating a hospital is like running a corporation, then a hospital relying only on financial markers, in particular the budget, to judge its success is a lot like a country relying on GDP to measure other aspects of life. It is cold, impersonal, and misses most of what is valuable. When we adopt this attitude, we rely on numbers and dollars to judge what is important, even sacred, in the care of our fellow humans. The assessment lacks any evaluation about the well-being of the people working in, visiting, or supplying services to the organisation. It does not give any understanding of the special place a hospital holds within a community, or the opportunity that the hospital has to interact with and improve many other aspects of society.

Measuring the level of success of a hospital in this way misses the great impact such an organisation can have on the values and life experiences of the people who pass through its doors. It also fails to grasp the vital role that a hospital can have in exemplifying inspiration, governance, wisdom, and sustainability.

Perhaps it is time to consider a more comprehensive assessment of a hospital's work and success, just as others have used measures other than economic data to judge a country's well-being. In 1972, the fourth King of Bhutan, Jigme Singye Wangchuck, stated that:

> *"The Gross National Happiness [of Bhutan] is more important than the Gross Domestic Product."*

Subsequently, the Bhutanese advisors and academics honoured and further developed his thought that analysis of a country's progress should be more holistic and based on criteria in addition to economic aspects of success. There was an emphasis on sustainable growth and focus on change that prioritised the well-being of Bhutan's citizens, communities, and the natural environment. This exemplary process ultimately led to the Bhutanese Gross National Happiness Index (GNH),[45] which is a tool that aids the Bhutan government in policymaking. It not only measures the subjective well-being, or happiness, of Bhutanese citizens, but also evaluates and encourages aspects of life that ultimately enrich people's lives.

The GNH Index informs decision-making and is based around the pillars of good governance, sustainable socio-economic development, cultural preservation, and environmental conservation. These elements are further broken down into domains of psychological well-being of citizens, health, education, time use, cultural diversity, governance, community vitality, ecological diversity and resilience, and living standards. Therefore, GNH becomes a comprehensive index through which all issues are considered, with the good of the entire nation in mind.

These broader views acknowledge that there are a range of factors that contribute to a country's well-being, rather than just GDP data. Such views have spread with production of other indices such as the World Values Survey,[46] Human Development Index,[47] and Happy Planet Index,[48] which also have a more holistic attitude when determining the progress and well-being of a country. The field of humanistic economics[49] arose from similar ideas with attempts to put people first, rather than the entrenched traditional economic theories focused on economic growth with lesser regard for population well-being. Humanistic economists argue that any institution, business, or corporation does not achieve true success through merely concentrating on financial data. The effect on people and the world is of at least equivalent importance to the effect on the bottom line.

Currently, when deciding on new treatments or styles of patient care, most hospitals make the final decision based on the 'business case'. Proposals that are financially beneficial get the green light. In practical terms, this boils the decision down to whether proposals are considered profitable or not for the hospital. Making the financial considerations the final and deciding factor creates an unconscious understanding that the dollar-cost is the most important element in management of the hospital.

It is time for Australian hospitals to alter the way we do 'business'. We can engage in further thought and discussion about how we evaluate and judge success within an organisation. Clinical outcomes are paramount of course, and close attention to sensible fiscal markers is vital. However, a different focus can also be employed. Consideration of other more comprehensive and nuanced factors should be implemented. This approach will enable decision-making that increases the well-being of the whole organisation. A conscious approach such as this will ultimately improve both clinical outcomes and also financial performance.

The high-level decisions of our health leaders can be made in a way that incorporates greater concern about the local community, governance issues, environmental concerns, sustainability, and the psychological well-being of the hospital staff. It is possible for us to draw up a charter that focuses attention on these areas and includes them as part of the lens through which every decision in a healthcare institution is made. This initiative will produce more balanced and inclusive planning and decision-making. It will allow an introduction and consideration of factors such as worker well-being, community integration, and moral responsibility. I'm confident this change in attitude and new approach will be supported enthusiastically and help in development of organisational pride.

By doing good, we feel good. Hospital management will experience empowerment through this process as they achieve greater and more encompassing goals. They will notice the effect of this shift, with the early signs being a more engaged staff and an improvement in the organisational climate. Implementation of such a matrix that considers other agendas within decision-making is overdue. Where attention is given, and what questions are asked, is where change will occur.

2.7 What of the Hospital Staff Well-Being?

Do hospitals currently give any thought to worker well-being? The answer to this is a resounding yes. Universally, hospitals want to promote well-being amongst the people who work there. Not only is there over-arching goodwill and care for the staff, it is also understood that happy and engaged staff are more productive with less problematic organisational behaviours.[50]

One difficulty is that assessing well-being is complex. Many institutions will have frequent surveys of workers' attitudes and try to assess engagement from these results. Often, the results – if not particularly reassuring – will lead to an external consultancy firm coming in to address the need for cultural change. Unfortunately, this approach seems to separate the issue of staff morale and well-being from the rest of the hospital's work. Having appointed a visiting consultant, management feels as though attention has been paid to the issue, even if this is seen by staff to be a cursory exercise rather than an intervention that causes lasting and valuable change. A further risk is that by using external contractors there can be an impression created that well-being of staff is not a core business of the hospital. A message is sent that poor morale within the hospital is a problem to be dealt with by others and able to be ignored by senior leadership.

With this overlay, the issue of staff well-being and happiness can be seen as outside senior leadership's remit and an incidental aspect of the workplace, rather than an integral consideration in every decision made by the hospital management. One measure of a hospital's success might be the degree to which each staff member has great trust and belief that the organisation has their best interests at heart. When each worker feels respected and valued, they will have more nourishing at-work relationships and interactions, and the flow on effects relate to beneficial organisational outcomes. Perhaps a hospital that achieved these goals could be judged as successful in at least one domain. My anecdotal experience is that success in these areas goes hand in hand with elevation of all other concerns.

If we return to the business arguments expressed by Friedman and others – that financial profit should be the sole aim of any organisational activity – we find that these opinions provoked other unexpected and interesting responses. While Friedman's opinion gave support to those businesses with an exclusively money-driven approach, it also added momentum to a rival view: that corporations should include social considerations in their decision making and interactions with their communities, with the aim of contributing to society in other ways. This movement, described as Corporate Social Responsibility (CSR), has gained traction in the last 30 years and is now the preferred way of business in much of the world.[51]

Through the agency of CSR, large businesses have realised that sole concentration on the 'bottom line' negates their responsibility to society and misses the opportunity to help create a better world. Corporations are realising that rather than just concentrating on income-generation, they have potential to do good. With CSR, a portion of the business expenditure is used for initiatives in the wider community and for the betterment of society.

Interestingly, firms that have adopted the CSR approach enthusiastically and authentically have benefitted financially; their services come to be chosen by consumers more frequently than less socially-minded competitors. Further to this, firms are now being urged to consider a social responsibility to advance people's rights to, and experience of, happiness – 'CSR for Happiness.'[52] Evidence is also accumulating that businesses with this attitude not only increase worker well-being, but may also become more successful organisations.

It is time to re-examine Australian hospitals and consider the responsibilities that each has to stakeholders, including patients, staff, and external contractors. We must take a broader view of the effects that any healthcare organisation has on the people both within it and on its periphery. Through this reappraisal, we may find new avenues to success.

2.8 Evaluating Ourselves in a New Way?

Is it possible to change the method by which success of a hospital is estimated? Can we produce a more thorough assessment of whether hospitals are serving both patients and the balance sheet, as well as the needs of workers, local communities, and wider society? This would include a broader view of important factors needing consideration in all decisions from management. To do so would require a significant shift in thinking. However, without encouraging and respecting different views, we cannot become aware of new and emerging opportunities and possibilities. As Albert Einstein said:

> *"No problem can be solved by the consciousness that created it. We must see the world anew."*

So, how to begin this process and see the world anew? Like many things, it starts with a commitment to change, then communication and dialogue, and subsequently requires guidance and leadership. Leaders need a preparedness and ability to make decisions through a different lens, with consideration of staff well-being and inclusion of the hospital's place in the community. In other words: trying to find benefits for all. Decisions could be underpinned by a deep sense of 'what is right'. The new matrix of decision making could be communicated to the staff and disseminated more widely. From that point, instead of decisions being centred around budgetary considerations and 'business plans', high level discussions would also ask:

- ❀ What is the moral governance?
- ❀ Are there any other motivations to consider?
- ❀ How does this impact staff and employment?
- ❀ How does this affect subjective well-being for the staff?
- ❀ How will this affect the local community?
- ❀ Are these actions environmentally and socially sustainable?

Instead of hospitals regarding the bottom line as the mark of success, similar to a nation rating itself based solely on GDP, it is possible to be more progressive and considerate of all interests. It is possible to give weighting to things that are hard to measure but crucial for people's well-being and happiness.

I propose that individual hospitals follow the lead of the Gross National Happiness Index and adopt a more comprehensive tool that creates the foundation for future decision-making. This would be an innovative method of operating. This unique assessment matrix could be referred to as the 'Hospital Sustainability Overview' and would be the lens through which all interventions were assessed.

Of course, managers and decision makers will attest that all these factors are already included in their thought processes when it comes to making decisions and taking action. I agree that bureaucrats do believe that they have the best intentions in most cases. However, I think the current system causes the broader, more inclusive and varied concerns to be pushed aside, ignored, or to become invisible. Without a specific framework that encourages every decision to be viewed with an eye to these imperatives, our finance trained executives will automatically revert to the usual, bottom-line dominated viewpoint. Without a new and enforced paradigm for taking decisions, 'business case' will remain the sole filter used. Without a mandatory new matrix, there will be an unconscious falling-back on the familiar style. Business as usual.

One of the initial steps will be to change the language that is used within our hospital and healthcare executive suites. Instead of exclusively discussing a 'business case', perhaps a term such as 'feasibility proposal' could be used. In this way, the words that are used shift the focus from purely financial aspects to a more complete assessment of the proposal. In meetings, the dollar-cost argument will still be voiced, as should thoughts on other broader considerations. Further, in the lead-up to a new financial year, in every healthcare institution there are meetings where 'budget bids' are placed by different departments. A bid is, in effect, a request for a sum of money from the overall hospital budget to support a new initiative or direction. But if the jargon changed slightly from business-speak and we instead term these bids 'innovation proposals' then within the meeting they are viewed in a different light. Although it may seem a small intervention, using different language causes us to make different value judgements. Words matter.

There will still be a critical part of the decision that revolves around cost, but there can also be thought and discussion around what is good for the whole institution, the people within it, and the community. Part of the debate may centre not on what is affordable in dollar terms, but instead on what is necessary for well-being or what is the optimal decision when thinking in an environmental sustainability context.

Use of a new decision-making framework with a more nuanced and comprehensive filter may lead to widespread endorsement of the concept within the hospital and in the staff. This type of thinking allows increased respect and trust to develop both within and outside the organisation.

2.9 Measuring What Is Important

I am certainly not proposing any less rigor in measurement of ourselves or diluting reviews of the clinical performance of our hospitals. Excellence in care and standards must be maintained and enhanced. I do not advocate a lazy, or 'touchy-feely' management style where anything at all will be accepted. Rather, I am suggesting even more fastidious attention to assessment and measurement. This includes more detail in the analysis of clinical data as well as including other components in organisational level decisions.

We need to know and understand ourselves and our organisations with greater depth. This understanding can come with a different filter and a new attitude. No hospital can tolerate laxity or poor work practices; however, we do need a more encompassing, comprehensive, and sophisticated measure of how hospitals affect everyone associated with them, from the patients themselves through to those with a community level association. It will be necessary to shine a fresh light on our performance at every level. Not just to identify 'offenders' or outliers with poorer than expected clinical outcomes, or to unmask poor financial performance, but also to drill down on extraordinary performance and outcomes. An extraordinary hospital must come from elevation of performance at all levels, with study and emulation of the best practices. This approach is more effective than concentrating on normalising, minimising, or hiding the poorer aspects, whether they be the time spent by patients in ED, financial performance, or even clinical outcomes.

Our hospitals can become exemplars to all organisations in how to care for staff and the world we live in. A positive hospital-wide attitude and new way of assessment and decision making can reverberate throughout an organisation, from both medical and surgical units, through to record keeping, cleaning services, food services, and so on. With the new filter, the initial assessment of where the hospital is at can be done in a manner that surfaces previously unrecognised strengths rather than as an exercise to find scapegoats for suboptimal results. With new attitudes, all can be rejuvenated. Once fear is taken out of the equation, data will be clearer and more comprehensive. A positive and inclusive viewpoint will result in the hospital exploring suggestions on improved practices that arise from those who know – the people doing the job. With support from management and development of feelings of belonging, pride, and unity, workers will lift to the level of performing at their best. Perhaps this can elevate the whole organisation to greater heights than we have risen to before.

2.10 Where to From Here?

Historically, public hospitals in Australia have essentially measured themselves in two ways: with clinical outcome data and using financial performance assessments. As we have seen, the clinical outcome data can be irregular, distorted, and flawed. The financial data can be rubbery and 'massaged' to fit with budgetary needs and fiscal expectations. Whether a particular hospital adheres to its arbitrarily decided budget certainly seems a limited assessment of the success of a hospital.

It is possible to slightly change the way we view overall performance of any hospital, while still maintaining rigour around clinical data and provision of accounting details to the Department of Health. Prioritisation of patient care will continue, even as the new decision-making index is implemented. Through introduction of a charter or index whereby an institution gives extra attention to being a 'good citizen', the factors involved in good citizenship come to the fore and grow in significance.

Are we brave enough to do something different? Will we aim higher? We can choose to go down the route of embracing a more positive, holistic view of success. We can foster hospitals that meld with their surrounding communities and are responsible and sustainable institutions. Or we can choose to continue the old ways, with decisions being exclusively dominated by financial considerations, without regard for our people. What will we decide?

{ex·ist·ing}

INDIVIDUAL EXISTENCE CAN BE DESCRIBED AS A STATE OF being that is independent of consciousness. Further, each of us are members of gatherings, teams, organisations, or coalitions. Every group will have its own collective existence, its own way of being. There will be a status quo, expectations, and behavioural standards that members adhere to. These conditions are fixed and unconscious. They continue as the norm and represent the established culture of that group.

The nature, experience, and culture of our organisations can seem unchanging and unchangeable – a day-to-day, never-ending existence. However, if we change the view of culture slightly from a fixed 'existence' to something more adaptable, the culture seems more amenable to modification. This is possible if we focus instead on the 'existing' culture – a set of prevalent conditions and behaviours.

In the systems that currently exist in healthcare, it can be easy to feel demoralised and assume that organisational cultures are impossible to change. However, change can always occur when we allow ourselves to consider new methods and unexplored ideas. Embracing different perspectives alters our existing thought patterns.

Should we view our organisational culture as an immutable existence, fixed as a permanent and unconscious state of being? Or could we instead consider culture as the existing way – the current mode of operation – and one that is open to change?

3.1 Success Resulting from Culture Change

Newcastle United is one of the biggest football clubs in the English Premier League... and also a perennial underperformer since the early 20th century. After the takeover of the club by Saudi Arabian interests in late 2021, the club was sitting second-to-last and facing relegation from the top tier competition.

A new manager, Eddie Howe, was appointed. Howe made a couple of player signings and some tactical modifications to the defensive set-up, but the main change noticed by club insiders was in the environment. Howe made a concerted effort to get to know all the players personally. He spoke to them directly, openly, and honestly. Increased emphasis was placed on discipline, dress code, and player interactions. Some of the words frequently used about the atmosphere engendered by Howe are togetherness, trust, and relationships.

It is acknowledged that Eddie Howe changed and bettered the Newcastle culture, but in the cut-throat world of professional football, this would mean little without improved results. However, together with the sense of a more nourishing club structure was a concurrent dramatic improvement in on-field results, with Newcastle rising up the table away from the relegation zone and finishing 11th for the 2021-2022 season.

It appeared that success for Newcastle United was related less to tactical alterations and more strongly associated with a poorly understood feature of any team or organisation – culture.

3.2 What Is Culture?

Culture is a word that we often hear applied to groups, organisations, and hospital settings. However, culture as a concept is very hard to understand and analyse. This is because what we refer to as the culture of an organisation may be everything that we witness, or even just what we unconsciously sense, when in a particular environment. Indeed, it is often referred to as the 'feel' of a workplace.

It can be hard to describe some of these feelings and sensations, but it's important to try. Culture is the dominant factor in any organisation, affecting every process and outcome and is considered the principal factor behind success. The existing culture is also the basis for how all people experience and remember their interaction with a particular group.

In any established group, there is an underlying culture or way of being that guides attitudes, behaviours, and performance of the group's activities. This culture is invisible and surrounds the team without an awareness of it in many circumstances. Due to the elusive, hidden, almost mysterious nature of culture, it resists understanding and assessment, and is difficult to alter or change.

When discussing culture, a parable written by novelist David Foster Wallace is often used:[53]

> *"There are these two young fish swimming along, and they happen to meet an older fish swimming the other way, who nods at them and says, 'Morning boys. How's the water?', and the two young fish swim on for a bit, and eventually one of them looks at the other and goes, 'What the hell is water?'"*

In the telling of this story, Wallace was not, in fact, referring to organisational culture. Rather he was arguing against moving through life unconsciously, without being aware of the wider world. However, the water parable does work well when considering organisations as the culture envelops all, even if it is not understood. Awareness of the existence of an overriding organisational culture may only come when it deteriorates to an intolerable level. The culture is the 'water'.

Organisational culture is also referred to as the 'personality' of the organisation that influences internal behaviours, or as 'the way we get things done around here.' This is an appropriate and helpful saying as culture arises in any organisation as a way of dealing with problems, both internal processes and the external pressures of getting the job done. The accumulated knowledge and patterns of behaviour that allow the 'job to be done' become a system of accepted norms and attitudes that guide thoughts and actions. These eventually develop into unconscious ways of operating and existing. This way of being eventually comes to exist without being questioned and is passed on to new members through education and observation.

The reason we use terms such as 'the personality' or 'the water' of an organisation is that organisational culture resists easy definition. This contributes to the difficulty in its understanding, assessment, and modification. Others describe culture as being the gap between what the written rules say and what the unwritten rules allow.

3.3 Culture: A Poorly Understood Concept

Dictionary definitions of culture include: "The way of life, customs, and beliefs" and "Attitudes, behaviours and opinions of a particular group".[54] These definitions describe some of what organisational culture consists of. However, they don't seem to encompass all that the culture within an organisation entails, particularly the emotive aspects of culture.

During the emergence of a functional culture in any organisation – one that that operates sufficiently well to survive – accumulation of resources occurs in the form of learnings and processes. On the other side of the ledger are operational needs. We might view any organisation's emotional state as a system of scales in which internal resources are balanced by challenges faced. When the challenges and demands rise too high, outweighing the positives or resources, the scales tilt down on one side and the organisation struggles and becomes a less happy place.

Perhaps all organisations have these constantly adjusting scales that alter with the ledger of challenges and resources. When the scales are permanently stuck, overloaded with demands and inadequate assets, the visible problematic evidence of poor culture may become apparent. This may be the point at which a hospital's culture is labelled 'toxic'.

Several models that aid in understanding the complexity of organisational culture have been produced with perhaps the most famous being Edgar Schein's model consisting of three layers of culture. These three dimensions are: artifacts, espoused values, and assumptions.[55]

Artifacts are the superficial things one witnesses – sees, hears, observes, experiences – when entering an organisation or interacting with a group. This is the level of revealed culture and will include the building set-up, dress style, modes of communication, and revealed behaviour. Occasionally, this set of observations is mistakenly assumed to reflect the overall culture (particularly when poor behaviour is witnessed) but should be more accurately regarded as the visible manifestation of culture, often described as the 'climate' of the organisation.

Espoused values are conscious ideas and beliefs of how the organisation operates, functions, and deals with certain situations. These values may be verbalised or written, and they underpin what is deemed acceptable and correct. For example, a company's website may state that it deals with all people equally and fairly, irrespective of race, gender, etc.

The deepest layer of culture is that of assumptions. Assumptions are the unconscious basis for how members of an organisation think, feel, and act. These assumptions are held because they have been in operation for a long time and are now taken for granted. Assumptions are the basis of an organisation's culture and inform 'how we *really* do things around here'. For example, a mission statement may include a declaration that the company treats all employees equally and does not tolerate poor behaviour, but it is implicitly understood by all within the organisation that a behavioural outburst will generate a different response and sanction depending on the seniority level of the transgressor.

Culture at the deepest, often unconscious, level of assumptions is ingrained. It informs all in the organisation of what is valued and what has no merit. It thereby confers and enables a sense of organisational identity. Therefore, attempting to change culture requires deep exploration of unconscious tightly-held beliefs.

A helpful visual model of organisational culture is the 'iceberg' model which has been used concurrently by many.[56] Within this model, the first level of Schein's culture framework is represented by the visible area of the iceberg. This relates to the artifacts of the organisation that are easily seen. The second level of culture, espoused values, lies just at the surface of the water, and relates to how we believe we operate and the conscious values that guide us. The deeper third layer of culture is submerged, and not visible. This layer makes up the larger part of culture and consists of the unrecognised assumptions that drive all behaviours, communications, and actions within the organisation. Culture has been described as what actions are performed and standards kept by people when no one is watching.

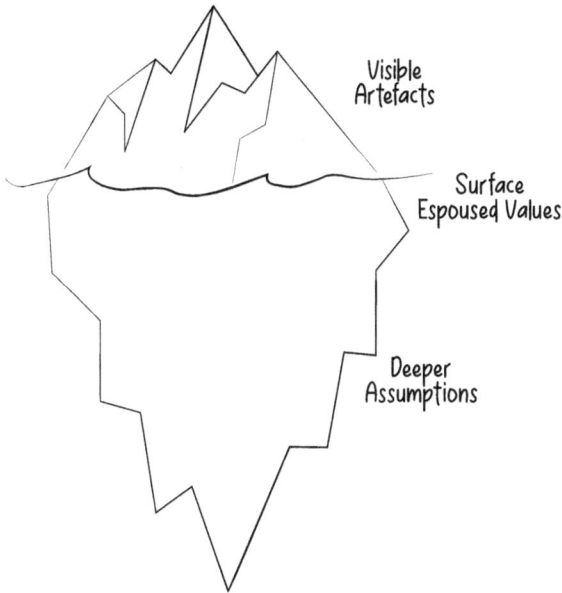

Culture was originally a term used in anthropology to describe the aspects of a particular society or group that were the most consistent, representative, and unchangeable. Similarly, organisational cultural assumptions are widely held, can persist for generations, and resist change. Culture becomes ingrained because it has worked adequately to solve internal and external problems. As such, it has developed a validity. Therefore, attempts to change culture will be lengthy, difficult, and anxiety-inducing. The fear, and subsequent resistance to change, will be partly due to the perceived loss of a system that has existed and worked, together with doubt and concern over what will replace the existing ways of being.

3.4 What Is Toxic Culture?

Most of the time, a hospital's culture is not thought of or considered. It is not part of our consciousness and remains invisible until problems arise. When the culture of an organisation does come to the forefront of our minds, the two descriptive words one may hear are 'good' or, more frequently, 'toxic'. Obviously, the quality of culture in a particular hospital is not a binary assessment – there must be grades of goodness or even toxicity. Is it possible to investigate what toxic culture really consists of?

Culture can be a difficult concept to pin down, and 'toxic culture' is also a term used without strict definition. It feels to be a visceral judgement, based on emotion rather than cognition, and seems to imply responses such as disgust with, or ill-feeling toward, the organisation. The emotive aspect gives a sense that harm has been done. Perhaps this visceral experience of culture is appropriate, for an organisation's culture is often initially 'felt' rather than cognitively registered.

Of course, the first step in reversing any overly negative aspects of an organisation's culture lies in identifying what these elements are. Unfortunately, currently there is no way to objectively measure a hospital's culture. The assessment remains subjective. However, large data series have been collected of employees' interviews when leaving institutions,[57] and subsequent linguistic analysis of this data has led to an attempt to identify what the predominant features of a toxic culture consist of.

Within this assessment,[58] the five components most strongly associated with a toxic culture were: a disrespectful workplace, non-inclusivity, unethical practices, a 'cut-throat' environment, and abusive behaviours.

Disrespect that was experienced or witnessed was found to be the strongest individual indicator of a negative judgement of culture. Non-inclusion could relate to minority groups, but could also apply to those not belonging to any particular demographic minority. The sense of being intentionally excluded from in-groups, cliques, or not being welcomed resulted in an assessment of toxicity.

Unethical and cut-throat behaviours may be more strongly related to the corporate environment than to hospitals, but this judgement reveals how any overly competitive situations are rated negatively. Once again, trust is critical to creating a harmonious workplace and good culture. Abusive behaviours witnessed in the workplace such as yelling, demeaning comments, or bullying are, unsurprisingly, one of the strongest indicators of a toxic workplace.

The flow-onthat results from these indicators of toxicity cause significant harm to an organisation. Cultural problems lead to increased absenteeism,[59] higher staff-turnover,[60] increased stress and burnout,[61,62] and increased physical and psychological ill health.[63] Other organisational risks of toxic culture are harder to quantify; these include decreased productivity of workers and reputational damage.

The costs of having a toxic culture are enormous and far-reaching – perhaps impacting every facet of the organisation. There are financial risks in addition to the human toll. Importantly, when considering hospitals with toxic culture, there is evidence of significant negative effects on patient care outcomes.[64]

Trying to cognitively understand toxic culture or define it in words remains difficult. Perhaps it is best considered in a similar vein to the way US Justice Potter Stewart famously discussed pornography in 1964 – hard to define but "you know it when you see it".[65]

3.5 Should We Care What Our Hospital Culture Is?

If we consider that any organisational culture has arisen and persisted because it accomplishes at least some of the desired organisational outcomes, then should we really be trying to change it? Some might argue that if the culture of a particular hospital currently achieves the most pressing goals of the organisation, then it needs no alteration.

This argument together with the recognition that culture change is difficult and protracted may lead to a belief that it is better not to try to change things. Leave them as they are. However, an organisation that is considering a culture change intervention is almost certainly doing so because they have a problem. Any organisation that thinks it may have a poor culture probably does.

Usually, recognition of cultural problems will have become apparent due to visible behaviours. The climate of the organisation will have become unpleasant. Perhaps this is exhibited through disrespect, bullying reports, outbursts, or unacceptable dialogue. These observed behaviours are intolerable yet will be accompanied by even deeper problems, which, if left unaddressed, will lead to related difficulties such as loss of staff, absenteeism, disengagement, and poor performance.

Within the current burnout epidemic, hospitals with higher rates of psychological distress in staff may also be those most affected by problematic hospital culture.[66] In some regards, this could be a chicken-and-egg situation. Businesses[67] and hospitals have found that the underlying culture is strongly linked to performance. In hospitals, of course, performance is ultimately judged on patient care and clinical outcomes. Therefore, assessment of culture is important[68] and there is an accompanying mandate to rectify identified problems.

However, not only do hospitals have a duty to optimise patient care, they must also consider and attend to staff well-being. Poor culture causes many unwanted effects. In addition to the high rates of psychological distress and burnout described in hospital doctors,[69] there are associated higher operational costs.[70] Furthermore, there are concerns over the future impact on young doctors of exposure to troubling behaviours seen in hospital cultures.[71]

There are many reasons to pay heed to hospital culture. All hospital workers are dedicated to the best possible outcomes for patients, and such outcomes are most likely to be achieved through creating and nurturing a supportive culture.

3.6 What Role Does Personal Integrity Play in the Development of Culture?

Recently, I was reading a news article about a 'cosmetic surgeon' who was facing legal charges over a liposuction procedure that had gone wrong. Apparently, he had obtained pre-operative consent from the patient – a young woman – to film the procedure and transmit the video to his millions of 'followers' on a social media platform. It was stated that this was not an unusual practice for this doctor, who would film these procedures accompanied by music and dancing, and then post them online for others to witness.

This report caused me great consternation. Are there not values that doctors universally hold? Of course, it is possible that my view of what is appropriate conduct is outdated. Perhaps it is wrong to assume that there are widespread and commonly held standards of behaviour. Was this liposuction operation a required medical procedure? Was it unnecessary but lucrative? Or was it advertising and a performance? Maybe it was something else entirely.

What it does show is a complete disregard for the patient and the practice of medicine, an absence of professionalism, and lack of dignity and self-respect. That even a tiny minority of doctors would partake in these acts is abhorrent. Could it indicate how our medical culture has degenerated – that any Australian medical graduate would contemplate and partake in this behaviour for financial and social gain?

Of course, we have always had outliers, or those who are seen to be on the edge of what is deemed acceptable behaviour. To me, though, this report seems to indicate that we have reached another, lower, level. How do we respond as a profession? The regulatory boards have dealt with the matter and the doctor has been banned from performing cosmetic procedures. Is that enough? Is a legal and regulatory response sufficient? That action is appropriate in dealing with the individual, but what of the profession as a whole? At what point do we, as a profession, feel a moral obligation to improve the situation?

Whenever that imperative arrives it must come with a concerted and purposive effort to build integrity. Solely paying attention to negative actions and eradication of poor culture does not, of itself, produce exemplary behaviours or outstanding culture. Reducing bad does not produce good, it just makes things less bad.

All doctors who have worked in a hospital are aware of certain challenges and problems that can arise within institutions. Sometimes, within a particular hospital, cultural problems may become apparent with displays of 'toxic' culture or climate. Those institutions will have their own ways of attending to the issues with varying degrees of success. However, to see these recent events around cosmetic surgery practices in the community setting feels like a new development. It is an unsettling wake-up call. This incident may be the canary that died from toxic fumes in the workplace. This report, and others like it, may be the danger sign alerting us to the need for attention to the atmosphere and environment of medicine.

To take a different slant, did this young doctor need to witness better examples and develop ongoing relationships with wise mentors? Did he lose sight of what appropriate behaviour is due to a paucity of connection with others in the profession? Does this indicate a problem with our systems, or is it merely a one-off?

It may be time to put standards of behaviour and culture at the forefront of our minds for medical schools, hospitals, and all healthcare institutions. Instead of believing in, and relying on, our perceived inherent goodness to serve us and passively create a thriving climate, this may be the moment to start actively building positive conduct and culture. The more these outrageous behaviours are tolerated and normalised, the less we will notice them. They will shift the bell curve of appropriate actions. If our standards are allowed to be lowered, then we can expect a corresponding reduction in respect from the public and our patients.

3.7 What Type of Culture Do We Want to Build?

I believe that if asked what type of culture they wanted to build, almost all clinicians would respond by describing an optimal environment with words such as: honesty, trust, integrity, best-practice, compassion, constant learning, supportive, values-driven, and kind. Themes of virtuous emotions and actions. I wonder if we see these qualities as frequently as we would like. And if the culture of any organisation consists of visible artefacts, espoused values, and unconscious assumptions, what would they be in a thriving healthcare culture?

In my opinion, the visible manifestations of this flourishing environment would be respectful interactions, friendly staff, and sharing of information and workload. Espoused values would be that all staff are treated equally and kindly, and all opinions are listened to and understood to be valuable. The underlying assumptions – those that create the most powerful part of any group's culture – would be that support is extended to inexperienced or struggling staff. This would be accompanied by the knowledge that in times when we are struggling ourselves, we will be supported. It would be understood that mistakes do occur, even with exacting standards of care, and that the errors are treated with forgiveness to facilitate learning. It would be a culture that allows, indeed promotes, respectful debate and disagreement so that all viewpoints build a more complete decision-making style. Elders would be revered and in return provide kind mentorship to juniors and newcomers to pass on knowledge. It would be understood that the highest standards are aspired to and that the maintenance of such standards comes from the unity and support of team-mates.

One day, during the early years of my specialist training, I was presenting a patient history to my consultant. We were at the patient's bedside with the residents and nurses also in attendance. The woman had had a pregnancy complication necessitating admission to hospital, possibly to remain for the rest of her pregnancy. The day before, she had been admitted under another consultant from our team and her management had been planned.

However, when we explained the clinical problem and the treatment plan to the consultant who was now on call, the plan for the patient's care was openly criticised. The initial management had not been controversial or unusual, but the consultant who had taken over on-call proceeded to change all the orders of the preceding specialist.

Through his words and body language, the second specialist denigrated his colleague's orders. It was implied that the current treatment of the patient was poorly informed and possibly verging on dangerous. Given that both specialists presumably must have had the woman's best interests at heart, this attitude was difficult to comprehend, particularly as the first management plan was conservative and conventional care. It was apparent that this display may have related more to personal differences between the two senior doctors, rather than to the medical management.

Of course, we all have different opinions, and clinical circumstances do change, but that was not conveyed in the second doctor's comments. These seemingly ego-laden situations can be incongruous and upsetting for junior staff and nurses, not to mention undermining the patient's confidence in the team.

The interaction would have been much more productive and educational if the second consultant had explained that he occasionally took an alternative approach, but that both were acceptable and safe. He could have spoken to the first specialist and discussed the case to formulate a collaborative team approach moving forward. This would have been a wonderful example of teamwork and shown a desire to optimise patient care for the junior doctors. It could have strengthened the bonds between the two specialists through exhibiting mutual respect.

The '70/20/10 rule'[72,73] of learning suggests that we develop our on-the-job learning with 70% resulting from self-directed learning by observation and dealing with challenges, 20% is from interaction with a mentor or senior colleague, and only 10% from formal instruction and education. Even unconsciously, junior doctors will be internalising, modelling, and learning the behaviours and demeanour of their superiors. This means that seniors in any industry have an immediate effect on the climate of their organisation, and also a delayed effect on future culture through the influence on their junior staff. Behaviours and values that are witnessed will be perpetuated.

We may be able to use the 70/20/10 rule to our advantage in the desire to improve hospital culture. By being aware of these effects and the legacies we can create, we can concentrate on exhibiting good behaviours – setting a good example, as our mothers would have said – and thereby help to embed excellent values into the senior doctors of tomorrow. Each kind gesture, supportive comment to a junior, or expression of thanks to a nurse creates ripples. These things are noticed. Each action, however small, affects others as well as ourselves. These behaviours create a more pleasant and collegiate environment, which also reduces tension and facilitates more creative thought.[74]

Perhaps we need to remember the ancient Greek proverb:[75]

> *"A society grows great when old men plant trees*
> *whose shade they know they shall never sit in."*

3.8 Is Strategy a Healthy Breakfast?

There is a famous saying in business circles that is attributed to American management consultant Peter Drucker: "Culture eats strategy for breakfast".[76]

This glib pronouncement does not mean that businesses, including healthcare institutions, do not need operational strategy. Rather, it denotes that if there are significant issues or poor performance within an organisation, cultural improvement should be preferred over alteration of strategy. It also implies that the best strategy will not count for much in an environment with poor culture. Indeed, a good organisational culture often negates the need for many strategy initiatives, as creative solutions to problems often arise and are implemented organically.

We have discussed the difficulty of defining, assessing, and understanding culture. But strategy is different – it is more easily understood, more visible, and better defined. Most definitions of strategy are something like, 'A long-term plan for achieving a goal or a result.' Within these words is the key to the difference. A plan is the result of a cognitive process has been thought out, and the goal or results are defined end points. Culture is sensed instinctively, and any changes, good or bad, can become embedded over the longer term with ongoing effects.

When considering the idea of strategy, we understand that it can be communicated, written down, and thought of as a linear path to success. Strategy is superficial, visible, and controllable. It is a process that has clear timing of implementation, and easily measurable success or failure. Strategy involves mechanistic change. Culture change is more organic. A change in culture will involve processes that are deeper, less visible, and more mysterious. To create successful culture change is harder but more permanent than strategy implementation, as it is part of the evolution of the organisation. Strategy change involves what an organisation does; culture change involves what an organisation becomes.

3.9 Better Culture Enables Us to Be Better People

The All Blacks – New Zealand's national rugby union team – are arguably the most successful sporting team ever. Throughout the history of international rugby, now a professional sport, the All Blacks have a win ratio of 77% from over 600 games. They have always been the dominant team. However, in the late 1990s and early 2000s, the team changed. There was less enjoyment in performance, a reduction in team unity and identity, and increasing alcohol abuse.[77] A new head coach, Graham Henry, was appointed at the end of 2003. His start to the job was rocky and, after a loss resulting in the All Blacks finishing last in the 2004 Tri-Nation Series, it became apparent that there were problems to address.

The All Blacks did not decide to change their strategy. They did not commit to a plan of altering the game-style or tactics. Instead, they decided to overhaul and reinforce the team's culture to re-examine what they stood for and what they represented. The All Blacks' culture change started with a deep exploration of themselves, how they interacted on a personal level, how they integrated as a group, and how each individual could create a stronger collective. There was an understanding that development and embodiment of each player's values would translate into a stronger team culture – "Better people make better All Blacks".

The process led to the All Blacks embracing a system that emphasised proud belonging to the jersey, and a joint understanding that a strong team facilitated strong individuals. It became a cyclic process, as those strong individuals devoted themselves to a strong team culture. Their culture resurrection was a deliberate, stepwise, slow process. There were bumps in the road with Henry being fortunate to retain his position in 2007 after a quarter final loss in the World Cup – the worst World Cup result in All Black history.

However, the deep culture changes eventually translated to on-field success. The All Blacks won the 2011 Rugby World Cup, under intense pressure on home soil. After this, Henry retired with the most successful coaching record of any All Blacks coach, and an 85.4% winning rate in 103 games.

The results of this profound culture change continue, even after Henry's reign. Since the loss in South Africa early in Henry's tenure, which precipitated the investigation and change of All Black culture, the team lost only 21 of the next 200 games, winning or drawing 89.5% of all matches.

Strategy change would have been easy in 2004 for the talented players of the New Zealand team. However, it is questionable whether the team could have generated the unprecedented success and ongoing change in values without the process that led to improved team culture.

In many healthcare institutions, it may be worth concentrating on improving the underlying culture instead of the organisational strategy. With an elevated culture may come a range of unexpected benefits.

3.10 Barriers to Successful Culture Change

Despite the rich rewards that a well-executed culture change program can produce, most organisations will not choose to go down that path even in the presence of acknowledged toxic culture. Some of the reasons are that culture change is long and hard, uncertain, and will meet resistance.

Perhaps the principal reason for inaction is that individually and collectively, there is a lack of courage. Instead, the decision is to opt for an organisational reshuffle, 'change of direction', or creation of a new management structure. It is easier to implement a quick, technical, and visible new strategy. These tactics will be applauded, as they are what management texts advise. Unfortunately, superficial change will not address the deeper entrenched cultural issues. As author John Steinbeck said:[78]

"Only mediocrity escapes criticism."

Organisations often allow fear to overcome the desire for sustained improvement and cultural change. This may be influenced by previous unsuccessful change efforts that led us to believe that future attempts are futile. The proposal of a culture change process will induce anxiety and fear in staff due to a loss of certainty. This produces resistance.

Although many of these same staff will have previously wished for a different workplace climate, they will be anxious about loss of the known reality in exchange for an unknown future. Some senior staff, including experienced doctors in a hospital setting, will oppose change vigorously, due to a subconscious fear of becoming less relevant in the new system.

Loss aversion is a powerful motivator in humans – we fear loss more than we desire gain.[79] To have a new system, an old system must be replaced, with loss of a known way of being. Even when the previous system was maladaptive, there will still be sadness and grief with the change.

However, the biggest fear that inhibits culture change relates to the nature of the process. A true culture change initiative, rather than a superficial technical 'solution', will involve self-exploration. Great courage is required to face up to the unconscious biases and unhelpful attitudes that drive action. Modifying culture requires investigation of ourselves, our relationships, and personal interactions. This can bring to the surface things that we would prefer to keep hidden.

Uncovering the deep cultural assumptions within an organisation will not occur until the senior leaders are prepared to explore their own assumptions. This requires bravery and honesty. It calls on an ability to delve into suppressed thoughts rather than resist going too deep for fear of what might be found. Discovering one's own biases, negative attitudes, and problematic behaviours is essential. Being able to start our own individual growth and change is the first step in modifying the overarching culture of the organisation.

Culture change starts with being open, honest, and curious. It requires deep listening. Culture change is about the 'soft skills'; that's why it's so hard.

3.11 Cultures Within a Culture

Within any overarching culture, there are smaller groups, or subcultures, that also exist. The climate of the overall culture is one thing, but there may be a different feel to the subcultures. These could be small subcultures that continually cause problems within a generally well-functioning larger organisation. Alternatively, some of these subcultures may be extraordinary performers within an overall poor culture; shining lights in an otherwise dull environment.

The tendency is to pay excessive attention to the negative performers – the poor subcultures – and try to 'fix' them. Negativity gets attention.[80] However, it can be argued that there is little movement towards success by studying failure, and that by concentrating on poor performance we only learn more about that.

Instead, it is possible to focus attention on the outstanding performers – the 'positively deviant' subcultures.[81] Much can be learnt from the hospital teams,[82] departments, and subcultures that have generated outstanding results. Of course, poorly performing areas need attention – particularly in healthcare – but by changing our focus a little, it is possible to lessen the overwhelming attention paid to the negative outliers and adopt a more balanced view. Investigation of the conditions that have produced the extraordinarily positive results may uncover factors and practices that can be extrapolated to advance the whole institution.

And of course, optimal culture will not come from tearing down everything that exists. In every organisation there are good features that must be retained and built upon as the foundations of the new way of existing. By recognising and promoting the good that is already present, the origins and history of the organisation can be honoured. It is appropriate to pay tribute to those that have gone before and maintain the heritage of the institution.

This individual variation is part of the reason that culture change in each hospital will be a little different. It cannot be formulaic. Each culture has developed with different challenges. Each has its own strengths and parts that have become maladaptive. Each organisation has had its own journey and history and will have stories of origin that must be treasured.

3.12 Are We Prepared to Pay the Price?

Everything in life comes with a cost, whether that is money, time, sleep, pride, or any number of other measures. As intelligent beings, we usually weigh up the cost-benefit ratio before making a decision. In situations where the benefit is uncertain, we are often reticent to invest our own resources for a chance at an unknown outcome, even if that future is potentially uplifting. For an outcome such as improved workplace culture, negative voices are often overly influential thereby preventing others from an imagined and desired future. In many hospitals, everyone wants to see organisational transformation, but many are not prepared to make any personal change towards this goal.

Hawthorn Football Club had been a powerhouse of the Australian Football League for over a decade when it entered the 1989 Grand Final against a fast, skilled, energetic Geelong team. At half-time, Hawthorn had a healthy lead, but the ageing champions were tired and injured from what had been a brutal and physical match. The

Hawthorn players sensed that their younger Geelong opponents could overrun them in the second half.

The half-time address to the Hawthorn players from Coach Allan Jeans included a parable about a young boy who had saved up all of his money to buy a quality pair of shoes. At the last moment, the boy decided to keep some of the money and purchase a cheaper pair. Unfortunately, the lower quality shoes fell apart after a short time. The crestfallen boy realised his error and that he should have 'paid the right price' for the better shoes. Jeans informed his players that success would only eventuate if they were prepared to pay the price required.

At three-quarter time, footage shows Jeans continually exhorting his exhausted players to pay the price that was asked. The Hawthorn players gave everything they had and held on to win a close game in what was arguably the greatest Grand Final ever. They became the Champions once more – they had paid the price demanded of them.

There are many opportunities in life, but all come with a cost. Often, we do not achieve success because we are not willing to make the appropriate investment of time, concentration, or hard work. Sometimes, the payment required is courage or honesty. Sometimes it's a willingness to imagine. We regret the things we don't attempt. We must pay the right price for positive change. Let's not forget that the current damaging environments in many institutions are also exacting a cost on their people's health.

In years to come, will we be regretting that the change we wished to see in hospitals did not occur because we weren't prepared to pay the right price?

3.13 The First Steps in Culture Change

Every significant advance in life, although viewed retrospectively as a 'breakthrough moment', is based on many other interventions, actions, or failed attempts. In actuality, great leaps forward are made up of many unrecognised small steps. This also applies in organisational culture change.

The wonderful culture of an exemplary organisation does not happen by accident, and the changes that led to this way of being did not come instantly with an isolated breakthrough or after a single intervention. Rather, the culture was established after many conversations and collaborations, multiple small acts of kindness, and time spent identifying the best way to meet and interact, and it may still require investigation of other failed culture improvements. The culture embeds and is further propagated by the ongoing actions of many individuals under the umbrella and guidance of the overarching organisation.

Notre-Dame Cathedral in Paris is one of the best known and most loved buildings in Europe. It is a magnificent sight to behold, impressive in both size and beauty. But it hasn't always existed in the current form. In the 12th century, the construction of the cathedral began, with plans and design drawn up. However, the construction took 300 years to complete. Due to the length of time involved, there were numerous changes to the plan, and the final product incorporates several different styles of architecture. Problems that arose during the building process required innovative solutions to be devised, such as the flying buttresses that support the outer walls.

Obviously, most of the workers involved with the building of the cathedral did not live to see it completed. These workers undertook their jobs, making small steps, brick by brick, with trust and faith that their actions were contributing to something that would eventually become extraordinary. Today, through centuries of hard work and many actions by many people, Notre-Dame stands as an outstanding symbol of French culture. The cathedral doesn't look the way it was originally envisaged, and the construction took much longer than planned, however it is an example of what unified belief and effort can create.

Once we create something that is cherished, it will then be fiercely protected. Just as the Notre-Dame fire of 2019 caused an immediate and determined response to fight the flames and subsequently rebuild, a great hospital culture will also be treasured and protected.

In our fast-paced modern world, we like to solve problems with quick solutions and an easily visible path to the end point. Culture building processes in hospitals and other organisations will not occur in this manner. It will not be a straight line from 'here to there' but, in the end, it will be worth it.

Just as the crest of a wave cannot exist without all of the water that makes up the body of the wave, outstanding organisational culture does not exist without all of the small acts that have led to that point. The first building blocks of culture change are those that relate to interpersonal interaction – the human aspects of the organisation. Ultimately, any positive cultural change will come from multiple small steps and repeated actions that seem inconsequential yet, over time, construct something to be proud of. It will relate to each conversation, how groups interact, how they respond to challenges, and how they support each other. Together, people within the organisation can build the necessary structure and the culture that is desired.

The word *culture* comes from the Latin *colere* and refers to the cultivation of soil and nurturing of plants. The results of any planting can be, depending on conditions, a flourishing crop, or stagnation and withering. Within our own cultures, we would all love to flourish and thrive.

{lead·ing}

ALL PEOPLE WILL EXPERIENCE LEADERSHIP OR BEING LED at times during their life. Whether this be in the school yard or in a board room, we have all had leaders in our groups and teams. Many of us have been the designated leader. Given that leadership is so ubiquitous, seemingly we'd all have a clear understanding of what makes a good leader. However, like many of the most important elements in organisations and society, leadership is poorly understood.

Leadership is felt at the unconscious and emotional level rather than evaluated cognitively. We 'know' when we are being led well or badly. Good leadership needs to include technical competence and proficiency with the prevalent systems, but must also encompass factors that are only experienced intuitively.

The emotional measures of leadership, such as how much trust the group places in the leader, have become neglected and under-valued. Perhaps these elements are diminished because they are less visible and harder to evaluate and comprehend. However, the emotional aspects of leadership are some of the most critical. These factors must come to the fore and be examined and developed if our systems are to change for the better.

4.1 What Is Leadership?

When I was first starting to be appointed to leadership positions within medical teams and hospital departments, I felt some anxiety. Who was I to direct and control these groups of educated and high-performing individuals? I started to research leadership theories and practices to improve my capabilities and alleviate my worries.

From the multiple shelves on leadership in any bookstore, it became apparent to me that leadership is a highly valued but poorly understood topic. I also found that there were many different approaches and answers to the question about what leadership consists of. Many of these bookstore texts, often written by an individual who had followed an unconventional path to success (which often also included becoming outrageously wealthy), asserted that their method was the only recipe to achieve your goals. However, none of them seemed to hold the secret to my leadership challenges. While all of the books contained insights and interesting anecdotes, it appeared that each organisational or group context would be different and require its own approach.

As well as edicts from billionaires, many of these leadership books were written by military leaders, detailing actions in battles and wars that were then somehow extrapolated to peacetime business situations, or leadership in other fields. This felt disingenuous when thinking of organisational leadership. A business or hospital is not at war with its competitors. Most of the messages didn't seem to apply. I wasn't at war, beginning a start-up, or concentrating on amassing a fortune. Despite the multitude of conflicting ideas, I didn't really apply any of the lessons learned from the leadership texts.

Oddly, I found that some of the best outcomes that I had with my team would be when I used techniques or styles of behaviour that were similar to those used when playing or coaching sports. The groups responded to being treated in similar ways. It wasn't so much control or detailed direction that was required, more so care and respect.

The medical teams needed to connect with each other just as much as a group of teenage athletes playing a sport did. The kids played better when they were treated with affection and allowed to have a sense of fun. The doctors performed for higher stakes, but also worked more effectively when they had a caring and enjoyable environment. It wasn't about controlling them – it was about relationships and guidance.

The realisation (which perhaps should have been obvious) was that there isn't a secret way to lead specific teams. All teams are the same, in many ways. The first factor in creating a great team and culture is as simple as being nice to people and treating them fairly and respectfully with clear communication. The doctors didn't want me to tell them how to do their job, they just needed a supportive framework around them where they could develop trust and feel part of a team in which there was regard for all members.

4.2 The Desire for Leadership

It is obvious that leadership roles are desired and prized by many in our society. People gain power with leadership roles in any setting and associate such roles with enhanced status and often increased remuneration. As humans, we have an unconscious mental shortcut that assigns other abilities to those in powerful positions, frequently assuming that due to their high status in one field, their opinions about unrelated topics also somehow have extra authority. Therefore, there are many reasons and attractions to leadership. People with certain personality characteristics – including narcissism – will be drawn strongly to leadership roles, even when they are poorly suited.

Each of us has an image or construct of the 'ideal' leader, ranging from an authoritarian figure who can bravely lead us forward through solo action and decision making, determination, and self-will, to the democratic leader who involves and consults many people before making each decision.

Leadership is a complex concept that encompasses many facets. It may sometimes be easier to consider what it is that leadership is not than to define what leadership actually is. Leadership is not just the job title, the position, a particular set of attributes, or an ability to organise and manage. Some of the areas encompassed by leadership include: setting cultural expectations, communicating, motivating, collaborating, directing, delegating, taking ownership of difficult situations, acknowledging responsibility for poor outcomes, inspiring others, dispensing consequences, recognising noteworthy efforts, giving directions, making sense of uncertainty, strategising, collaborating, expressing gratitude, forgiving, counselling, and supporting.

Further, leadership is about directing focus onto areas that need or deserve attention. These may be organisational goals, improvements, corrections, or modifications required, as well as areas that warrant praise due to unusual or unprecedented success, exemplary effort, and behaviours valued by the organisation. The leader must have the requisite skills for the position within the appropriate industry and must have clearly held personal values which are congruent with the desired culture of the organisation. The leader must also have an ability to create and share goals with other members.

When I think of the consultants, directors, or heads of units who influenced me most during my training, I must wrack my brain to discern who gave the best advice on surgical technique, or who I obtained certain theoretical knowledge from. However, I have immediate recall of how I felt with each of my 'bosses', and what emotions they stirred in me. Some of the lessons I learned were from those I didn't want to emulate. The best learning was from those whose behaviour I admired. These people were kind, not only to patients but to juniors, nurses, and all staff. I felt great affection for these leaders, and I worked harder for them as I was determined not to let them down. When around good people, we behave more virtuously, with the opposite also applying. The best leaders – those I wanted to be like – were honest, kind, and fair.

As leadership research increases, it is more frequently recognised that emotional intelligence correlates with leadership effectiveness. This does not just imply nicety, but also kindness, empathy, an ability to register the emotional states and needs of other people, and a willingness to try to assist. These qualities are part of the rich mix that constitutes wisdom. Wisdom implies a level of intelligence, both cognitive and emotional. It also requires self-regulation of emotions, which allows the use of different and appropriate styles of interaction according to circumstances and the people involved.

Wisdom has long been recognised as an important virtue in a leader, with both ancient Greek and Chinese philosophers having similar sayings along the lines of, 'With power must come wisdom.'

The current challenges to hospitals are causing many organisations to consider their culture and try to increase organisational pride, foster staff well-being, and produce a flourishing environment. This is more than merely trying to continue with a current strategy, or business as usual, which only requires technical management or transactional leadership. These hospitals are also examining their leadership structures.

Evolving into a thriving organisation requires a more inspired transformational leadership style that engages the emotions and imagination of staff. This is where curious, appreciative leadership prioritises development of people over development of buildings or organisational processes. In this environment egos can be controlled in order to collaboratively create the desired vision. With this style, the leader does not need to control everything. They are more responsible for helping to unify, envision, and facilitate. The leader does not have, or need to have, all the answers. The leader encourages a vision and invites others to collaborate with the detail. In this structure, a leader will be content helping to trace an outline and stepping back to allow others to add the colour.

4.3 What Qualities Should a Leader Display?

As all people are different, no two leaders will share identical qualities in their makeup. Throughout history, the personal qualities of charisma, confidence, and extraversion have been suggested as the ideal qualities for a leader. It has been surmised that people will unite behind a (usually) male of this type. This is the basis for the 'Great Man' leadership model.

More recent organisational thinking is that the best leadership – that which creates unified teams – involves a less individualistic and aggressive style.[83] The qualities needed for this type of leadership are empathy, balance, and an ability to listen. These factors, when combined with drive, intelligence, and personal technical skills, are a rare combination. Sometimes, great success can come for a group that is led by someone who lacks traditional leadership attributes but has good interpersonal skills.

A cricket team consists of eleven players, and each player's individual results contribute to broader team success. The usual method of choosing the captain, or leader, of the team is to select the team and then pick the captain from these individuals. In higher level representative teams, the best eleven players available are selected and the captain then chosen. In a cricket team, there will usually be six specialist batsmen (who will contribute the majority of a team's score), a wicketkeeper, and four specialist bowlers. Some of the bowlers may be able to bat a little and contribute runs, and some of the batsmen may be able to bowl a little.

In the 1970's, an international Test cricket quality batsman would be expected to have an average score, or 'batting average', of at least 35 runs per innings. An average of above 40 runs per innings would indicate a high-quality batsman, and above 50, an outstanding performer. However, in the late 1970's, the English cricket authorities had a dilemma. Their captain, Mike Brearley, was clearly a poor performer in his role as opening batsman. Over his entire Test career, Brearley batted 66 times for an average of only 22.9 runs per inning – about half of what would be expected in a high-quality performer. Over his 39 Test match career, he never scored a century.

Yet despite his relatively poor individual statistics, Brearley was a prized member of the team, for Brearley was an outstanding captain, arguably the greatest ever in English Test cricket history. His leadership facilitated strong performances from the other players of the team and allowed them to operate at their highest level. Brearley was not in the best eleven cricket players in the country but came to be selected for his captaincy skills rather than for his batting ability. When he retired as the English captain in 1980, his own batting record was mediocre at best, but the English team had enjoyed great success. Despite Brearley underperforming with his individual contribution, the overall achievements of the team were impressive. Statistically, Brearley is the most successful English Test cricket captain of all time, winning 18 and losing only 4 of his 31 matches in charge of the team.

Cricket is a fascinating sport which is sometimes considered an individual sport involving a collection of solo performers who just happen to be members of the same collective. Scores are cumulative of each player's contribution, rather than the score being generated collaboratively. Occasionally, individual performances and records overshadow the achievements of the group. In this setting, Brearley's England team was one of the most interesting cricket sides ever. Instead of eleven outstanding performers where each player is judged and ranked for their personal accomplishments, Brearley was able to create a group dynamic where personal achievement came to be considered less important than collective results and, thereby, team success was attained.

4.4 Who Should Become the Leader?

Within many organisations, including medical departments in hospitals, the position of leader is often allocated to the best performer within the team. The individual with extraordinary personal results within the field is somehow believed to also have the abilities to lead, nurture, and guide others. This extrapolation is made automatically, but on examination seems an unusual assumption. Perhaps, if consideration is given to the appointment, the reasoning may be that all the other team members and juniors admire the extraordinarily gifted member, so they will give unqualified support to the appointment.

However, in any field, the best individual performer may have risen to that level by being solely focused on their own performance. To develop superb technical skills is often a solitary pursuit and may come at the expense of development of interpersonal skills that are critical for leadership. The highly competent performer will occasionally encounter difficulties with the required shift from a very self-centred view to adopting an other-centred perspective. This individual may not possess the ability, or even the desire, to create a harmonious team. If promoted from within the group, the prior interactions and relationships that occurred on the journey to becoming the outstanding performer of the team may undermine the ability to lead the same team. Indeed, this type of appointment could end with both a disgruntled team and lower standards of individual performance from the star who is now also wrestling with leadership duties. The old saying is: 'to become a good leader, first you must be a good team-mate.'

It may be instructive that, in English cricket, after Mike Brearley resigned as Test captain in 1980, the next captain appointed was Ian Botham who was at the time perhaps the world's leading cricketer. Botham was an all-rounder; a match-winner with both his batting and his bowling. He was an exciting and charismatic performer, and one of the greatest players ever. It was assumed that he would be the star player who would lead by example, and that the team would unite behind him. Unfortunately, things didn't work out that way. During Botham's tenure as captain, the team played poorly and Botham's own performance, perhaps weighed down by having to concentrate on others due to his captaincy duties, deteriorated dramatically. After 12 matches in charge as Test captain with no wins, Botham resigned from the team's leadership. Brearley was asked to come back as Test captain, which he agreed to. Immediately, the English performance improved, and after three victories enabling a come-from-behind series win against the Australians, Brearley retired once more. During his brief return, Brearley continued with his relatively mediocre individual performances while Botham, freed from the pressures of captaincy, once more became a match-winner.

4.5 The Type of Leadership

Within our world, there is a widespread and understandable lack of confidence in leaders at all levels of business, society, and government. Reports of unethical behaviour and focus on personal gain have eroded community belief and trust in the leaders of many institutions. When there is frequent evidence of organisations displaying greed and questionable moral standards without any concern for care of less powerful individuals, the community, or the planet, it is unsurprising that there is an associated growth of mistrust. Too many leaders appear entirely self-focused. Many appear more concerned about the size of their bonus payments than of the health, safety, and well-being of their workers. Leadership sets the tone for any group, and in some respects, a widespread lack of honourable and wise leadership has been to the detriment of humankind.

In recent times, it has become recognised that personal humility is an important characteristic of exceptional leaders.[84] Perhaps Harry Truman, who served as US President from 1945 to 1953, was ahead of his time when he said:[85]

> *"It's amazing what you can accomplish*
> *if you don't care who gets the credit."*

This quote seems to promote the opposite of narcissistic, self-centred leadership which seeks personal glory. An attitude such as Truman's will not result in diminished pride about achievements nor a decrease in allocation of praise for outstanding individual contributions; there is instead an implied understanding that the success will be enjoyed by the whole team, rather than the leader choosing to bask in the glow of others' achievements. Within the quote is a sense that team goals and the achievement of objectives that result in the common good are rated more highly than individual goals.

Indeed, some desirable qualities and traits for a leader, such as humility, may be characteristics that cause one to resist promotion to leadership positions. But it is crucial to note that humility is neither submissiveness nor a belief that one is unworthy. Rather it is a personal quality that acknowledges that no individual has all the answers. In some ways, humility demonstrates greater intelligence and wisdom.

The most well-known research into the importance of humility in leaders may be that of Jim Collins[86] who, in 'Good to Great', found that one of the main factors in the unusual event of a good company transitioning to an extraordinary company with sustained exceptional success, was having a leader who was assessed as a 'Level 5' leader. The difference between a Level 4 leader and the uppermost Level 5 related to personality traits which were surprising as they went against the conventional wisdom of the time. Prior to Collins's research, it was assumed that a hard-driving, charismatic, glamorous leader was the secret to success. Instead, Collins's team found that part of the leap in a company's fortunes was related to the leader having both professional will and drive combined with empathy and humility. The humble leader, rather than the 'Great Man', was the key to developing outstanding culture, teamwork, and performance. Indeed, rather than a 'Great Man', the qualities of empathy and humility combined with professional excellence are often seen in today's great female leaders.

Despite Collins's widely referenced work, increased humility of leaders does not appear to have become commonplace in western societies where individualistic qualities, self-advancement, and desire for personal status are still encouraged. This leads to those with narcissistic traits and a desire for personal glory to seek leadership roles more frequently than others. Combined with a human predilection to be attracted to excessive self-confidence, this often ends in poor leadership and dysfunctional teams. More self-focused leaders will have a communication style that is based on directing, demanding, and delegating as opposed to questioning, listening, and supporting. The result will be a group with poorly connected management rather than a team with engaging leadership.

With the thinking around the advantages of humble leadership, there is a saying that those who push themselves forward and actively want to be in charge should not be allowed to become the leader. A more sophisticated way of deciding on leadership positions could be through assessment of which potential candidates would garner the respect of the team, and also have the above desirable personal qualities. Perhaps these individuals can be identified, encouraged, and supported to aspire to leadership roles.

More humility in the leader, rather than self-focus, is certainly important to the development of team spirit and positive emotion within an organisation. However, rather than the presence or absence of humility being the sole measure of an exceptional leader, this aspect of personality may simply indicate the existence of high emotional intelligence within that individual. It is possible that humility may be the marker of a broader set of characteristics, abilities, personality traits, and admirable qualities that combine to make up an outstanding leadership candidate.

These leaders are able to consider different viewpoints and alternative opinions without feeling threatened, and they are regarded highly. As the Chinese proverb states:[87]

> *"A little fragrance always clings*
> *to the hand that gives the roses."*

4.6 The Importance of Trust

Sometimes in life, it seems logical and sensible not to trust anyone or anything. As humans, we are never more vulnerable and exposed than when we give trust to someone. One definition of trust is: "Choosing to risk making something you value become vulnerable to someone else's actions".[88] Being vulnerable, allowing exposure, and taking personal risk are not easy or comfortable. The problem is that without trusting others, we cannot find happiness, connection, and fulfilment in our lives.

Similarly, at work, without feeling trust, we cannot create or nurture relationships, feel joy, or be uplifted. In low-trust work environments where no one feels safe, innovations are not made, and honest feedback and truth is not shared. Information becomes protected and siloed. This leads to a culture of half-truths, lies, and silence. These are the environments in which meetings consist of some participants pushing for initiatives motivated by self-interest, others making arguments based around fear of losing resources, and a further group remaining unengaged and largely quiet.

Under current global conditions, uncertain economic circumstances, and tense political outlooks, society wants to believe in and trust our leaders. The increasing challenges to hospitals of excessive demand, pandemics, and burnout mean that healthcare workers also long to believe in hospital leadership. But at the same time, trust in leaders is at an all-time low which contributes to poor attitudes and behaviours. This further erodes organisational culture, causing a spiral of increasing stress and suspicion. Leadership is key to reversing this. The level of trust that staff have in their organisation's leader directly correlates with commitment, performance, job satisfaction, and intent to leave.[89] Authentic leadership and 'doing what is right' allows integrity and belief to grow.

So, with all these positive effects within an organisation when there is a trusted and trustworthy leader – how can trust be generated? Firstly, it may be wise to acknowledge that trust takes a long time and many actions to develop but can be dissolved in an instant. The word *trustworthy* gives us the initial indication of how to create a better climate. The leader must be worthy of someone else's trust. Integrity is essential. The leader must be authentic and live the values that they preach. There cannot be a gap between the words and the actions of the leader. Building trust comes with a combination of the leader's words, actions, style of communication, and expressed emotion.

The trusted leader will be reliable and consistent. They will be open and honest in sharing information. Competence will be shown by meeting expectations and problem solving. All actions, words, and behaviours will be infused with compassion and empathy. Of course, not all decisions that the leader makes will be greeted with universal approval. Nor should they. All leaders have to make hard decisions that will occasionally adversely impact some. However, an authentic leader will explain the decision-making process honestly, help others understand the reasons for the chosen direction, and apologise for and try to mitigate any unwanted human impacts.

Leaders of this type will create trust, for staff know that both their best interests, and those of the wider organisation, are considered in the planning and formation of strategy. These leaders foster cultures of enduring positive change. These are the leaders people come to regard with admiration and love.

4.7 The Need for Love

The senior consultants who impacted me most during my training nurtured me by giving guidance and encouragement. My observation of their ways, techniques, and behaviours helped direct my development. They allowed me to learn from mistakes, protected me from making major errors, and assisted if things did go wrong. They appreciated my diligence and were thankful for the ways in which I cared for the patients and interacted with staff in their units. I think they may have felt affection for me. I certainly look back on them, decades later, with love and gratitude.

The best teams always seem to have a loving and loved leader. Perhaps it's essential. This style of leadership allows strong bonds and connections, enjoyment at work, and also provides a platform if difficult feedback is needed.

In hospitals, we often hear the refrain, "See one, do one, teach one". This is used in joking reference to the method of educating and passing on technical skills. Along the same lines, given that we model and unconsciously imitate the people we admire, it is possible that the affectionate and caring ways of outstanding leaders are passed on, in a recurring cycle that promotes compassion. One wonders why this isn't the norm. Why is it remarkable when experienced senior people behave in kind ways? Shouldn't that just be the way we all interact? Perhaps just as common sense is often uncommon, common decency can be rare.

It is said that the kindest gift is time – especially time to truly listen. This may be the method by which these outstanding leaders operate and excel – by staying curious and listening to the members of their team. Being aware of what is communicated with body language, and both listening to what is voiced and hearing what is not said. Instead of the common comment, often delivered in a passive-aggressive manner, that one is 'saying what needs to be said', the authentic leader will listen with empathy and bravery and 'hear what needs to be heard'.

4.8 Who Is On the Plane?

One of the most underrated dimensions of leadership lies in decision making around whom the leadership group is comprised of, and what leadership roles are allocated to which individual. These steps are critical to organisational success. Sometimes, one of the critical strengths of the best leaders is their ability to recognise, accumulate, and promote talented and balanced people, those with whom they can work cohesively, to together create a high-functioning team.

In some ways, who is within the leadership team, the makeup of the team, and the interactions of the group can be as important as who the leader is. If we consider the leader as the captain of the aeroplane, then the leadership group also reside within the cockpit. While the leader may be the aeroplane's captain, the wise leader will realise that he or she is not the only gifted pilot or navigator. The leader's most important role will sometimes be as the organiser, delegator, and enabler of team functioning. In certain situations, the leader will not be holding the controls of the aeroplane while taxiing down the runway.

Through empowering others, a stronger bond of trust and respect is developed, and skills are built. Of course, empowerment of others involves giving away some of one's own personal power. This is where the saying, 'The single most important job of a leader is to produce more leaders, not more followers' becomes relevant. Through the empowerment of others, sharing responsibility, and creating connections of honesty and trust, a powerful team that provides thrust and momentum can be created.

In any organisation, there will be negative voices and cynical opinions that can slow progress. To continue the aeroplane metaphor, these people increase drag. They can be viewed as either flaps on the wings of the aircraft, or chocks under the wheels. Flaps increase drag and slow down the plane, but also have useful functions in flight. Chocks are triangular blocks placed under the wheels to prevent any movement of the aeroplane while on the runway. The chocks must be removed to allow the aeroplane to commence forward motion. In an organisation that has become immobilised due to certain people and their actions that inhibit progress, a decision must be made as to whether these individuals are beneficial to the group or an unhelpful obstacle.

Negative voices are useful at certain stages of organisational development. They can be critical to alert the importance of careful decision-making around the path forward. They make rash choices less likely, but sometimes they can impede all action. When these people are able to become integrated, valuable team members, then they will play an essential role in the organisation's ability to elevate. However, if the negative views are persistent and merely represent self-interest rather than the good of the organisation, then they do not allow for any organisational growth and development. If, over time, they are unable to adopt the overriding views of the organisation and instead remain a block, they must be removed – they're no longer helpful as they obstruct motion and acceleration.

At times, the humble leader may need to be the skilled pilot flying the plane through difficult terrain, often the intelligent navigator plotting a course, sometimes they must act as the kind cabin crew, and occasionally must be the decisive leader who realises that surplus baggage has to be jettisoned. The wisest leader will recruit, develop, integrate, and inspire a crew who can independently operate a complex aeroplane that is able to accelerate and then elevate.

Over time, the humble leader blends into the team and provides overview and guidance. In this way, the leader embodies the words translated from Chinese philosopher Lao Tzu:

"True leaders may be hardly known to their followers
Next after them are the leaders the people know and admire
After them, are the leaders that the people fear
After them, are the leaders that the people despise
But the great leader is the one that after the work is done,
the people say 'Oh, we did it ourselves.'"

4.9 Medical and Hospital Leadership

When we think of hospitals, we often conjure images of patients in operating theatres, emergency departments, or hospital beds. However, in addition to patient care, a hospital is a large complex organisation with many other processes and outcomes. The occurrence of disease and injury is unpredictable in any community, and while a hospital endeavours to provide best-practice care for each patient, it also operates under relatively fixed financial constraints with a co-existent, somewhat unknowable workload.

These two sometimes-competing interests of financial

accountability and clinical care can occasionally lead to confusion and internal dispute over how to best manage a hospital. Is a hospital primarily an institution devoted to the care and treatment of patients, that also has to pay attention to budgetary concerns? Or is it primarily a business that just happens to be in the healthcare industry? Of course, it is both of those things and more, yet medical care and the running of a hospital can be very expensive, and the balance between the clinical side and the business concerns can sometimes be difficult.

For example, if there is a spate of patients with a very rare cancer for which there is a new, expensive drug treatment that has slightly better outcomes than the less expensive alternative, should the institution supply the more expensive drug to all of the patients without regard for financial constraints? Or should it attempt to still provide excellent care with the less expensive option and allow funds to be saved for treatment of other patients, other conditions, and other initiatives? There are obviously multiple factors that must be examined in this somewhat unrealistic and simplified scenario, including ethical, social, and political viewpoints.

Further to these discussions is the occasionally uneasy equipoise between executive management and senior medical management. Often, there are two streams of power and influence within the hospital that seem to run in parallel rather than in tandem. Occasionally, they meld well; sometimes, less well. In this situation, who should have the final say on significant strategic directions for the hospital? The senior executive, the chief executive officer, or the most senior doctor, the chief medical officer?

Poor communication between these groups can result in situations where the doctors believe that the administrators do not give due thought to clinical care and the needs of their patients, while the hospital executives consider the doctors financially naïve and ignorant of all the detail behind any decision. Without understanding the other's perspective leads to disharmony, disrespect, and eruptions of outrage.

Many hospital executive members have come from a nursing background, with others originally working in financial professions such as accounting. Surprisingly, it is less common for executive members to have medical training, and rarer still to have doctors in the executive group who have previously had clinical practices. While it is entirely appropriate that hospital executive management contains those with nursing experience and those with financial expertise, it would seem sensible to also have experienced medical input incorporated into the process of high-level strategy development. After all, the core business of any hospital, or any healthcare institution, is looking after patients. In my experience, hospitals that have had wise and clinically astute medical staff in senior executive roles have felt more functional and collaborative, and have generated less frustration amongst senior doctors.

A common point of dispute is when busy doctors with heavy clinical loads, are unable to make it to meetings scheduled in business hours at relatively short notice. The meeting times may suit the administrators but not the doctors, particularly if they have a practice outside the hospital. The doctors then feel disrespected, underappreciated, and occasionally undermined. Even worse can be when the doctor takes time away from their clinical duties to attend the meeting, but the issue of critical concern was not covered in depth and decisions deferred, thus making it a waste of their time. On the other hand, the administrators can rightly feel aggrieved that they have to constantly make allowances and meet out of hours to comply with the doctors' wishes.

There is empirical research showing that having an appropriately trained doctor as the chief executive officer leads to a higher performing hospital,[90,91] however, other research suggests that while having a doctor in the top leadership group is important, there is no significant difference in hospital performance if the CEO is medically trained or not.[92] Perhaps the most salient lesson from research into the makeup of a hospital's senior leadership group is that top management does equate to better hospital performance,[93] however this is largely related to effective communication and information sharing practices rather than the particular background of individual executive members.

In many instances, the problem within hospitals is that the leaders don't actually lead in one sense. Oftentimes, the executive leaders concentrate on day-to-day management and dealing with problems and crises as they arise. This is appropriate, particularly with current extreme demands. But this is management – not leadership. With exclusive focus on immediate business, and dealing with issues as they arise, there is less attention paid to new opportunity or vision shown for potential exciting new directions. There are no discussions or proposals for innovative ideas or creative solutions. There is no engagement of the staff or exhortation of the hospital community to elevate. Many just follow what is done everywhere else and manage according to what is thought to be expected, what is routine and standard. This isn't a surprising management strategy. No one gets criticised for doing what everyone else is doing. But it isn't leadership. Can any manager convince themselves that without time to think, dream, create, or contemplate alternative viewpoints they are truly able to envisage what the organisation could become?

This should not be taken as a criticism of those hard working and overloaded individuals. Their jam-packed diaries don't allow a different way. And much of what our healthcare leaders must do is necessarily management. The job requires this. But not all of a leader's role can be management. Some of it must be leading – strengthening bonds, setting examples, motivating and inspiring others, helping others create, thinking and dreaming of better ways. Perhaps this is more an indictment on the systems, expectations, and styles of work that we have allowed to become the norm. Unless we are prepared to be imaginative, brave, and different, it will be impossible to become excellent or visionary.

4.10 The Secret to Becoming a Leader

When many of us rise in seniority and start to assume leadership roles, we follow the same path. We read leadership guides and manuals, we watch TED Talks, we explore the importance of performing a daily 'twenty-mile march,'[94] try to become more effective by establishing 'seven habits,'[95] and suppress hunger while we are ensuring that we 'eat last.'[96] We try to begin with understanding our 'why'[97] and attempt to 'lean in.'[98]

These are all inspiring messages with outstanding lessons. But reading a book or having a position title does not make one a true leader. We may consider ourselves the leader, but can someone really be described as a leader if they don't have committed followers? Without followers, or at least colleagues who are collaborated with and consulted, perhaps the real position description is organiser or manager. Staff do not choose to be led or become followers because of which books someone has read. They listen to and line up with those they trust and feel affection and respect for.

Perhaps we don't need the books. It may be better to just reflect on how our own memorable and treasured leaders have treated us in the past. In some ways, we already instinctively know what is required, if we are brave enough to admit it. Deep down, we all know how to look after others, build mutual positive regard, and help create happy and functional teams.

The mentors and very best leaders that each of us has been associated with created a feeling of nurturing, and a sense of being understood. There were, of course, non-negotiable areas relating to performance standards and behavioural guidelines, but even these were learnt in an overarching framework of kindness. To give these gifts to others will be to get them back. The leader in title, who treats others with affection and care, will become the leader with devoted followers.

{com·mu·ni·cat·ing}

ALMOST ALL HUMAN INTERACTION IS BASED ON INTERPER-
sonal communication. Communication informs and influences most
behaviour and is also the method of enacting change – both within
ourselves and in others. The style, frequency, and content of communication will be the factor that dictates the success of leadership,
group culture, and teamwork. As such, communication within any
organisation is of paramount importance. This communication may
be verbal, non-verbal, or electronic. Silence can be a type of communication, as can a lack of response to written messages via email, text,
or other means.

All communication modes can be used in constructive interactions with information sharing, instruction, guidance, support, and
affection. All forms of communication can also allow us to criticise,
demean, isolate, ostracise, harass, or bully. Choosing to adopt either
a positive or negative style of communication is a decision that each
of us makes multiple times every day. Each episode of communication will influence the interpersonal dynamics and relationships of
the group and organisation. Over time, the dominant communication style becomes established and accepted without questioning.
The structure, feel, and sentiment of communication – whether with

a positive or negative valence – will embed and be unique to each organisation. Viewed in this way, every single instance of communication is important.

5.1 The Value of Listening

Very early in medical school, it is taught that most diagnoses are not made by physical examination or through tests and investigations. Rather, the correct diagnosis is made based on the patient's history. In other words, what the patient tells the doctor. Even in cases where there is a difficult diagnosis, when one goes back and reviews the patient history, there may be a clue that was overlooked, and then caused delay prior to establishing the right diagnosis and instituting the appropriate treatment.

So, in order to facilitate this process of diagnosis, one would assume that doctors must be expert communicators. Unfortunately, the reality is something quite different. When doctor-patient consultations were analysed in 1999, it was uncommon for the patient to be able to complete their initial statement or presenting complaint without being interrupted by the doctor within the first 25 seconds.[99] Recent data has confirmed these findings[100] but, concerningly, the time to first interruption has become even shorter. On average, only 11 seconds had elapsed after the start of the consultation before the patient was interrupted.

Doctors are highly intelligent but time poor. It may be assumed that they can quickly redirect the conversation or focus the patient in order to rapidly make a diagnosis and create efficiency in care. However, an earlier interruption reduces the chance of accurate diagnosis.[101,102] If medical students are taught that the patient's history is critical, and the evidence supports this, why doesn't it happen?

Like the rest of society, medical practice is changing. The pace of life is increasing. But despite larger cities, better transport, and increased ability to connect quickly via electronic means, in modern society many of us have less direct human interaction. Are we all becoming less skilled at communication?

With the preponderance of technology, concerns have been raised about a reduction in attention spans,[103] particularly due to the effects of cell phones. Could the early interruptions in consultations relate to an inability to concentrate? Unfortunately, we can't lay the blame for our bad manners and poor medical practices on cell phones. Reports of physicians interrupting patients within 30 seconds of a consultation go back to the 1980's,[104] prior to the existence of mobile phones.

Concurrent with the decrease in time to first interruption over the last 40 years[105] has been an erosion of patients' trust in their doctors.[106,107] This reduction in trust is problematic as patients with a higher level of trust in the doctor-patient relationship have improved clinical outcomes.[108]

It isn't surprising that patients lack trust in a therapeutic relationship when they are interrupted so quickly while discussing their medical problem. The behaviour certainly seems rude and could be interpreted as indicating a lack of compassion. However, doctors are regarded almost universally as being kind and compassionate people. Could this style of interaction be explained by doctors being so pressed for time that they can't allow a patient to speak about their complaint for longer than a brief instant?

Again, this explanation is not supported by evidence. In analyses of the consultations where there were earlier interruptions, there was no difference in total consultation length than those without interruption.

Perhaps the way that doctors are trained has led to this style of practice? Does the constant pressure and stress of medical school produce anxious practitioners who jump in quickly if they feel things are unwinding too slowly? Do doctors feel that they need to dominate the conversation? These questions are difficult to answer yet need to be considered.

Within healthcare systems, much time and money is spent trying to increase optimal care and throughput. Efficiency can relate to making earlier and more accurate diagnoses. More rapid and more successful treatment of patients leads to a shorter duration of inpatient care and less use of limited resources. It is possible that the most dramatic improvement in hospital efficiency could be generated not by an expensive software package, or by better access to diagnostic imaging, but by improving communication.

One of the solutions to many of our current healthcare problems may come down to human interaction. Perhaps a profound improvement in medicine and hospitals could be achieved with attention to the seemingly simple act of listening.

5.2 Before We Speak

Many people enter a conversation with a preconceived idea of how it will go. We constantly make assumptions. Our brains will often jump to conclusions based on experience, previous interactions with a particular person, our current emotional state, and our own agenda and aspirations. Sometimes our interactions may be influenced by feelings of arrogance, contempt, or bravado; other conversations may be constrained and tentative due to feelings of anxiety, fear, or uncertainty.

A discussion can have many functions, but two of the most important are an exchange of information and the development of a more trusting and mutually beneficial relationship. However, in some organisations and in some interpersonal interactions, information can be regarded as a currency of power. In a poor culture, data and information can be protected and withheld, used to further one's own aims, or to negate the progress of others. Connections will not thrive in this unhelpful scenario.

Further, within any conversation, a sense of not being listened to or valued will hinder a relationship. Without mutual respect, the relationship cannot become a trusting and supportive one. Often, these poor communication characteristics will play out time after time. The elements of poor interaction can occur even before the conversation begins. After these exchanges both people will leave having had their prior negative assessment of the other reinforced.

In the New Testament, Jesus is quoted as saying, "It is easier for a camel to pass through the eye of a needle than for a rich man to enter the kingdom of God".[109] This is an unusual metaphor that has generated much discussion. It has been claimed that there was a small side gate into the walled city of Jerusalem that could allow access and entry at night when the main gates were closed. This small gate was known as 'the eye of the needle' due to its size. For a loaded camel to enter, it would need to have its packs removed and to stoop down. In other words, it would need to lose its baggage. And only the wealthy would own a loaded camel. Therefore, for a rich or proud man to reach 'the kingdom of God', he would need to 'lose his baggage'. This presumably meant being able to cast off arrogance, hubris or self-pride, and preconceived attitudes. He would need to discard bias and become humble.

A similar state exists with communication. To achieve truly worthwhile interactions, we need to be able to cast off our preconceptions, already-formed opinions, and attitudes. We need to enter the conversation curious, prepared to learn, and ready to share. This is to both participants' benefit; we can't learn without listening and hearing other views. As Irish playwright George Bernard Shaw said:[110]

*"If you have an apple and I have an apple and we
exchange them, we still each have an apple.
If you have an idea and I have an idea and we
exchange them, then we each now have two ideas."*

5.3 Embracing Curiosity

Medicine is a very conservative profession, and there is occasional
reluctance to accommodate new ways. This resistance can result in
attitudes that quickly end discussion about innovative ideas. Some of
this scepticism is entirely appropriate. Unproven techniques should
not be embraced too quickly, as hasty adoption could lead to patient
harm. The flip side of this is that the system can become staid and
resistant to change – a conservative wall of pride and arrogance can
be erected. And in some cases, those who do see things differently
can pay the price of ostracism by the establishment.

Barry Marshall was a medical registrar when he, together with
pathologist J. Robin Warren, became interested in stomach biopsy
specimens from patients with peptic ulcers. These specimens also
identified bacteria in the biopsies. At that time, the cause of peptic
ulcers was universally thought to be due to stress and associated
with lifestyle factors such as smoking and spicy food. It was taken
for granted that the acidity of the stomach would kill all bacteria.
Therefore, the organisms identified on the biopsy specimens were
undoubtedly contaminants, at least according to the prevailing view.

However, Marshall and Warren became convinced that the aetiol-
ogy of the ulcers was related to the organism that had been isolated.
Marshall's theories were pilloried by the medical establishment
which continued treating the patients with long-term medications
to reduce acid production in the stomach. Marshall's career suffered,

and he endured public ridicule. Eventually, the scorn drove him to induce his own peptic ulcer by drinking a culture of the organism, subsequently named Helicobacter pylori,[111] and then successfully treating himself with antibiotics rather than antacids. After years of opposition to his ideas in Australia, Marshall set up a laboratory in the US. Today, standard treatment of peptic ulcer throughout the world involves microbiological culture and treatment for Helicobacter. In 2005, Marshall and Warren were awarded the Nobel Prize.

As a medical student in the 1980s and a hospital resident doctor in the early 1990s, I recall the scorn with which Marshall was spoken about by consultants in the tea rooms of operating theatres. How dare Marshall challenge the accepted wisdom of the establishment? Due to the attitudes of my senior colleagues, who I assumed to be all-knowing, I developed an opinion that Marshall must indeed be a crackpot, despite not having analysed his research myself, or even having a full understanding of the arguments.

A personal lesson that I take away from this is the great influence, even when unspoken and unconscious, that senior colleagues have over less experienced staff. The medical profession that didn't listen and was too proud to countenance new ideas reinforced these attitudes in junior doctors.

The resistance to listening and the arrogance in assuming that what was taught was indisputable were poor examples of communication and culture. Experienced doctors allowed a lack of personal humility to hinder wider understanding of the true pathogenesis of a medical condition, delaying effective treatment for many people. This inability to overcome entrenched attitudes before entering a conversation can inhibit innovation. Without mutual positive regard, effective exchange of ideas can't take place. And unless we listen and remain curious, we will never learn anything new. To move through the barrier to a more informed and better way, we must first shed our baggage.

5.4 What Is the Style of Our Dialogue?

John and Julie Gottman are internationally renowned relationship experts who run the Gottman Institute – an organisation dedicated to strengthening relationships.[112] The Gottmans have conducted decades of research on the stability of relationships. Through observing a couple's interactions over a short period of time, Gottman's methods can predict with 90% accuracy which couples will separate or divorce in the following six years.[113] The negative behaviours most predictive of relationship difficulties are criticism of the other person, contempt, defensiveness, and 'stonewalling' which is seen as emotional withdrawal from the interaction.[114]

In contrast, successful relationships are identified by the couples' behaviour being gentle, positive, and supportive of each other even in conflict. In other words: they are kind to each other. Within the happy marriages or relationships that endure and thrive, John Gottman found that the ratio of positive to negative comments was always greater than 5:1. At least five positive comments or affirmations for each negative comment. For those relationships that were toxic and doomed to fail quickly, the ratio was less than 1:1. Less than one positive comment for each negative. And many relationships will be languishing – neither thriving nor quickly dissolving. Not toxic, but slowly eroding.

It's not just in marriage that the positivity ratio in communication is important. Similar results are seen in children and youth sports coaching. Those teams who are coached with a style that has greater than five positive comments to each negative comment will gain skills more quickly, be more engaged, and achieve more sporting success.[115,116]

Within business organisations, a similar assessment of the positivity-negativity ratio has been applied to communication. The higher the ratio, and the more positive the style of intra-organisation communication, the more successful the business.[117] In those organ-isations that have a communication style with less than a 1:1 ratio of positive to negative comments, the business will be failing.

Of course, an unhappy marriage can dissolve to end the distress; a disgruntled young sportsperson can elect to leave a team overseen by a critical coach. Even a private business can go under. But what about a hospital? Public hospitals must endure and, even in a neg-ative environment, the hospital must continue to function and treat patients. Perhaps it will just be a less happy place.

An opposing argument that could be raised when discussing positivity rates of communication is that hospital environments – especially groups of doctors – are not youth sports teams or mar-riages where tenderness is required. And public hospitals are not businesses. Many doctors may argue that hospitals are filled with highly trained specialists where a cold, dispassionate attitude is nec-essary. They may assert that a critical slant is necessary to maintain standards and vigilance so that mistakes will not occur. This opinion can initially seem convincing, but it flies counter to the experience in professional sports in the US, where similarly highly trained and driven individuals are focused on success and eradication of mis-takes. In professional sports, poor results are also open to criticism and even more obvious.

Within professional sports teams in the US, the ratio of positive to negative comments from coaches to players has been found to be critical to success. Team results are improved when a positive-negative ratio of around 5:1 is applied to communication.[118] Even in the hardened ranks of the American NBA (National Basketball Association), the most successful team dynasty ever, the Chicago Bulls coached by Phil Jackson found that a drop in positive com-munication between coaches and players led to disharmony in the group and poorer performance.[119]

Suggesting that attention should be paid to increasing positive communication styles within hospitals and medical teams will provoke comments that not everything that occurs within hospitals is positive. There are poor clinical outcomes, and occasionally mistakes are made. This argument, which is completely valid, will reference life's harsh realities and suggest that pursuing a more positive attitude may gloss over or diminish the significance of important factors which must be dealt with. This is, of course, true. Hospitals perform real and serious work. However, negative outcomes can never be hidden forever, and will not be knowingly ignored or overlooked.[120] Our natural tendency as humans is to have a negativity bias which can lead us to be over focused on poorer outcomes. The result is that in many hospital environments, rather than ignoring negative occurrences that need attention, we overemphasise the unwanted mistakes and erode the confidence of colleagues who need support.

All facets of medical practice can be viewed more effectively in a trusting and connected team that has good relationships. Mistakes and negative outcomes are more openly investigated in an environment with good communication. Acquisition of skill is higher in teams where mistakes are reviewed, and learning is facilitated in a positive way rather than in teams where mistakes create shame and punitive behaviours. Breakdowns in teamwork lead to undesirable patient outcomes, and most commonly these failures result from inadequate communication.[121]

From an organisational point of view, a hospital that has overly negative communication styles, in addition to being a less happy place, will have greater absenteeism and disengagement, and find more difficulty in the recruitment of quality staff. As in relationships with higher rates of negative communication, emotional distancing and withdrawal leads to silence and lack of information sharing.

It appears obvious that effective communication is critical to high-functioning teams. This involves a positive and supportive framework where information is freely available and discussed, and questions are encouraged. This is even more critical in industries where mistakes can lead to physical risk or death.

Since the 1960s, the NASA (National Aeronautics and Space Administration) space exploration program has been viewed as one of the pinnacles of human endeavour, combining the best of human intelligence and ingenuity with cutting-edge technology and personal bravery. As well as appearing to be an admirable organisation, NASA has been an inspiring concept. However, in 2003 the NASA space program was changed irrevocably after the space shuttle Columbia broke up into pieces as it returned to earth, resulting in the deaths of all seven astronauts. The Columbia shuttle had previously flown 28 missions into space. The space shuttle program was suspended, and NASA undertook an extensive review into the disaster. The review's findings indicated that poor internal communication, fear of sharing information, and silence, were part of the disaster's causation.[122]

Despite the multi-billion-dollar budget, incredible knowledge, and mind-blowing technology, the program faltered due to breakdown in effective communication. This type of poor communication and silence, with the devastating effects it can wreak, has been extrapolated to the health industry.[123] Better communication and the support and kindness that we give each other not only binds us together in effective teams, it also affords increased safety for our patients.

Who knew? Communication *is* rocket science!

5.5 The Importance of 'Good Morning'

Some years ago, I was sharing consulting rooms with several colleagues. We all worked both in the private system and at the local public hospital. One of the doctors, let's call him Dr A, had his consulting room just next door to mine. Our paths would cross frequently if we were both consulting on a particular day. Dr A was a talented surgeon, but he could also be moody. The rest of us tolerated this and occasionally had a private chuckle about his moods.

At one stage, however, Dr A stopped communicating with me. As we both arrived in the morning, I would offer a hello or other greeting, and he would pass in silence. The first few times, I wondered whether he had heard me speak. Previously, he had been variable in his responses, sometimes offering words and occasionally only a grunt. After this silence continued, I realised that it was deliberate. I wondered whether I had upset him, or if something else in his life was troubling him. My practice was busy, and I wondered if there was an element of jealousy even though Dr A also seemed to have enough work.

Eventually, I stopped saying good morning also. We passed each other in silence. Our lives operated in parallel without any direct communication between us unless it was necessary for immediate patient care. It was awkward and unpleasant and clearly not the best situation as far as team functioning was concerned. I became aware of reports that Dr A was also grumpy in the hospital with juniors, nurses, and occasionally with patients. Looking back, it was interesting how many allowances were made by us all for this behaviour. Around this time, Dr A decided to leave our group practice and set up his own solo rooms down the road. This seemed to make him happier within the hospital for a while, and it certainly lifted the mood within my own rooms.

By this time, I had become the clinical director of the public hospital department and when, six months or so later, Dr A had made a series of major clinical decisions that were questionable the director of medical services (DMS) and I made an appointment to discuss the situation with Dr A. These clinical scenarios and treatments had been presented at a unit-wide meeting, and the discussion had led to a change in policy over these admittedly difficult situations. Dr A did not attend this departmental meeting, as had become his habit. The morning of our appointment, Dr A did not arrive and therefore the DMS and I went down to his rooms.

After presenting the data and asking for feedback, Dr A became agitated. We left after informing him of the new policy and protocols. A couple of months later, Dr A secured a position in another location and moved away. There was a palpable immediate improvement in the camaraderie and feel of the unit. His anger, unpredictable moods, and outbursts had led to fear in some staff and a tense atmosphere that did not allow the junior staff and nurses to perform their best work.

Since then, I have wondered many times whether the situation could have been handled differently. We worried about Dr A, and the possibility that he was struggling emotionally or even depressed. He had resisted all attempts to create a situation where we could find common ground and had distanced himself from opportunities to admit to weakness or problems. My feeling now is that rather than talking in general terms or 'dancing around the issue', I should have faced up to the difficult conversation earlier, and informed Dr A that his difficult behaviours were creating distress for others. I also think that I ought to have told him that the lack of a simple greeting in the morning felt disrespectful. I'm not sure whether this approach would have worked, however I think that a little more bravery, honesty, and even bluntness would have been better than allowing the situation to silently persist.

I have seen and heard of similar situations in other contexts. It may be that a brave conversation not only clears the air but also allows those such as Dr A to be able to communicate their feelings – something they may find difficult. Importantly, even if we are having the worst day ever, a simple greeting or hello to another lifts our own spirits and shows respect to the other team member. We can all choose to be the one who makes the first greeting.

One difficult person can change the way an entire workplace is experienced by all. Even for those not directly involved with the Dr As of the world, the feeling of tension is unpleasant. Greetings, common decency, and the use of names are simple gestures that make a difference to how we feel at work. These should be standards that are not negotiable. Indeed, they are measures that we ought to hold ourselves to. While we may sometimes believe that our moods and the way we communicate are solely our own business, they are not. Behaviour that should not occur becomes the business of all. One person's poor communication can affect the whole team and the environment.

5.6 The Stories We Tell

For most of human existence, history resided in the form of verbal records. Tales and information handed down in spoken rather than written words. For example, the Indigenous Peoples of Australia transferred and passed on their history and culture verbally from generation to generation for tens of thousands of years. The Dreaming, or dreamtime, was passed on by elders and allowed for a persisting understanding of the world and its creation. To transfer this information accurately required deep listening and sophisticated methods of discourse. Perhaps this aspect of human history and evolution, with verbal retention and handing-on of information, is why we instinctively find stories so powerful. We can connect to them in a personal, human sense.

In modern society and current day hospitals, we still like to find meaning in events that have occurred. We still take incomplete or vague information, and try to create understanding and context, or a story, around it. This can unwittingly lead to the circulation of incorrect information and unsettling or damaging rumours. Clearly, staff need to be informed about developments, and a unified and accurate understanding is important for morale.

Hospitals can attempt to facilitate organisation-wide information sharing and harmony through a 'sense-making' process whereby a leadership group will try to collectively interpret unexpected events or situations. The practice will involve exploring different perspectives of a situation to help all come to a shared view[124] which can then be disseminated. Sense-making not only helps with unified organisational understanding; it can also aid decision-making and facilitate system change. Increasingly, in a VUCA (Volatile, Uncertain, Complex, Ambiguous) world a process such as this holds many advantages.

In institutions, the sense-making process should not take the form of a modern-day business meeting. It can be set up with a different feel and aim. As well as investigating events, the process should explore the emotions that were provoked. When considering this style of practice, perhaps we can take note of ancient wisdom and create a type of Indigenous 'yarning circle'[125] where all participants are respected and have equal voice – a forum where all are deeply listened to.

One of the many problems with modern-day meetings is that the meeting does not represent a collaborative idea-sharing event, but rather an opportunity to dole out information without interpretation or discussion. In some meetings, the participants may not feel valued or safe enough to raise concerns, which indicates poor relationships and a lack of trust. Attendees can leave such meetings without a clear understanding of what occurred, but with a belief that their time was wasted. The tendency is for each to then unconsciously create their own story of what transpired. Often, these interpretations will result in stories that are unhelpful to the organisation such as, 'He is a power-grabbing so-and-so' or, 'This organisation does not care about wasting my time'. Ideally, any meeting should spend the latter part coming to a shared agreement and understanding of the content discussed. Otherwise, different viewpoints can become damaging reports or rumours.

American systems scientist Peter Senge discusses how organisational culture can be hostile to new concepts unless there is a safe environment or 'container' to speak about them in.[126] This container can be a room that is visualised as a transformative vessel that allows space for the creation of new ideas. It protects the emerging tender thoughts until they are more developed. As Senge acknowledges, established systems are naturally hostile to new ideas. Therefore, creation of new concepts and new styles of practice must be protected and sheltered until mature.

Within hospitals, we can create this container – possibly a specific meeting room where listening, respect, and trust are spoken about and are valued practices. And within this room a new meeting style can arise that allows discussion about the creation of an improved reality. In these meetings, innovative concepts can be safely discussed, planned, and allowed to flourish. An environment where there are no 'stupid' ideas or questions. A place where a new culture can arise and be protected until it has strong enough roots to be able to withstand attack. This place would allow safety for sharing information and planning alternative approaches. A place to create a new and exciting story.

5.7 Appreciating Other Songs

At Australian football matches, the end of the game is typically marked by the winning team's theme song being broadcast over the sound system and enthusiastically sung by supporters of that club as they rejoice in the success. It is a great tradition. However, at some point, years ago, I realised that I had changed. Now, instead of singing my own team's song in victory and staying grumpily silent in defeat, I happily sing the song of whichever team wins, even if it isn't the team I support. I enjoy the words of each song and the act of celebrating the game. It isn't that I don't care if my team wins or not. I still strongly support my own club; it's that I have realised that the game is more important to me than any individual club. Without other clubs to play against, there would be no competition. And if my team won every single game, there would be no suspense, and no resultant joy accompanying the victory. In that sense, all supporters must appreciate all clubs, and to some degree, support the other clubs also.

Within organisations, including hospitals, oftentimes there will be meetings where all attendees seem only concerned about self-interest. At these times, the saying, 'The squeaky wheel gets the oil' comes into play. It commonly appears that the loudest, most obnoxious opinions seem to be rewarded with greater resources than others who have a more dignified approach. As the leader of my department, I wondered whether I was remiss if I didn't whinge and create havoc to best serve the interests of my own unit. These were not behavioural styles that I wished to adopt, and I realised that the loudest leaders often had poorly functioning teams. It became apparent to me that these leaders were more transactional in their outlook than transformational. This was the reason their teams didn't gel. Unfortunately, with the lack of humility shown, it appeared that they would never be able to become outstanding leaders.[127] However, these voices were not only disruptive, but also too often rewarded.

It seems that the only way this too-frequent scenario does not play out is when the chairperson can recognise that allowing over-whelming self-interest is not in the best interests of the meeting or the organisation. Even better if the concept of 'no pitch' meetings are encouraged. Within this framework, participants in the meeting cannot push their own agendas, and all attendees are trying to work together for the betterment of the organisation as a whole. The 'no-pitch' concept can remove much bickering and jockeying for resources. This style of meeting removes the self-interest that often comes at the expense of the overall good.

Without all departments flourishing, the hospital or institution does not achieve the same level of success, irrespective of where the resources are allocated. There are times when it is acceptable to push one's own department's agenda, but more often the right course of action is to consider others and the needs of the whole.

Sometimes the right thing to do is to sing the other team's song.

5.8 Practise to Become Lucky

In the late 1970s and 1980s, an Australian footballer named Peter Daicos played for Collingwood. Daicos had an uncanny ability to thread goals from impossible positions and to cause the football to bounce at surprising angles to go through the goals.[128] He did it week after week, repeatedly performing feats impossible for any other player. When asked about his luck, he replied, "It's funny, the more I practise, the luckier I get".

Hospitals that have outstanding communication styles are not just lucky. The 'luck' has come from every single conversation, interaction, 'good morning', or greeting.[129] It results from years of meetings where all participants were listened to. The luck has been generated by every positive comment, and it is strengthened by every occasion when strongly held attitudes can be shed and all present in a conversation can remain curious. With time, these small occurrences have created a communication style that now appears effortless and is adopted by new members to become self-perpetuating. It isn't luck; it's practice.

{be·com·ing}

THE PROCESS OF CREATING TEAMS FROM GROUPS OF INDI-
viduals can seem mysterious. The path to becoming a unified group,
or a team, is not clear. What are the steps and the ingredients? Does
the process need to be planned, or is it best to hope it will happen on
its own without conscious attention? If the transition to becoming a
team is possible, when will it occur?

Perhaps the first task is to understand what a team actually is. It
isn't just a group of people arbitrarily put together. It's about individuals with different abilities, roles, and tasks who are all jointly committed to a common goal or mission. The team will have shared emotion
and purpose rather than individual motivations and aims. It requires
the group's desired outcomes to be melded with, or even identical to,
those of each individual. More than that, the team needs to provide a
well of affection and acceptance that members can add to and draw
from, all while understanding that others 'have their back'.

It could be considered that a group cannot become a team without
there being a joint purpose or goal. There must also be a co-existent
system of operation between the members that defines interpersonal
interactions as well as strategic planning. Finally, it is essential to
have a positive emotional commitment of all members toward everyone in the team.

It is often hard to identify the exact point at which the group coalesces to become a team. However, when it happens, it leads to a joint understanding that both integrates and empowers the team members and creates a unity in which the team can accomplish extraordinary goals.

In the current healthcare crisis, formulation of higher functioning teams is an essential part of the solution. The importance of teams cannot be overstated. Good teams improve patient care and organisational outcomes, and – most critically – provide essential individual support for clinicians.

6.1 Teams and Systems

Life was tough for our ancestors during the last ice age. Humans had to forage more widely for limited seasonal plant-foods, and smaller game became sparse. With reduced sources of nutrition but higher caloric demands due to the cold, humans began to hunt larger animals. Woolly mammoths, the ancient precursors of modern elephants, were large animals that had potential to provide lots of food. However, the mammoths had evolved to cope with the freezing conditions and had the protection of their enormous size, travelling in herds, and being armed with dangerous tusks.[130]

Any individual trying to kill a mammoth with a makeshift spear undertook significant risk of death. Close proximity was required to throw the spear with enough force to pierce the animal's hide. Even then, a single spear would be unlikely to bring down a mammoth. Better results were obtained when a large group of hunters banded together in an attempt to slay a mammoth.

It is difficult to know the exact hunting techniques used, however, the preponderance of bones and pieces of weapons at certain sites have led to theories[131] that herds of mammoths were stampeded over a bluff, or that the hunting groups developed a plan of separating one animal from the herd with spears and torches, forcing the animal to move along a certain route with a hidden deep pit into which the mammoth would plunge and be trapped, injured, and able to be killed. The mammoth's size guaranteed ongoing sustenance and survival for some time.

This hunting party could be considered the first human team. The tactics, communication, collaboration, and execution were the system that facilitated the success of the team.

Similarly, the greatest invention of the past 50 years is neither a product nor an entity, it is a system. This system – the internet – is an enormous network of interconnected computers that produces unfathomable power. It is a system that facilitates learning, collaboration, information sharing, and creativity. We each use it multiple times a day.

One hunter cannot kill a mammoth, and an isolated PC cannot contain all the world's information. However, with connection, interaction, and cooperation, functional teams with great systems can achieve large and impressive goals.

6.2 Starting to Build

A recent Harvard Business Review article entitled, 'Do We Still Need Teams?'[132] argued that teams were a thing of the past, and that teams should be rebranded, or renamed, as 'co-acting groups' – described as a loose confederation of employees who dip in and out of collaborative projects.

Some of the reasoning behind the piece is clear, particularly for businesses with altered physical working arrangements after COVID. However, this assertion appears poorly supported by research and seems to be a retrograde step. If these suggestions gained support, they could create risk within the healthcare setting.

Much of what is currently wrong with hospital culture relates to an underlying lack of relatedness and personal connection.[133] Of course, no one plans for this. However, over time, with less interpersonal interaction, poorer relationships, and larger work demands, people find themselves working in siloed and isolated environments.[134] They begin to only concentrate on their own immediate duties. There is less collaboration and a diminishing sense of team support. These factors are largely invisible and develop slowly, however they can grow to be implicated in behavioural problems in the organisation, such as petty bickering and detachment. Disengagement, arguments, lacking unity – no one would want to describe their favourite sports team in these terms. And yet medical teams play for higher stakes.

Humans are social creatures with an innate desire to form connections and create groups.[135] This drive that originally gave survival benefits persists. People usually function better when they are with others. Unfortunately, even with increased 'connectivity' in the technologically rich present, there can be increased isolation and loneliness. Without authentic human interaction, our basic psychological needs are not being met. This can contribute to widespread unhappiness, anxiety, and depression[136] in our workplaces.

It is a sad fact that many people feel lonely at work, including in large organisations.[137] Even in hospitals, where one may assume that a shared purpose would unite people, many feel disconnected and alone. For doctors, the competitive climate that medical culture occasionally promotes can also contribute to loneliness becoming more prevalent.[138]

Even in a group who don't believe that they can come together to form a team, having people who are lonely or isolated is undesirable. It is a failure of the group members and the leaders. This situation not only has detrimental effects on the isolated individual it also diminishes group output. In healthcare, having fractured groups who purport to be a team is unacceptable as the flow-on effects impact upon the patients.

It seems unnecessary to question whether high-quality teams improve patient outcomes in hospitals. Of course, our instinctive response is that we all believe in the value of teamwork in improving patient care. Fortunately, our intuition is also supported by evidence.[139] The multiple positive outcomes of successful healthcare teams include improved patient outcomes, organisational benefits such as reduced costs, and increased life satisfaction for individual team-members.[140] Thus, we have both the human instinct to come together into groups, and evidence that high-quality teams achieve better results. Perhaps consideration of how to build better teams is a more appropriate suggestion than calls to abandon them.

6.3 How Do We Create a Team?

Some teams appear to come together effortlessly, while other groups cannot seem to coalesce even with major interventions devoted to the task. The process of forming functional teams can be one of the hardest tasks within an organisation.

Becoming a successful team happens more easily when members establish good communication patterns and acknowledge the qualities and abilities of colleagues. At that point, a common purpose seems achievable. But, although it sounds very straightforward, the unfortunate reality is that teams that are both happy and successful are uncommon. This is not due to mutual exclusivity of these two markers, but because excellent teams are rare. Therefore, outstanding teams must be cherished and further examined for clues around what it was that allowed the group to coalesce.

Perhaps, rather than a hospital team, we should consider what is required in the formation of a successful sporting team. Within sports, success is more easily defined, and the necessary ingredients appear more visible. Sports teams rarely achieve success without unified commitment to a team goal and positive regard for all team-mates. Overly individualistic self-focus, or a dominant ego, weakens the team ethos.

Medical groups can be a little like high-level professional sports teams. Most of the individuals are talented operators with great skill and self-belief. Each group of doctors will belong to a team or unit that has joint responsibility for many patients. Within this structure, however, are also many instances of individual decisions or actions that a particular doctor can take. These outcomes, for instance with surgical procedures, can also be easily tabulated and analysed, as can the overall departmental data.

Cricket seems to be the sport that most closely parallels special-ist medical teams within hospitals. As previously alluded to, while a cricket team consists of 11 team-mates, in some people's eyes the team is actually a group of 11 individuals. Players are judged on their individual achievements (such as runs scored), and the team's total score is cumulative of each player's individual tally, rather than coming from joint team achievements. Indeed, each delivery bowled is essentially a one-on-one contest. Within the construct of the sport of cricket, individual statistics are highly scrutinised.

However, many of the greatest bowlers of all time, the highest wicket-takers, largely operated in tandem with a particular bowler from the other end. This other bowler was not as successful in terms of wickets taken but played a different role. This 'less-successful' bowler kept pressure on the batsmen through tight reliable bowling which restricted run-scoring. The build-up of pressure from slow scoring often led the batsmen to take more chances against the star bowler and resulted in them losing their wicket. In this instance, who deserves the glory? The wicket-taker? Or the bowling partnership? Or perhaps the fielders who saved runs, also generating pressure? Tight fielding, saving runs, and taking catches all add to team success.

Within a hospital, who deserves recognition? Should it be the surgeon performing an operation? Attention could also be directed to the role played by the anaesthetist maintaining the patient's oxygenation and life support while anaesthetised, or the theatre nurses handing the appropriate instruments at exactly the right moment. There is also the critical role of the GP who first diagnosed the problem, and the dietician optimising the patient's nutrition status to facilitate healing. Clearly this list goes on. There is obviously a large group of people, constituting a complex system, involved in every episode of care for each patient. The overarching goal of the organisation is for the patient to be cured, to heal, and to recover. The system by which patients receive care requires the input of many individuals with different complementary skills. What is the term that we use to refer to this system? Most would call it a team. Just as with sports, medical team success is dependent on many factors and many people, not just one. If any of the roles are not performed well, the outcome is less successful.

Returning to the cricket analogy, what if the team is not united but still has several established world-class performers? Recognised champions or stars who make the newcomers 'earn their stripes' before begrudgingly accepting and integrating them into the team. In this scenario, an inexperienced player who does not feel valued will be more nervous, and therefore will most likely not perform at the peak of their abilities, perhaps leading to a dropped catch. However, in a team where a young player is immediately accepted as a full member upon selection, with their qualities recognised, the debutante will feel more relaxed and possibly able to stretch a little more, enabling a difficult catch to be taken. Another wicket for the star bowler, and the resultant outcome of team success.

A saying often heard in youth sports is, 'There is no 'I' in team', which implies that one's own agenda and desire for personal recognition should be set aside and the team goals be considered paramount. While this may be true in team sports, is it so in medicine? If we consider medical teams in a similar light as a cricket team, perhaps the most venerated surgeons, for example, would be the 'high-flyers'. Within this environment, like cricket, if the whole team is not performing optimally and smaller steps are missed, it impacts team success. And then the most vaunted performers will be at risk of poorer outcomes for their patients. Unfortunately, within medicine, there can be an external sense that self-interest is causing individuals to compete against other members of their own team. This reduces success for both the individuals concerned and for the collective.

Perhaps a better saying that allows for individual goals and striving for personal excellence while still recognising the need for tight and supportive team bonds and an overarching desire for group achievement is:[141]

> *"The strength of the wolf is the pack,*
> *and the strength of the pack is the wolf."*

6.4 New Members

Previously, when recruiting new team members, I always thought it was wise to keep the words of famous explorer Ranulph Fiennes[142] foremost in one's mind:

> *"Whenever feasible, pick your team on*
> *character, not skill. You can teach skills;*
> *you can't teach character."*

These words felt as though they resonated with truth. If I ignored my initial negative gut feelings about an applicant, and approved their employment, I usually regretted the outcome. The instinctive rapid thinking that created wariness about a potential employee usually proved correct. Perhaps this is because consideration of qualities such as character, or personality, are hard to consider with rational thought. These judgements are usually more of an emotional, subjective type of assessment. Decisions of this nature may be best thought of in that way, rather than as cognitive, slower processes such as consideration of an applicant's academic merit or the quality of a resume.[143]

The pronouncement of Fiennes still seems to carry merit even when considering senior appointments. The 'essence' of the person who is employed, whether framed as character or in some other terms, will dictate how well they integrate and communicate with the team. It may be the deciding factor as to whether the person becomes a trusted and valuable member of a cohesive group or someone who just works in the department without enhancing the spirit of the organisation. This person may become the new appointee who, disappointingly, fails to meld into the team and instead becomes one of a loose association of employees. One of the members of the aforementioned 'co-acting group'.

However, with junior members or appointments, I now believe that Fiennes' view is not strictly accurate, and that a different approach may be more appropriate. It appears to me now that character can be taught or, perhaps more accurately, unearthed and allowed to flourish. In a culture where new team members feel valued with a sense of belonging, they will lean into the underlying expectations and support. In this way, they will adopt the behaviours and communication styles of the existing culture. This will allow the new appointee to perform with all of their training and skills.

Most of the ways that people behave are dependent on the prevailing environment. New appointees will usually adopt the language and communication styles of the organisation and group that they join. Most of this process is unconscious, again revealing the importance of leadership style and the dominant culture. This adoption of attitudes and behaviours starts even before the member begins employment. It starts at the initial interview. While the candidate is being assessed, they are also observing and developing an unconscious understanding of how the organisation functions.

During the induction process, the values the organisation espouses will be communicated to the new member. These lessons will be absorbed through both what is said and what the newcomer observes. In an organisation with poor induction processes, where the newcomer is not 'made to feel at home' the lesson learned is that respect has to be earned with time, isolation is acceptable, and poor communication is the norm. However, in a great team, the two factors of what is said and what is done will reflect similar values. The manner and tone of speech, the words, and the actions, all marry up and demonstrate both the culture and character of the team, and our own strengths. New members absorb these lessons and examples.

In the words of Aristotle:[144]

> *"We do not act rightly because we have virtue or excellence, rather we have these because we have acted rightly. We are what we repeatedly do. Excellence, then, is not an act but a habit."*

6.5 Strengthening Bonds

The importance of leadership feedback cannot be overestimated. Kindness, balance, support, and wisdom are essential qualities that a team needs from its leaders; without them, a group will not excel. The leader must recognise and appreciate what each team member brings to the group, and ideally this is spoken about and disseminated publicly. 'Praise in public, challenge in private' is a useful phrase to keep in mind. However, of equal importance in generating a highly cohesive group is enabling the team members to appreciate each other.

At the end of 2021, as the Covid-19 lockdowns and restrictions were easing in Australia, it became clear that our obstetric department team could meet in person as a group for our usual December celebration. These dinner meetings were always eagerly anticipated, however, this year, I hadn't had time, or indeed inclination, to arrange any presentations. In fact, the very thought of arranging another meeting left me with an overwhelming sense of exhaustion. I asked the group whether we should go ahead with the event, secretly hoping that they would decline. However, there was great enthusiasm to meet and have dinner and the usual fun night, so I booked our regular venue.

When the date rapidly arrived, with growing trepidation, I had come up with only one activity. This would be an activity that was unfamiliar to most of us, including myself. My sense was that it would either be a roaring success or a complete disaster. After the usual end of year comments, I stood in front of the group of around 50 doctors and senior midwives holding a container full of individually wrapped chocolates.

"In this bucket, I have three Lindt Chocolate Balls for each person" I began, "The first is for yourself. This is to recognise all the hard work that each of us has done, and the resilience that we have shown after a tough couple of years. So, the first chocolate for each person is to honour themselves" – I paused and then continued, "The other chocolates are to give to two other members of our team. These are for special efforts that you have noticed, to express thanks, to acknowledge hard work, or to publicly appreciate someone who has gone above the usual excellent standards to do something amazing. The only proviso is that we each come to the front and present our chocolates, telling everyone what the recipient has done that is special."

I presented my own two gift chocolates, one to a junior doctor who had been struggling with the pressures of work but had lifted her effort. With persistence and dedication, she had become a reliable and valued member of the team. The other I presented to an extraordinary senior midwife who was a wonderful leader. She combined efficiency and compassion to both staff and patients in an admirable mix. I stepped back.

There were some moments of quiet. I sensed a reticence to be the first to participate in the process. Finally, just as the silence was becoming uncomfortable, a doctor rose and came to the front. Taking chocolates from the bucket, she presented thanks and chocolate to two others in the group. Soon after, the enthusiasm for the activity became infectious. Some wanted to present a second round of chocolates. Eventually, every member of the team had risen, one by one, and thanked, recognised, appreciated, and honoured, others in our team.

There were affirmations given that night which were heartwarming. There were comments and anecdotes that I had not heard before, and perspectives I hadn't considered. In the end, all of us seemed to be aware of how fortunate we were to belong to the group. We felt joint pride, mutual respect, and gratitude. With the team's ability to be brave and open on that night, many bonds were strengthened.

6.6 Communicating Expectations

Within my department, we had always employed fewer registrars than many similar sized units. This was deliberate, with the intention being that our registrars would have busy surgical loads, with an ability to learn and perfect skills. Our desire was to provide excellent training to a few, rather than less satisfactory training to many. The flip side of this strategy, however, was that the consultants were busier, awake and working at night more often than if we had a larger number of junior staff. With fewer registrars, the consultants and registrars developed a close working relationship. We got to know each other very well. Through the course of a training year in our department, the registrars progressed from being our juniors to becoming our respected colleagues and friends. Many ex-registrars returned to work as consultants in our unit later in their careers.

Our style with juniors was intentionally supportive and relaxed, rather than overbearing and directive. This way of interacting seemed to be appreciated; our registrars respected the way they were treated and enjoyed the structure of the jobs. They absorbed our style and remarked on the friendly interaction between members of the senior team. Universally, our registrars were thankful for the opportunities they were provided with.

Then, one year, things changed. Our happy equilibrium was disturbed with the arrival of a registrar who complained throughout the year about almost everything. Everything their predecessors had enjoyed, this registrar appeared to experience as a source of discontent. For cases in which we, the consultants, thought supervision and support were required, we were judged to be over-cautious. When we tried to give autonomy in decisions, we were accused of being laissez-faire. Where we felt that we had been relaxed and friendly, the feedback was that we were not formal enough. There were similar complaints about the organisation, pay office, and the like.

The senior team found this situation distressing and confusing. The job that we had crafted – a sought-after position – did not seem to be valued. Many discussions took place between the consultant group to discuss the issue, and many meetings were held with the registrar in question. We became aware that in previous hospitals, and in other positions, similar problems had surfaced for this registrar.

At the end of the year, we had two choices. We could decide that this was a one-off problem, and that the discord most likely lay with the personality of the individual concerned and our inability to find common ground. This appeared to be the obvious response. However, we decided that we would try to learn from what had transpired and attempt to use the learnings to improve how we did things. We carefully examined all the information obtained from the registrar's exit feedback. There were many criticisms that we didn't think were accurate, but we tried to look at even the most outlandish of these, asking, "We don't think this is true, but what could it be true of?".

One lesson that we drew was that where we had been letting registrars settle in and slowly absorb and understand our culture, some misunderstandings had arisen. Our style was to allow the registrars to observe the behaviours and relationships within the department and come to understand the department organically, rather than being directed about how to view our unit. The method that had served us well had let us down in this case. This realisation led us to expand our induction interviews and more traditionally inform the registrars of expectations and protocols. We did not want any further situations where there was confusion over the job structure and how we saw it best performed.

There were fears that with this more formal approach we would lose the 'feel' of the job that had developed over many years, which involved a supportive and nourishing learning environment. We worried that we would become too directive and dictatorial, rather than allowing some personal crafting of the role by each registrar. We also wanted the values that we held dear to continue to be considered and respected by our new registrars. With this in mind, we developed a 'Reflection Tool' that we asked our registrars to fill out at the beginning of their term with us. We used this tool as a further part of our 'on-boarding' procedure.

Within the document, we had 12 areas that we thought were important to be a competent and compassionate doctor within our specialty and our hospital. The individual strengths ranged from surgical and obstetric skills through to categories such as interaction with peers, interaction with juniors, and integration with the wider community. There were descriptive notes around each characteristic, for example, the descriptor for the characteristic of 'Relationships with peers' states, "Maintaining collegiality and demonstrating generosity in sharing opportunities for training and learning". The 'Emotional resilience' characteristic is further described as, "Ability to process challenging events and environments, including adverse clinical outcomes and communication challenges, without impacting ability to continue daily activities".

Instead of rating or scoring oneself on an independent scale for each area, as is done in some other self-assessment tools, we designed our document such that the registrars would number each area from 1 to 12, with 1 being the area that they felt that they were strongest in currently. With this framework, every area was numbered. There had to be a 1, and there had to be every other number up to 12. This structure meant that there was no right answer. Indeed, this is the reality of each of our lives as we all have strengths in all these areas, but some may be more developed or evident at any one time.

The Reflection Tool allowed thinking to occur about many aspects of clinical medicine that our team felt were important. We followed up the registrar's completion of the document with discussion and contemplation about the results with a member of the senior team. The Reflection Tool was repeated at the end of the term for each registrar and often the results changed markedly.

For our unit, spending time thinking non-defensively about negative feedback led to profound change and improvement. The difficult and confronting exercise of challenging ourselves was ultimately beneficial. Perhaps unsurprisingly, with the greater communication at the start of the term, we did not have any further dissent or behavioural issues with future registrars. The Reflection Tool allowed a further and separate style of communication, fostering generative discussions and legitimising dialogue about vulnerability and other sensitive areas. Using this tool, we could further inform juniors on the factors that we saw as important, and the ongoing need that each of us has for self-evaluation and reflection was met. Production of the Reflection Tool required an honest appraisal of ourselves. It forced us to define what we saw as essential qualities and enabled us to recognise that all feedback has value.

6.7 Creating Unity

From the outside, any group that operates under a joint banner or collaborates within the same structure could be viewed as a team. However, those on the outside have no knowledge of the relationships between the individual members. Without tight bonds, including positive regard or affection, a group isn't a team; it's just a collection of people placed together. There is no unity and no common purpose.

Depending on the size of a particular organisation, there may be only one team, or there may be many sub-groups or teams that make up the whole organisation. Each of these smaller teams will have their own unique identity.

Earlier, we considered a Harvard Business Review article[145] that suggested organisations should be embracing loose affiliations of individuals rather than aspiring to develop true teams. Again, I believe that this attitude is misguided. Particularly in health, the opposite is needed[146,147] and must be worked towards. Instead of 'loose affiliations', we need more groups that support, trust, respect, and are friendly to each other. True teams. Groups whose members feel allegiance to team-mates and commit to joint goals rather than individual success. The group members will know if that is how their team operates and feels. Those 'inside the tent' will recognise whether there is an authentic sense of 'we' and 'us'.

Most organisations and groups of a certain size will proudly point to a mission statement – a set of words describing grand and virtuous visions and aspirations. However, within the group these statements may be regarded as lip-service only and may breed cynicism when the written goals are compared to a different reality. The mission statement can be an extremely powerful emblem if it describes lived values and actions, but it can also become a screen to hide behind. If the statement describes an ideal that is never lived up to, it feels empty and meaningless.

The specific words chosen for a mission statement will never generate organisational pride or create higher functioning teams. However, a truly believed mission and a joint purpose can help to elevate all. The desired future may begin with a credo of beliefs and goals but, more importantly, must also be reflected in actions with visible evidence of the organisation's values.

Pride is defined as a deep satisfaction in one's own achievements, or the achievements of those with whom one is associated. To foster genuine organisational pride, both these factors of individual and group pride are required. Individual members must feel pride in their own efforts and results, aiming to achieve personal excellence. They also must be able to experience delight with the achievements and work of others within the group. Without being able to rejoice in the success of others and the overall group, the members are simply a collection of competitive individuals who just happen to be situated under the same banner.

To develop a high-quality team, all members must 'buy in' to a shared ethos and have a belief that all the other members also feel the same ownership and joint purpose. Everyone must have the same sense of belonging and understand that their fellow members also want to belong and operate under the same codes.

When teams gel, the result can be inspiring. In some groups, there is a point where things suddenly become somewhat magical. In my opinion, this is not an inappropriate use of this word. 'Magic' describes both the moment and the feeling. It's the point in time where all members have committed to joint values, are supporting each other and the wider construct of the group, and there is a shared sense of togetherness. It is impossible to understand how and when it will happen, or if it's even possible for this to occur in any particular group but, when it does materialise, it feels like magic. Stirring, powerful, and not fully understood. It is the time that the group members coalesce and become a team. And it is also the moment when there is a joint realisation of this coming together. When everyone 'gets' it.

The wonderful feeling at the recognition of team unity is instant and uplifting. It's the point where the wheels of the aeroplane lift off the runway. Enough impetus has been generated to allow ascendance. Instead of a group of individuals in the aeroplane travelling down the tarmac, they are now a team that has elevated. Together, they are flying.

6.8 Creating an Identity

At the point that the group becomes airborne, they form a united collective. Thoughts and emotions have changed from solely being focused on what is good for the individual, to revolving around what benefits the whole, and what is good for team dynamics.

Once lift-off has occurred, it can be useful to have a new and unique language referring to the team and the shared mission. Some choose a new term or nickname that applies to the team, either used only within the group or sometimes also communicated to the wider world. New language, or new names, can indicate that a brand-new entity has formed, as though arising from what has come before. This new language can help foster belonging and pride.

This creation of a 'new' entity, or a new way of being, was performed very effectively in the Australian Football League in the late 2000s. Ross Lyon was the coach of St Kilda,[148] a team often referred to as the Saints. Within press conferences, as with many good leaders, Lyon would refer to his team as 'we' or 'us'. However, at one point, he changed his language and began describing his team in the third person. He, and subsequently other team members, began referring to the group as "Saints-Footy". For example, Lyon might say, "That performance is not what we would expect of Saints-Footy" or, "That's the way Saints-Footy wants to play defence".

This way of speaking about the team seemed to create an identity that encompassed the competitive aspect of the sport as well as other non-football factors. This entity involved an emerging culture, upstanding values, behavioural expectations, and principles. The term seemed to encircle and include the players and coaches as well as the club officials and helpers. The emergence of 'Saints-Footy' gave a feeling of an organisation that all those involved in were proud of. Perhaps this way of communication was unintentional, but the punchy moniker combining the usual nickname of the team with the activity, seemed to imbue the organisation with a fresh image of vitality, self-respect, and oneness. It implied a tight group with a unified vision. It was a credo that felt like a lived and believed mission. Unsurprisingly, this coincided with a time of great success for St Kilda.

6.9 Adhering to the Vision

Creating a joint team structure with shared values and codes of behaviour is very powerful. When the team is flying, new horizons and possibilities can be seen and aimed at. However, if the collective vision ever wanes or is breached, it becomes easier to lose momentum and bring the team down. The behaviours and standards must be continually upheld by all the members, otherwise the espoused statements will feel inauthentic. Disparity in team behaviour and attitudes will pull on the organisation like gravity.

A recent example, also from the AFL, illustrates this. One of the star players for the Collingwood Football Club has had several off-field incidents both in Australia and overseas that have involved drunkenness, aggression, and other troubling behaviours.[149] The reports of these incidents have described behaviours that transgressed the professed and desired culture of his team. The player's brilliance on the field had perhaps allowed leeway in the sanctions imposed by Collingwood. However, with repeated misdemeanours, the club was unable to turn a blind eye. To do so would devalue and undermine the commitment to established shared values from all other team members. It would suggest that there was disparity between the espoused values and the reality. To overlook repeated poor behaviour creates discord and weakens team spirit and culture.

The player involved was not alone as a young man who became involved in poor behaviours, however, this difficult situation could be compared with and considered through the lens of a group of doctors in a hospital. While the behaviours of the doctors will, most likely, not be so extreme, how should the organisation respond to the individual who flouts team and organisational rules? Even within professional organisations such as hospitals, poor behaviours can sometimes be overlooked in those who have outstanding technical ability. Some individuals get away with incidents that may be dealt with more harshly if exhibited by a less talented person.

The behaviour, whether positive or negative, of all team members influences team identity. An organisation that does not encourage and demand the best will get what they settle for. At this point, the functioning of the team will deteriorate, and members will begin acting in an individualistic manner. The team will essentially dissolve to the loose collaboration of co-acting agents with each following their own idea of what is acceptable.

However, with this difficult situation comes opportunity. The way the group leadership deals with the transgressing individual is critical. Teams that honestly, courageously, and promptly display a firm manner that listens and attempts to understand without softening the non-negotiable expectations and standards can further embed a culture of success. With this action, the team recognises that the grand mission statement is more than just words, it is a document of lived values.

Those who have been in a team that takes off and flies know the joy that is provoked. A shared sense of pride in what the group has achieved and the team that the group has transformed into. There is now a sense of unity, from where great results can ensue. Once that point has been attained, the team principles cannot be allowed to weaken. They must be even more vigorously cherished and protected. Not many teams take off, and once a team achieves elevation it can make inspiring journeys.

6.10 The Path to Becoming a Team

The premier health services that deliver outstanding results to patients and their communities draw on the best practices in medicine and also pay attention to excellence in human relations and organisational systems. The top hospitals in terms of patient outcomes are usually also those that optimise staff conditions and well-being.[150,151] Part of this results from providing stable, friendly environments that people enjoy being in. Most of us want good relationships and to belong to an inspiring organisation.

In recent times, our societies have become more individualistic and increasingly driven by materialistic goals and attitudes of self-interest.[152] Concurrently, many modern hospitals and clinical departments in resource-rich countries have inadvertently allowed the importance of team building to slip. As group dynamics have eroded, problematic behaviours are increasingly recognised. For the good of all, it is time to give more thought to building stronger teams.

Everyone is familiar with the pleasure of being with a group of friends; people who respect and like each other. These are individuals who enjoy each other's company and gather with mutual regard and appreciation of their friends' personalities, experiences, and skills. The positive emotions generated produce inclusion and togetherness, and the bonds become closer and stronger. These groups also provide compassion and support to each other if one of the group members is struggling.

A group of friends is one version of the ideal team: a collection of committed, talented, supportive members. Adding a group purpose overlaid on the individual roles can deepen relationships and connection. Groups can and should be friendly coalitions that meet with support, respect, and humour. They can cooperate and support each other to achieve higher aims. The challenges of difficult work situations will seem more easily navigated in collegiate teams. We must change the question from, "Is this good for me?" to, "Is this good for the team?".

{be·long·ing}

BELONGING APPEARS TO BE A SIMPLE CONCEPT; WE USE THE term without much thought. Upon further examination, it becomes more complicated. What does it mean to belong? Belonging seems to convey an emotional as well as cognitive understanding of a relationship. It is more than just wearing the same uniform or being in the same location. Belonging implies feelings of being valued and respected, and a joint acknowledgment by others that one is an accepted member of the group. This carries an understanding of reciprocal relationships. However, these subjective external connections are open to contemplation. Is belonging an all-or-nothing phenomenon, or are there degrees of belonging? What is the scale? Does a more valued person belong in a group more than a less respected one?

This sense of belonging involves both internal and external assessments of interpersonal relationships. What of belonging to a place or a country? Is this just an inner belief or does it also relate to intrinsic respect for a geographical area – and is a reciprocal relationship required? Does the place need to value you also, in some sense?

In whatever way we describe it, belonging is an important part of human well-being; belonging not only to places but also to constructs such as groups, teams, and alliances. We all have an innate need to belong[153] that has arisen through evolution, with those who belonged to groups or tribes having increased survival and improved reproductive capability.[154] Belonging gave safety and access to resources, allowed communication and connection, and facilitated positive emotions and creativity. Belonging promotes collective unity and group success. In any team, group, or institution that wants to function at the highest level, a shared sense of belonging is required. This applies to healthcare in Australia today.

Belonging is still essential to us today;[155] it enhances our psychological and physical health. However, in increasingly individualistic, isolated, lonely societies and institutions, the experience of belonging is less often experienced.[156,157] The importance of creating a feeling of belonging to our teams and within our organisations has been underappreciated. Similarly, we all need to feel that our organisations have connection to society – we all, intrinsically, want to be good 'global citizens'.

As children, we often hear that it is the simple things in life that are the most important. Perhaps belonging is the most complex simple thing there is.

7.1 Belonging to People

After completing high school and being accepted into medicine at the University of Melbourne, I attended the registration day with a sense of excitement. I felt that I was about to begin an interesting and fabulous path. I was looking forward to making friends and meeting companions for this journey. But as I stood in line to register and met several people who would become my fellow students for the next six years, the only things that seemed to be of interest to others was where we had gone to school and what score we had achieved in our year-12 exams. Within the group, internally, we were already being ranked and judged.

Over the next couple of weeks, I realised that I felt little common ground with my cohort. I didn't think I belonged in this world, and I certainly wasn't part of the tribe. Almost everyone else had attended expensive private schools or select-entry high schools that were almost as well resourced. No one lived in the same outskirts of Melbourne that I did, and none of my peers took the same train line out to the northern suburbs. Later, as I came to understand the wealth and privilege of the schools that so many of my fellow medical students had attended, I felt envy. How I would have loved to have played football or cricket on their manicured green playing fields. How I would have loved to have sat in their auditoriums or swam in their indoor swimming pools. I had attended my local high school, where I had been happy, not really understanding that this different world existed.

Before I attended university, I had known that my family weren't rich. But now I came to understand that we were actually poor. At that time in Australia, attending university was free. That was a fortunate event of timing; otherwise, I wouldn't have been able to attend. Most people leaving my school went out and sought work rather than pursuing tertiary education.

My university years were not particularly happy ones for me. It seemed to me that I didn't belong and shouldn't be there. I felt that I was a fraud and I made limited connections. The level of uncertainty that I felt could become disabling. Around the same time, I suffered a bad injury and ceased playing football. I let my relationships with my team-mates slip. On the weekends, I tried to keep my school friendships strong and reconnect with my old mates. Unfortunately, this led to too much drinking, which weakened my studies, and further made me feel like an imposter. When I went to university and compared myself to the rich kids, I felt ashamed of where I lived, the clothes I wore, even the style of my haircut. To this day, the chip on my shoulder from long ago can cause me to feel anger when doctors show greed or entitlement.

But of course, it wasn't the other students' problem, it was mine. I just couldn't find a way to establish common ground and to connect. I had a belief that I wouldn't make friends, so I didn't. And my misplaced pride and self-righteousness wouldn't allow me to let anyone know I was struggling. Everyone else in my course knew they belonged, or at least it seemed that way to me. I realise now that probably wasn't the truth. It's possible that many of us were isolated and struggling, feeling alone and without a sense of belonging, but we all pretended otherwise.

Throughout university, I had to work on weekends to be able to survive financially, even though I was still living at home with my parents. I had a variety of jobs, but the main one was working as a nursing aide at a residential nursing home. That meant I got all the messy jobs. I cleaned up doubly incontinent residents, showered people, dressed them, brushed their false teeth, made beds, and fed those who couldn't feed themselves. Funnily enough, I enjoyed the work… apart from on mornings when I had a hangover. It felt like honest work. And in the black humour of the staff, I laughed more than I did with my medical student colleagues. I felt more at home, possibly because I felt like a valued part of a team.

After graduating from medicine and becoming a doctor, I went to work as an intern in a large general hospital. I wasn't sure what to expect as I still had a sense that I was an imposter. But after drifting for some years, I suddenly felt as though I had found my place and that I belonged again. Instead of being a student and dealing with topics theoretically, I was suddenly in the real world. Instead of feeling judged about my clothes, background, or car, this was a workplace where I was judged by how diligently I worked and how well I performed as one of the team. One strength I had was that I could work hard. The work ethic I had developed meant that I could work harder and longer than many of the people whose lives I had envied. Suddenly, I realised that I could be a valued team member.

As an intern on the wards at night, I recognised the relief of my colleagues when I arrived early, ready to take handover and get to work. I sensed the gratitude of nurses when I responded quickly to their calls regarding patients whom they were concerned about. I experienced joy when I successfully achieved intravenous access on patients with 'difficult veins'. I felt valued when I managed the ward efficiently and allowed the registrars to grab some valuable rest. And I felt the support and thanks of a wider team when I managed to complete my ward duties and then help out in a busy emergency department.

Although I was a junior doctor, I still had significant responsibilities to attend to and decisions to make for the good of my patients. I had a well-defined role. There were clear expectations of what I needed to do. By getting through my tasks and making sure my patients had thorough care, I settled into the team. Working hard and being a team member. Supporting my team-mates, performing my role. Helping to engender a team spirit. These were things that I had done all my life within sports teams, and it felt natural and right. I wasn't lost any more. I knew that I belonged.

It's a powerful feeling when you have a sense of belonging, camaraderie – almost kinship at times. This is what gave me enjoyment at work, and what is required for the production of teams with common goals. Many of our institutions lack this critical element. Producing a system where bonding of people to others is valued will be essential in the creation of the teams and organisations we want to see.

7.2 Creating Relationships with Others

When I look back on my time at university, I feel some sadness. Although there were many good things that occurred, and lots of good times, I feel that my student experiences were curtailed by a lack of connection, an absence of a sense of belonging. It seems like a lost opportunity. There could have been so much more than just 'getting through' and passing. Life could have been more rewarding for all of us if we had felt that we were more inter-connected. If we had all felt part of a larger team or community, rather than separate groups, cliques, and individuals.

Associated with this lack of a common unity while I was at university was an underlying feeling of competition. An understanding that we were fighting against the people around us for approval and grades. Of course, there was a desire for good marks – we were probably all 'Type A' personalities after all. Even in the early stages, some students already had their eyes on certain specialty careers. What wasn't appreciated was that our career trajectories would be at least as powerfully influenced by how we worked, and how we interacted with our superiors and teams in hospitals, as our results in medical school. Our relationships with superiors in the 'real world' dictated our references, which determined future opportunities. I know many people, myself included, who had unimpressive marks in medical school, but then performed well in the workplace and were accepted into the career path of their choosing because they were good at the job and at being part of a team.

Years later, when I attended a reunion, I knew for sure that the feeling that I had always harboured about the lack of camaraderie at medical school was true. It wasn't imagined. I wasn't alone in my feeling a lack of collective cohesion. Once more, on the night of the reunion, there was quite a fragmented group. There was the dominant 'popular kids' clique, almost exclusively from white, wealthy backgrounds. There were also lots of smaller groups, and then individuals without many friends. It stayed like that all night. Even as the drinks flowed, there wasn't much movement between groups. Left to our own devices, most of us stayed with 'our' group from the same demographic. Anglo-Saxon origin, Chinese background, and so on. We could have learned so much more from each other, not just about medicine but about life, by integrating and mixing both on the reunion night and many years earlier. On reunion night, even after 20 years, many people didn't speak to others in the room. There was no common unity within the cohort. No team. No sense of community.

Should there be? There are obvious challenges to connecting with people from different backgrounds, cultures, and social strata. But really, in a cohort of medical students, we all had more commonality than difference. If we had all been willing to develop a greater sense of connection with the whole group, then we could have all had a much more enjoyable time. If the collective integration of the group had improved, it would have been to the benefit of us all. Perhaps none of us ever developed the skills to allow this to happen.

In my own work life, I have seen teams where newcomers who are quite different to the other members join the group. If these people are welcomed, made part of the team, and made to feel as though they belong, the whole team becomes richer and stronger. However, if there is no formal effort to welcome and integrate or induct the new person, then the team stays fragmented.

Some of the greatest longevity and happiness levels in the world are seen in Okinawa, Japan.[158] One of the contributory reasons has been surmised to be the *Moai,* which are friendship or social support groups that begin when very young children are allocated to a group of usually around five. These groups are expected to stay together for life, meeting regularly for catchups, companionship, and support. The individuals do not choose each other as friends, they come from different backgrounds, and they are expected to have different life journeys and trajectories. But they stay together and grow to love each other. In some ways, it seems like a second family. These groups strengthen the bonds within their communities. They still have their biological families, and their own chosen friends, but the *Moai* extend their networks and enmesh the individuals within a group.

Could there be a role for a system like this in medical schools, beyond the usual cliques? A system where people of different backgrounds make a commitment to the group to stay in touch, support each other through their professional career and extend the networks to strengthen the overall community? Or even at the level of our hospitals and hospital communities? Could groups be formed with representatives of the whole workforce? Not just the usual senior doctors with senior doctors, nurses with nurses, domestic staff with domestic staff, and so on; but a cross-cultural group, straddling many differences between members, with the point being a desire to forge stronger bonds within the hospital community. True teams value all members. Teams where members are valued create bonds between people who then feel a strong sense of belonging.

I know that this may feel like pie-in-the-sky thinking. It is unlikely to occur in a modern hospital or persist even if it did begin. However, our initial reactions to these proposals may reveal some truths about ourselves and our communities. Perhaps first we must examine why it feels unlikely to successfully form groups from diverse backgrounds. Why is it that we don't feel comfortable with others from different demographics? Can we only be friends with people who are a rough replica of ourselves? Can we only associate with those who drive a similar car to ours? How can we break down these assumptions and barriers? If we aren't prepared to try to form relationships with those who seem different to us, then we are less likely to be able form tight, cohesive, and high-functioning teams. For any organisation to thrive, we need to be friends with people within our own small group, and there also need to be relationships and connections beyond these groups. Those groups which manage to create common ground between members who initially seem quite different are those who operate in happier and more productive teams.

In addition to bonds between members of smaller teams, the most successful organisations promote interactions throughout all layers. This aids development of wide-ranging respect and appreciation for all team members involved. These connections and bonds cement the feeling of team and community. Not everyone in the organisation has to have close relationships, but without recognition of the connection with others beyond our own small sphere of influence and expertise, our organisations will be colder and more impersonal. It is possible to create tight intra-team connection, relationships outside our own small professional groups, and recognition of the connection with others who are also part of the wider organisation. It is possible for all to share in the understanding of belonging.

7.3 Belonging to a Team

When I was growing up, a common refrain in all the sports teams that I played for was, 'A champion team will beat a team of champions.' This saying seemed to urge us to create tight bonds and support each other. To put collective goals ahead of individual aspirations. To sacrifice personal glory for the good of the team. It indicated that if part of our effort was to support others, we would all improve together; the sum of the whole was greater than that of its parts. These days, a term often used in professional team sports is 'role player', which implies that if everyone sticks to the team ethics, team goals, and adheres to the plan, collective success will be more likely. The saying appears to be valid, judging by what is revealed. In top-level team sports, we often see a collection of the world's best players in a group that does not seem to achieve the success we expect. This is despite the individuals achieving significant personal acclaim, awards, and achievements. However, at the end of their careers, despite the personal accolades, these outstanding players often lament not being part of team success, or achieving team goals such as a championship.

One example that illustrates the importance of a champion team is in the story of Michael Jordan, possibly the greatest basketball player in history. Jordan was drafted to the Chicago Bulls from college in 1984. Immediately he was a standout, winning the National Basketball Association (NBA) Rookie of the Year Award. He continued his extraordinary form setting scoring records and achieving incredible feats. Over several seasons, Jordan was the league's highest scorer, and he was voted the Most Valuable Player (MVP) one year. Jordan was a sensation off the court as well, having his own footwear line and starring in movies.

However, despite these individual accolades, the club did not achieve overall success. The Bulls appointed Phil Jackson, previously an assistant coach, to the head coaching role in the 1989-1990 season. Jackson understood that for team success to ensue, his star player, Jordan, had to become less dominant to allow others to shine as well.[159] Jordan would have to integrate into the team a little more.

Under Jackson's wise leadership, Jordan came to see the truth of this argument despite initial hesitation: "I wasn't a Phil Jackson fan when he first came in because he was coming in to take the ball out of my hands".[160] However, the team improved even while Jordan's own scoring output dropped. Over the next ten years, with a more team-oriented and less star-centred approach, the Bulls became the most successful club in NBA history. With the champion player becoming a more integral part of the whole unit, others were able to further develop and perform more defined roles, ultimately leading to championships and glory for the team. Interestingly, with less of a dominant role but a better team around him, Jordan's personal success also increased, winning a further three league MVP awards.

It is fantastic for an organisation, or a team, to have outstanding performers if the stars are also committed to the team ethos. But if the rest of the team is merely a supporting cast and not valued, overall success will not be achieved. For team success, the gifted performer needs to integrate and occasionally relinquish the limelight, rather than having a solely individualistic attitude.

This can be the case in hospitals too. Amongst doctors, there are often large egos at play within a department. Sometimes, there are specialists who see themselves as the more important performer, perhaps the 'MVP'. In that person's mind, the rest of the team may be the supporting cast and they view their own achievements and attitudes as being of paramount importance to the group and the organisation. In actuality, the reverse may be true, as these overly self-focused individuals can cause reduced morale and drain the emotional resilience of the team. In this setting, the hospital department becomes less effective. It is important for all to recognise that if the whole unit can thrive and become renowned as a top-quality group, then career advances and personal achievements are increased for everyone.

As for those who are seen as less important in the group – perhaps the newcomers or those in less prestigious positions – they are also integral to any success. These people are also members of the collective and must be valued as equals in this regard. Although their individual roles may be less visible, they are still critical in team-goal delivery. In addition to their formal job descriptions, some of the outcomes that these people may produce could be the intangibles of team-cohesion, friendliness, openness, and creating bonds. All members of the group can become role players in a championship team.

7.4. Belonging to the Program

So, how do you get people, such as outstanding sportspeople or doctors, to put their own personal agenda slightly to one side and commit to the team? How do we make a team of champions into a champion team? The first requirement may be wise leadership with a broad overview of the whole group.

The leader needs to have the empathy to be able to combine each person's aspirations into the group dynamic and the group's goals. It seems that to develop a top-notch team, the leader must have great regard and affection for all the individuals in the group. Indeed, in my opinion, a leader must have a type of love for their team-mates. In an outstanding team, these same feelings will be shared amongst all the performers in the group.

I'm sure that to some people, using the word 'love' in this regard seems to be excessive. I disagree. Sure, you can have a good team without this quality, but not a great and enduring team. It's necessary to have affection, respect, and admiration for your team-mates. It's also important to support them in times of difficulty, always think the best of their actions, and to take joy in their successes. The description of all of those feelings and attitudes combined sure sounds a lot like love. The best teams often feel like families.

It's part of the leader's role to emphasise and make everyone understand that the bonds between the team must be tight and nourishing. This lesson will be conveyed with words and actions to result in a dawning realisation amongst the team that the environment has evolved to become better, more functional, increasingly supportive, and happier.

To develop deep affection for a person, first you must know them. Not just their name, but things about them such as their background, interests outside their profession, and journey to get to this point. Forming friendships with others will often involve developing a non-judgemental awareness of each other's weaknesses or vulnerabilities, as well as each other's strengths.

In some groups that don't integrate well, the superficial differences between group members can become the factors that separate them. However, in successful teams, this same diversity draws people together. Someone else's quirkiness, funny habits, or unusual interests are not seen as being weird or strange, they are not to be frowned upon or disparaged. Instead, these eccentricities are celebrated. They are the unique individual characteristics of that person, who is an important part of the team and, by extension, your life. These peculiar characteristics are something to enjoy and relish. Their non-uniformity is part of what makes the team embrace and love them. Why is there such a difference between groups that resent diversity and those that embrace it? It could be that teams that find difference and diversity enriching and uplifting are more other-focused than self-focused. In these other-focused teams it is recognised that unique qualities are brought into the team by those who seem different to oneself. Once more, putting one's own ego to the side for the sake of the whole is beneficial to the group.

With these inclusive attitudes, suddenly the organisation has bonds between different types of people. Instead of people only associating with those who are similar, there are now associations with others who are slightly different. Life becomes more interesting for all. The organisational relationships are broader and more open. They facilitate creativity. We grow as individuals. The community becomes stronger.

7.5 Creating Inclusion

The term 'diversity and inclusion' is bandied about in today's organisations but can sometimes feel insincere. The goal of enabling all people in any society to feel represented within an organisation is something worth aspiring to. All would agree with that. In practice however, the process often seems to involve bringing in people who look slightly different to the majority... and then having them adopt the identical attitudes, behaviour, and culture of the rest of the organisation. They are expected to look different but not think differently. If those from varied backgrounds exist in an organisation, but varied opinions are not listened to, tolerated, or valued, is this really inclusion? The organisation that is brave enough to encourage and hear diverse views and non-judgementally consider these opinions will develop into a more accepting workplace, ultimately one that becomes beloved by those within and looked at with admiration from outside.

In maternity care, there can often be an invisible, and sometimes overt, 'turf war' between obstetricians and midwives. This can create tension within a unit, to the detriment of morale and patient care. In my own unit, we had the added peculiarity of a significant team of GP obstetricians (general practitioners who also provided care within the hospital to pregnant women and labouring mothers). This was unusual in a large maternity unit. We also had a full cohort of specialist obstetricians, specialist registrars or trainee specialist doctors, and GP registrars or trainee generalist doctors. Therefore, there were many sub-teams within the larger team.

In addition to these professional differences, the specialist obstetric workforce was a varied and disparate group with many different cultures and countries of origin. This variation carried a risk of poor integration between individuals and within the group. With this in mind, we consciously aimed to become inclusive and united; to know each other's stories. This would allow our team to generate intra-group familiarity, empathy, and affection.

One of the ways we worked on this was through the structure of our Perinatal Morbidity and Mortality Meeting. Most large maternity units will have a regular PNMM where they review cases of interest, often involving poor outcomes for mother or baby. These events are rare, and distressing to all involved. When I was undertaking my specialist training, these meetings in tertiary centres had always commenced with a statement that the meeting was all about learning and optimisation of outcomes, rather than a 'witch-hunt' to find culprits to blame. However, after the preamble, the meetings usually descended to an exercise of finger-pointing and assignment of fault. The potential power of the meeting, in terms of education and support, was lost in the atmosphere of fear and recrimination.

Our unit instead made a determined effort to be balanced and kind during our meetings. We also tried to be inclusive of all staff. There was thorough analysis of poor outcomes, with rigorous questioning and desire to understand how to improve. We held an understanding that doctors and midwives who have been involved in poor patient outcomes will frequently be emotionally devastated. They will have agonised over and reviewed all their decisions many times before the meeting. It's a time for analysis, learning, and support. It is not a time to condemn those who have made conventional decisions and tried their best but have been conspired against by fate. In this setting, curiosity with regard to flaws in the system will produce understanding and bring the team closer; finding fault in individual actions will lead to division and strain that weakens the group.

Without this type of overview, the guilt present in these cases can become shame. Guilt means that you think you made a mistake. It usually leads to attempts to learn and do better. Shame can lead to you believing that you are inadequate, with intrinsic flaws and deficiencies that can't be rectified. Feelings of shame can result in lying, covering up, and hiding future poor outcomes. Once more, words are important and what is said, and how it is conveyed, at these meetings is critical. There is a great difference between thinking that you made the wrong decision, a mistake, even that you were at fault, and believing that there is something wrong with you, or that you are faulty.

In our PNMMs, which were great educational exercises that drew on all the expertise in the room, whether that was midwifery insights, general practitioner, or specialist opinions, we developed a comprehensive view of the particular problem from both hospital and community perspectives. In this setting, the team grew together and developed trust, even when discussing difficult subjects.

Due to the high emotions that ran through these monthly meetings, we decided to make the December meeting each year more about team bonding rather than case review. We touched on this earlier – the meetings consisted of dinner at a venue with facilities for presentations. They were attended by all of the maternity team, as well as the physicians involved in obstetric medicine, the anaesthetists involved with our patients, and our paediatricians. Over the years, we had many funny presentations about obstetrics, medicine, holidays, as well as quizzes and performances. We would have a 'Christmas Collection' where one of our team would briefly discuss their favourite charity, often a local one, and a collection bucket was passed around to take donations. This gave us a sense of our own privilege, gratitude for our lives, and an eye to the wider community outside our own group.

One of the most memorable Christmas meetings occurred one year with the theme being upbringing and culture of attendees with parents from countries other than Australia. One obstetrician in our team had come from Vietnam as a young child. It turned out that her family were refugees from the Vietnam War. We heard her amazing story, embellished by photographs, of her nuclear family leaving the extended family back in Vietnam, unsure of whether the boat would be shipwrecked or attacked by pirates, and a subsequent landing after many days at sea. After some time in a refugee camp, the family was resettled in Australia. During the talk, both the presenter and many in the audience became emotional. I will never forget that talk. We all understood her a little more and realised where her humanity and bravery stemmed from.

These sessions allowed us to unite as people with shared emotions. Being able to see someone else's path, the difficulties that they have encountered, and areas where they felt vulnerable helped us to connect and strengthen our bonds. These meetings, together with other initiatives, allowed us to develop affection for each other.

Most of the time, we don't get to choose the people we work with. We have no say in the make-up of our team. The same happens in families – we don't get to pick. Within our families, we support, protect, promote, and help each other. There are disagreements, and we don't always like our family members, but in most circumstances we continue to love them and look after them. The best hospital teams operate in the same way. There may be differences of opinion and squabbles, but the best teams have a strong base of mutual respect and affection to rest on. Occasionally, putting aside our individual goals and choosing to be part of the group is necessary to build something special. This attitude will not weaken us as individuals – rather it strengthens all of us as a group. The best hospitals and top departments recognise that the desired outcomes will not come from a talented group of individuals, but from a champion team.

7.6 Belonging to a Place

A sense of belonging isn't usually cognitively analysed. It's something that is felt and understood unconsciously. However, the empowering feeling of belonging has multiple inputs. From the viewpoint of healthcare, it involves the people one is with, the team, the standards and culture of the organisation, and even the physical structure of the buildings and the location of the institution. One can feel affinity for all of these elements.

In late primary school and high school, my family lived in a modest weatherboard house on the grounds of Gresswell Drug and Alcohol Rehabilitation Centre, where my father was the deputy superintendent of nursing. We had moved there partly because a house with nominal rent was provided with the job. There were several large psychiatric hospitals on the same grounds, and they all shared a green space of hundreds of acres which was partly fields with some native bush.

I spent a lot of time outdoors in the bushland and loved the tranquillity it afforded. The space and nature were also good for the patients with their various challenges, but eventually the land was sold off to developers by a state government who claimed that the patients would be better served in general hospitals in built up areas. The hospitals were closed, and the lands were cleared and turned into housing estates. I had moved out just before this occurred, as I was now working as a doctor, and my parents moved to the country before the development began.

More than 20 years later, after the death of my father, I was in Melbourne and decided to revisit my old home. As I drove into the area where I had lived, I felt immediate disorientation. I had known that our old house would be long gone, but every single thing had changed. There were no natural features that I remembered, there were no sights, outlooks, or vistas that I recognised. There was no familiarity at all. The road we had lived on remained in name, although its course had been shifted. I couldn't even be certain where our house had stood. There were many other new streets with big and impressive houses. The whole feeling was strange and unsettling. The site of much of my childhood and teenage years seemed to have vanished. It didn't exist anymore. Had I really lived here? Instead of the expected nice nostalgic drive, the day had become distressing and unpleasant. This was the one place that I had strong memories of growing up, and now it was gone. Where was I from and where did I belong?

I drove around a little more and found a gate leading up a dirt track to an area that had been behind our house. I recalled hearing that the developers had been stopped from putting houses in this area on the hill because of a particular rare bird species that lived in this one spot only. I trudged along the path, still disoriented and upset, trying to find my equilibrium. As I walked, I saw a tree that looked strangely familiar. Then it all became clear; I recognised the big old gum tree. When I was a teenager, I used to come up here in the football off-season and do sprint training along this track. Memories flooded back. This was my 'start tree', and up ahead was my 'finish tree'. During those sessions, I would sprint between the trees, about 40 metres apart, and walk or jog back to the start to sprint again. I had spent a lot of sweaty time up here.

A calming sense of home and familiarity flooded through me. I instantly felt happier and more settled. It was as though I had managed to find my way out of a bad dream. I did belong here. I knew the land, the bush, and the trees. Everything was okay.

Those moments were possibly the first time that I really understood the importance of belonging somewhere. Belonging to a place. My family had emigrated from England with me and my brother as young children. My sister was born in Australia. We had no other relatives here and we had moved around a lot. This area had been the place where we stayed the longest. To find it gone and unrecognisable had been shocking. But my feeling of home up here on the bush path and with the trees was visceral. I felt a sense of gratitude to these trees.

I started to think more about how important the concepts of land and Country are to Indigenous people. A sense of belonging to land, Country, place, is closely associated with well-being in Aboriginal people – more than it appears to be for those with non-Indigenous backgrounds. The colonisation of Australia, which has led to the displacement of First Nation peoples from their homelands, has affected their well-being for generations. There may be a little of this in all of us. Perhaps we all need a sense of belonging to a place.[161]

In a similar though less profound way, could this concept also be of relevance with our hospitals and institutions? How do we begin to understand our place in the world?

Perhaps our institutions can give attention to the country they are located in. Rather than an 'Acknowledgement of Country' which at the beginning of many meetings can become a hastily said, superficial sentence, there is scope to truly explore the origins of the land the hospital stands upon. What was this area used for before? Who were some of the important figures for the traditional owners of the land? Can their descendants have a role in the hospital now? Imagine hallways decorated with artwork from these people – giving a link between the current buildings and their occupants to those inhabitants of the same land thousands of years before. Similarly, the history of the hospital and how it has developed to serve the community can be reflected in words, photographs, and images. Paying attention to this history allows a connection to the land under our feet.

7.7 Buildings That Inspire Belonging

It's wonderful to feel affinity and belonging at work with our close group – our team. Is it also possible to feel this same sense of affinity for the structure and the buildings that house this team? I have certainly previously developed affection for hospital buildings I have worked in. Was it related to the people, or the teams, the work, or the location? It's hard to separate them.

I performed most of my specialty training at one old and revered hospital where the building was dated, and a little crummy in sections. I loved it there. Tradition seemed to flow through the building, infusing everything we did with a sense of history. There was a junior doctors' section, and the resident medical officers had quarters complete with kitchen, lounge, and bedrooms. This stood close to the labour wards, so that we could be called quickly in an emergency.

The halls of these quarters were lined with photographs stretching back almost a hundred years. Under the photos were details of those within the frame – the previous resident doctors – young men and women who were now our ageing consultants. In even older photos, there were images of legends of the profession about whom we had read in textbooks. As we would run through the corridors to attend a complicated birth, it felt as though tradition was peering down at us. We felt part of a chain. We were the present, and we had a link to the past.

That hospital is no longer present. It now exists with the same name, but in a different form and with an altered location. An up-to-date building with the necessary modernisations. I sometimes wonder whether the photos survived, and whether they are still displayed. I wonder whether that wonderful feeling of being part of something more far-reaching than ourselves has persisted for the current junior doctors of that institution.

Allowing people to have a sense of working in the present and having a vision of the future while being cognisant that we are building on foundations established by our predecessors is a powerful tool. It encourages increased pride in the institution, both in the work the hospital does currently, and a feeling of belonging to an important chain of history.

Hospitals are places where doctors and many others spend a lot of time. We create many positive clinical memories, but we also remember difficult and challenging cases and times. We remember the people around us and the place. We remember whether there was a sense of affinity with our colleagues, the hospital culture, the community, even the physical surroundings. These elements can all contribute to the way we feel at work. If these are positive feelings, it helps us to integrate and creates a sense of belonging. We become absorbed into the hospital's heritage.

7.8 Belonging to the Community

A couple of years ago, I was grocery shopping when I saw a lady I recognised. I had met her a short while before in the hospital. She'd had
a terrible mid-pregnancy stillbirth. We talked briefly and her grief
was palpable after this tragic loss. As we parted, we hugged – relative
strangers both affected by an unfair and traumatic event. Recently,
again in the supermarket, a young couple with a pram approached
me. It was the same woman, but this time she and her partner had a
healthy newborn, only one week old. Within the couple's happiness
was mixed some sadness and intense palpable relief. As we discussed
how difficult and stressful it is going through pregnancy after a previous unexpected tragedy, she continued to smile but tears came to her
eyes. Again, we hugged.

These experiences are not uncommon for those of us who work
in maternity care. In all the joy and excitement of new life, there are
some less happy outcomes. Seeing this emotion in the daily setting
of life outside the hospital reinforces how important the jobs we
have as clinicians are, and the significance of the systems around
us. Occasions such as childbirth are some of the most important a
person will have. These events are critical in people's lives. Seeing
people outside the consulting rooms, clinics, and hospitals reinforces
what is real in our own lives. This is our community and these are our
people. The ones we serve.

Every hospital will be a relatively large institution within its
community. Perhaps this is why we can sometimes become a little
seduced by our own importance. With the glamour of cutting-edge
medical treatments and the latest technologies, it is easy to forget
that we are caring for people rather than cases, and that these people
belong to the same systems and communities that we do. The modern
view of a hospital being a shining ivory tower, somehow separate to
the surrounding world, is flawed. A more thorough sense of where

and how we belong is essential. This comes with an understanding that effects ripple out from us to the community but that they also occur in the other direction.

Another example that emphasised the importance of our place in the wider community was when my unit needed a new portable ultrasound machine for a delivery suite. The previous machine had aged and now had poor image quality, not meeting the standard required for emergency care in modern obstetric units. The hospital was reluctant to spend the required money, and the issue dragged on for many months, creating angst among the obstetricians and potentially poorer outcomes for some women.

After hearing of this situation, a registered club in our area donated the funds to procure the machine. When the machine arrived in our delivery suite, there were photos taken by the local media with representatives from the club in attendance together with some clinicians. As I spent time with and thanked the club's chairman and CEO, I also explained how the new machine would benefit patients of the unit and provide safer care.

After this, both gentlemen recounted their own stories about interactions with the hospital and our maternity unit. They recalled the births of their own grandchildren. Their memories and the knowledge that their gift would help others gave them joy. In turn, we appreciated their generosity and recognised how their gift improved our service. These interactions were complementary. As in many things, it's a circle.

7.9 We All Belong on the Same Planet

In our world, there are many global environmental concerns. Our hospitals, as complex systems, have direct and indirect effects in many of these domains.

Within the operating theatres, technological advances have enabled endoscopic 'minimally invasive' or 'keyhole' surgery to be commonly used for many procedures that previously required open operations with an extended hospital stay and convalescence. Part of the surgical equipment for these procedures can include expensive single-use-only items of sleek industrial design. Similar instruments exist that are re-usable, but perhaps not as beautiful or enticing. The use of the disposable items can add up to thousands of dollars of extra expense for a single procedure.

If there is a clear benefit to a particular patient, then the more expensive equipment should be used. However, there are other considerations. The single-use items are discarded in contaminated waste and contribute to landfill. Their production has embedded costs in manufacturing of materials, energy, and transport. The more disposable instruments we use, the less we require re-usable instruments which can be cleaned and sterilised. The CSSD (Central Sterile Supply Department) that exists in every operating theatre complex will then have less work, which may impact local jobs.

In some instances, surgeons will insist that the range of disposable instruments they may require in a procedure be opened prior to commencing the operation. Occasionally, once the views of the operation site are established, it is decided that the operation is not necessary, or unable to be performed in this manner, and abandoned. These instruments of high cost, that can be opened in seconds, are all discarded.

Everyone within the systems has an influence; we can all increase sustainability in our practice. We can all contribute. Even the most esteemed surgeon is part of the system rather than being above these concerns.

On another occasion, at an executive meeting, it was proposed that our hospital kitchen and cafeteria be downgraded. The organisation would then bring in pre-prepared meals at reduced financial cost. The large catering organisation would truck in meals six times per week. They would be heated up for patients and staff. Thankfully, after a discussion about the importance of keeping local jobs, eating fresh food, and reducing our carbon footprint, the motion was declined. As well as providing healthcare services to the community, each hospital has a duty to its employees to treat them fairly. There is also a responsibility to the wider community. Loss of these jobs, even at initial reduced cost to the organisation, would not be consistent with these aims.

We must all be conscious of our effects on others, our effects on hospital behaviour and attitudes, and our effects on the surrounding community and world. Our hospitals are important pillars of our communities. With our responsibility comes privilege, and with privilege comes responsibility; the two are intrinsically linked. It is important to continually consider our roles and values, and to aspire to the highest standards in all decisions we make.

{im·ag·in·ing}

WOULDN'T LIFE BE DULL WITHOUT OUR IMAGINATIONS? Being able to imagine different paths, options, and futures is one of the best qualities we possess as humans. Imagination has led to great advances for humankind with amazing technological inventions. Imagination is also part of what allows us to see someone who is suffering, conceive a way that their circumstances could be improved, and then guide us in acting to help them with compassion.

Curiosity enables us to try new things and see mistakes and errors as minor setbacks and steps on the road to success. After being knocked down by a challenge, imagination is what underpins the determination to get up again and try a new approach.

Imagining, and having a vision, can be an individual occurrence, however, when the same vision is also held by others, a powerful movement can begin. Imagination can allow a group to unite and take major leaps forward. Is this the time for our healthcare leaders to start imagining, envisioning, and reinventing?

8.1 Contemplating Change

In 1963, Dr Martin Luther King delivered one of history's most extraordinary speeches,[162] calling for an end to racism and discrimination in the United States. Within the speech, King described his "dream", and engaged his audience's collective imagination. What he could envision with his concept of a different world and an alternative possible future helped many people in America to move from an understanding of 'the way things always were' to a vision of 'what could be'.

Without an ability to look at things differently, change is never possible. And what becomes possible can never be recognised without new thoughts, questions, and viewpoints. To persist and create something of worth requires an ability to bravely countenance a new future. Exciting possibilities are often scary when first considered.

Leaps of progress do not come with a fixed mindset, feeling trapped by convention, or believing that nothing can or ever will change. When we do tell ourselves change is not possible, are we voicing a belief, an assumption, or a fear? Could our negativity bias and loss-aversion prevent us from exploring new outlooks, even if the present is far from satisfactory? Perhaps one factor in why a problematic healthcare culture seems permanent and unchangeable relates to our own fear; are we too scared to contemplate a new way?

To consider altering the status quo requires great courage. Not only is the future unknown, but the current systems will resist change as well. Proposals of organisational change can induce resistance and attack from those less willing to consider innovation due to anxiety about loss of their own personal power or relevance.

A common early criticism of any proposed change will be that the new initiatives are unclear – plans that are not sufficiently intricate or precise. These people need detail, partly to alleviate unease about how the changes affect their personal situation. Unfortunately, these persistent negative voices often delay and eventually overwhelm positive change initiatives. The resistance causes a response that reduces bold imagination and leads to more meticulous description of planned change in minute items. This alters the process from one aiming at potentially wonderful futures to a procedure based around planning overly detailed and mechanistic management. No longer is there an uplifting and energising discussion about creating transformation; it is now a dialogue about production of transactional processes.

Is it an unrealistic concept to have a dream about what is possible for hospitals? Is it too touchy-feely, or airy-fairy, or any other denigratory saying that implies foolish naïvety and overly emotional idealism? Should we be more concrete in our thinking? Interestingly, Dr King's uplifting speech that created a movement and changed a nation contained words such as 'dream' rather than 'strategy' or 'business plan'.

A vision implies imagination, and it also describes something that is seen or visualised. An architect's initial sketch, an outline, or an ability to see a dot on a map that is somewhere we wish to travel to. Occasionally the longed-for future won't be easily seen; perhaps it's more of a vague image or understanding. The vision might not be clear enough to see, it might be something more instinctive and emotional. An inner knowing. And the future that is yearned for might not be seen but felt.

8.2 The Hospital as a Village

A hospital is a large and complex institution wherein many professions and trades are performed. These not only relate to the clinical care of patients with medicine, nursing, and allied health, they also include food services, electrical services, plumbing, engineering, IT, financial services, gardening – the list includes most occupations. Many products and services required by a hospital are supplied, produced, or modified within the institution. In some ways, the hospital community could be considered a village.

Within a village, everyone has an interest and responsibility in keeping things running and making the environment as pleasant, safe, and enriching as possible. If an individual member of the community is struggling, it affects the overall well-being of the village; all the residents must look out for each other. For example, if the baker in the village cannot work effectively, the rest of the people have no bread. The baker's ongoing well-being affects all. Similarly, it is in the village's best interests to aid in the training, happiness, and retention of the baker's apprentice.

One of the strengths of the ideal village is in the way it embraces difference. This grows the cultural makeup that makes life more interesting. There is a common understanding that diversity is stimulating and enjoyable. That human differences can unite, instead of divide. The community also holds shared goals of excellence in all areas of work and provides for the future as well as the present.

Outstanding training exists in the hospital/village for students of medicine, nursing, and allied health professions. In addition, given that a hospital is such a large and complex institution requiring input of most professions and trades, it is possible to aim for excellence in all the jobs. For example, within the cafeteria and hospital kitchens, the highest-quality chefs could be employed, who then train outstanding apprentices. Indeed, training and apprenticeships could be created in many areas such as electrical trades, carpentry, or landscape gardening.

Some villages have incredible appeal. Beauty, calm, order, good vibes. All people wish to have a beautiful workplace. For a hospital, there is beauty in multiple dimensions – interior and exterior beauty, and also functional elements such as how the care is delivered, how the work flows, and how the staff interact. The overall allure of an organisation relates largely to the emotion of the institution, the communication, and the culture. Some hospitals – many hospitals – have a beautiful 'feel'. In these institutions, there is an almost palpable sense of caring and 'goodness'.

The initial appreciation of any hospital will begin with the external appearance. The architectural design could encompass an exterior of awe. However, the design of the hospital must also facilitate the work necessities and the flow of the systems. Ambulance access, both road and helicopter, easy safe access for all patients and visitors, staff accessibility, and an uncomplicated way to get to work are all important. These invisible elements reduce frustration. They won't produce engagement of themselves but will facilitate an underswell of affection towards the workplace.

8.3 A Beautiful Village

In 1992, Mexico City was the world's most polluted megacity. Soon after, the Mexican government began a program to reduce pollution levels. When refurbishment of the existing hospital Manuel Gea Gonzalez occurred in 2013, these environmental and sustainability concerns were incorporated into the design and build. A striking exterior 'double skin' was part of the final construction. Interlocking white geometrically shaped panels produced diffusion of light and air currents thereby lowering direct sunlight and hot air hitting the windows which led to reduced cooling costs. And this eye-catching look has further sustainability aspects: the tiles have a titanium dioxide covering which absorbs pollutants when activated by daylight. The 'skin' can absorb the pollution emanating from 8,750 cars per day.[163]

Beauty is not only about visual aspects and applications, but also relates to concepts and motivations. The exterior of the hospital we imagine can also incorporate enticing gardens and access to nature. Vertical gardens can be used to increase visual beauty, improve views from the interior of the building, and reduce cooling costs due to the thermal properties of the plants. There can be a rooftop garden with vegetables grown by the hospital gardeners being used as produce in the hospital cafeteria. These plants could have their pollination aided by beehives on the roof, with the honey produced available for purchase within the hospital. We are only bound by our own imagination.

The optimal institution will induce pride in unexpected ways. Waste from the cafeteria can be diverted to on-site composting to be used on the hospital gardens. A reduced-plastic environment with, for example, no plastic cutlery, is preferred. In building and construction, attempts to incorporate recycled materials can be prioritised. Pride is fostered through thoughts and actions.

Often, the interiors of hospitals have many smooth hard surfaces, including floors. This is required for cleaning purposes but gives rise to oppressively noisy spaces. Sound diminution will be a priority as quieter and more peaceful environs aid patient healing,[164] staff performance,[165] reduce stress, lower cardiovascular health risk,[166] and allow creativity to flourish. A peaceful environment in meeting rooms is essential.

In addition to subdued environments being beneficial for patient recovery, access to nature also optimises healing. The field of evidence-based architectural design has found a striking relationship between access to natural views and improvements in patient recovery. Patients in hospital rooms with windows recover more quickly than those in rooms without windows. If the window has a nature view, recovery is even faster. Even just pictures and photos of nature views are beneficial if no windows are available. In a room without windows, a solitary indoor plant aids healing.[167] In many workplace environments, the presence of indoor plants and water views has been shown to reduce tension and anxiety.[168]

Creating beauty and realising dreams of design in our hospitals is possible. These dreams are achievable. Places of healing that are also beautiful can and should exist. Places where the best of human nature can be fostered. And places where great things happen in the care of our fellow humans. As Michelangelo said:[169]

> *"The danger lies not in setting our mark*
> *too high and failing, but in setting*
> *our mark too low and achieving it."*

8.4 Planning the Village

Any imagined future can seem to be a blurry point somewhere far away in the distance, without a clear path. Indeed, the imagined future might seem so different and aspirational that it often appears impossible to reach. When goals feel unachievable, it's easy to quit. The amount of work required can seem so great that it results in immobility – taking no steps. No clear direction in which to move.

Without a clearly envisaged route, it is common to become scared and frozen. Under these circumstances, the present situation starts to feel safer, more certain and known. Even though the current circumstances and environment are intolerable, now it feels even more frightening to pursue change. So, things don't change, and people stay where they are. Due to fear, uncertainty, and the resultant immobility, the toxic state is allowed to persist.

This can be a problem for hospitals. Sometimes, organisations are languishing in a state of unhappiness, but unable to move to make the break-through. Not managing to generate the courage required to change. Not taking any steps towards an improved future.

These hospitals end up with partial, 'band-aid', solutions that address only the most obvious manifestations of poor culture. They lurch from crisis to crisis, without really altering at all. Suddenly, years have passed. Sure, the hospital has continued to function and lots of patients have been treated successfully, but the aspirations of what the institution could have become have been forgotten and left behind.

So, how does a journey to a new and brighter future become a possibility? How does it begin? To travel to any unfamiliar destination is more difficult than simply choosing to stay in the current location. Moving in a new direction requires energy, desire, and commitment. Any dream or vision, however enthusiastically embraced, does not have an obvious route. The path is not signposted, and it certainly won't be a straight line. There will be twists and turns, sometimes doubling back or a retracing of steps. There will be unexpected obstacles. The journey will not be rapid or smooth. It will be questioned, and frequently misunderstood. But it will be worth it.

8.5 Facing Obstacles

When faced with ongoing, seemingly insurmountable challenges, the importance of positive emotion and mindset should not be forgotten. Optimism, hope, and an ability to find moments of joy in trying circumstances aid resilience and allow the creativity required in finding innovative approaches and solutions.

In 1914, Ernest Shackleton was already a famous polar explorer, having been knighted for his achievements. However, Shackleton had also failed on two occasions to become the first man to reach the South Pole, having been famously defeated in the quest in a 1911 'race'. Shackleton had turned his attention to a planned cross-continent crossing of Antarctica from sea to sea via the South Pole. This undertaking was known as the Imperial Trans-Antarctic Expedition. His journey began in August 1914, just as the First World

War was commencing, with Shackleton being urged to proceed with his quest by the First Lord of the Admiralty, Winston Churchill. The expedition was to fail in its grand objectives but ultimately turned into an incredible tale of heroism, survival, and leadership.[170]

Even before Shackleton's ship, the Endurance, made it to Antarctica, it was met with unexpected heavy pack ice. This ice eventually trapped the Endurance firmly. The crew decided to winter on board and recommence when the ice abated. However, the ice began to tighten. It would eventually crush and destroy the ship. The crew disembarked and camped on the ice for months before it began to melt and become unstable. They then escaped on salvaged lifeboats and navigated treacherous seas to reach an isolated rocky outcrop – Elephant Island – surviving in freezing conditions on meagre rations and occasional penguin or seal meat. The chance of rescue was virtually nil as Elephant Island was outside any shipping lanes. Shackleton and five of the crew rigged up sails on one of the 20-foot lifeboats. Despite poor navigation tools, they would attempt to traverse 800 miles of open sea to reach South Georgia Island, a sparsely inhabited whaling outpost.

Miraculously, this feat was accomplished. Unfortunately, they landed on the uninhabited side of the island. Shackleton and two other men tied themselves together with rope, put screws through the soles of their boots to fashion makeshift ice climbing shoes, and made a non-stop 36-hour trek over rocky mountains and glaciers to cross the island. Eventually, the men on Elephant Island were rescued and returned home, two years after starting their quest. Shackleton's leadership saved all of their lives.

During unexpected events and incredible risk and hardship, Shackleton had to set aside the original goal of exploration glory. His mission now became the need to save his men. His unique leadership has many lessons. Shackleton drew up duty rosters to keep the crew busy. All men, officers included, equally shared all physical and menial tasks. All men participated in the creation of entertainment and fun during the evenings. There were dress-ups, music nights, and funny haircut competitions. After disaster had struck, Shackleton realised that "The enemy was not the ice, but to deal with morale ... and the human spirit".[171]

In all subsequent analyses of Shackleton's feats of leadership, the main themes to emerge were that the crew knew of his affection for and dedication to them. The men were made to feel more important than the objective. And the most common features spoken about were Shackleton's positivity, unflagging optimism, and vision.

8.6 Finding the Way

Beginning a journey requires a plan. However, travel to a desired and imagined destination may not be based on what is already known or on established processes and understanding. The map to these types of endpoints may not be factual and precise like a road atlas. Some maps can only be based on emotions such as hope.

Hope-mapping starts with a vision of a longed-for future. Once the vision is established, to travel there requires visualising potential pathways and the initial steps. Without the commitment to action, there isn't any real hope of change, more just wishful thinking. Plotting any journey requires a defined plan which must incorporate both the vision as well as an understanding of how the process will commence. The map created will include a desired future that has defined wishes, goals, and aspirations. The map will be based on emotion. However, it will also reflect our understanding that determination and willpower are required as well as a visualisation of potential pathways – the first steps to begin the process.[172] Our guidance will come from an understanding of what emotions are motivating us and what will produce optimal culture as well as concrete plans of initial actions.

When looking at any map, being able to understand one's current position is crucial. Just as for any individual contemplating personal change and recognising the need for honest self-assessment, imagining a new organisational future involves a similar requirement for brave examination of people, processes, and systems.

Of course, to achieve lasting change within an institution such as a hospital is not something one person can do alone. The whole organisation must be engaged. This is the power of the hope map. The vision will be created by people uniting and jointly imagining a new future. Collective understanding and enthusiasm are generated at the same time as honest appraisal of current circumstances. The open self-reflection at the beginning of the process is what starts the change in the culture. After this process of defining where we are, an introspective and kind scrutiny commences. We will jointly decide where we want to be. As the climate shifts, an organisation-wide journey can be embarked upon.

Many people on the inside of healthcare institutions will recall other aborted proposals and failed attempts at change. However, instead of abandoning hope due to previous failure, these efforts provide lessons and help inform the new approach. Rather than the usual deficit-based approaches to change, there exists an opportunity to change through building on existing strengths.

The final destination will not be about amazing architecture or an impressive assembly of bricks and mortar. It will be about culture and relationships. It will be an institution with standards of excellence including positive communication styles, a place where interpersonal interactions leave all feeling good. We can all imagine belonging to that system. We all want to commit to a mission like that.

8.7 Appreciating the Community

Change programs with problem-based focuses are an understandable approach. These techniques have the advantage of quickly focusing attention on weaknesses that need to be addressed. However, this style of change management only lifts an organisation from a negative state to a functional level. This approach will not stimulate aspiration or creativity. It will not elevate the organisation beyond what is acceptable and mediocre.

An alternative approach could involve investigating the current position with a desire to encourage and grow the existing positive qualities. This would be a different change paradigm that alters the focus from eradicating bad to fostering good. Furthermore, the process of exploration is not solely about identification of deficiencies but also about finding the best qualities in what already exists and promoting these.

With respect to cultural change in hospitals that are suffering with 'toxic culture', Appreciative Inquiry (AI) may be a beneficial systems-change initiative.[173] Appreciative Inquiry is exactly what the words indicate; a curious questioning process and style that appreciates the results and findings that are uncovered and revealed. The undertaking of an AI process leads to identification of the best aspects of any situation with a desire to build on these strong points, rather than a change process with sole focus on eradication of unwanted elements. The AI intervention attempts to engender wide engagement and to hear from all voices, rather than just the usual opinions. This is a strength of AI; it enables novel and unusual perspectives, which can facilitate fresh insights. Innovative ideas and advances often come from unexpected and previously unheard sources.

The incorporation of AI-style questioning into a systems-change initiative can foster engagement from a previously disenfranchised group. The technique of AI has been validated in multinational companies and the US military,[174] as well as in hospital settings[175, 176] including during a pandemic.[177] Appreciative Inquiry allows a gradual, evolutionary, adaptive model of change, rather than a programmatic plan. The technique draws people together and forward, with hope of moving to what is desired, rather than staff feeling pushed or threatened into accepting anxiety-provoking change.

Of course, the other meaning of the word 'appreciate' refers to growing value. Indeed, organisational resources can increase with the AI process. Importantly in health, the process is balanced with acknowledgement of the need to address real and pressing problems. Throughout the initial inquiry phase, negatives are not ignored or overlooked, but are dissected in a modified light that, rather than apportioning fault, will allow meaningful information to emerge and growth to occur. During the process, attention to current problems is vital. There is essential ongoing activity with daily running of the hospital and associated ongoing 'housekeeping'. This allows the organisation to 'keep it real' even while evolving.

In fact, the process of closely studying a subject or system causes change in the entity due to the examination alone. During the process of questioning, attitudes shift, and a new reality is created. With AI, inquiry and change intervention are interlinked, rather than being separate processes. The style of questioning and analysis causes increasing awareness of strengths that increase further as attention is given to them. The new attitudes also change the way all in the organisation consider and deal with emerging challenges. The questions that are asked, the manner of asking, and where attention is directed dictates the change that eventuates.

8.8 Co-Creation

Oftentimes in organisations that are struggling, some individuals will sense a need for change. These people can feel that they are alone, and that others do not share the same sense of possibility or vision of what their groups could achieve. Sometimes, it feels easier to not say anything; just do your job and go home at the end of the day. With this mindset comes a life where work is to be endured, and home-life seen as when 'real' living begins. Of course, the two are not so easily separated. This attitude can also lead to personal disengagement and dissatisfaction. In this environment, the organisation further stalls. But when discussion is started, it is often found that the areas of complaint are shared, and the places for improvement are recognised by others. When these factors and situations are jointly explored, they become opportunities for the group to collaborate on, connect through, and plan for success.

At the end of the 2006 AFL season, Geelong Football Club were in a difficult position. After being besieged by severe financial difficulties for a number of years, the fiscal position of the club was slowly being resurrected. However, on field success – the ultimate measure for all football clubs – also eluded Geelong. The last premiership for the club had come more than 40 years earlier. Great hopes had been held at the start of the 2006 season, after they'd accumulated a talented list of players and had finished the 2005 season with encouraging performances. Unfortunately, the 2006 season was a disaster. As the season progressed with poor performances, the club internally unravelled. There were relationship breakdowns, poor behaviours, and power struggles that divided the coaches and the fitness staff. The club was a place of unrest.

After the season ended in ignominy, CEO Brian Cook spent much time undertaking a review of all processes. There were many negatives that could have been addressed with the usual style of simple sackings and censures, but a different approach was taken. Cook spoke to more than 60 people, at all levels within the organisation, and also to stakeholders outside the organisation. The players faced truths about required standards and eventually rewrote their own code of behaviour. Some staff were not re-employed, and others had duties reassigned.

The organisation set aside previous assumptions and re-imagined themselves, beginning with a thorough and honest self-examination. Cook made many recommendations to the Geelong Board which reflected a desire to build on what existed and create a new way. The recommendations were adopted and the co-creation of a new culture began.

Through courageous and confronting self-assessment, with associated acknowledgement of existing strengths, the aspirations of what the club could become then became reality. Geelong won the premiership in the 2007 season, beginning an unprecedented period of success. The club became financially successful, built a new stadium, and developed an organisation that all were proud of.

Being brave enough to imagine a new future and then following up with truthful and complete evaluation of the current situation is difficult. Most organisations either can't dream big enough or aren't sufficiently fearless and honest to travel this path. But, when done properly, there is treasure at the end of the journey.

8.9 Resurrecting a Struggling Village

To use the analogy of the hospital as a village once again, it is possible to imagine a flourishing community where all are thriving. Where there is understanding and respect for each person's roles and responsibilities. All the villagers are friendly and no one is allowed to become isolated. The focus and discussion of the community does not centre on someone's weaknesses or struggles, instead there is recognition and celebration of each other's unique gifts, abilities, and strengths.

However, in our hypothetical happy village, things have not always been this good. Some years ago, within this village, relationships had become strained, and the very essence of the village became clouded. While the businesses in the village were still functioning, they weren't excelling. They were languishing.

It was agreed that the situation was unacceptable, and that things needed to change. A decision was made to review the way the village operated and the way the residents interacted. It was decided to do this in a particular way that analysed everything about the village and aimed to build on and encourage the best of what the village was and what it could become.

All residents were involved in the process. The vision was collectively developed. Initial anxiety around change led to some becoming sceptical and obstructive. Subsequently, most of the naysayers, upon seeing the benefits of change, became firm advocates of the new reality. Others who could not accept change moved elsewhere to seek other opportunities.

When hoping for a new future, whether for a village or a hospital, the journey can be long and uncertain. With a unified approach, success is more likely. Although the destination has been envisaged, all must know that the route to becoming an outstanding performer in any field will be circuitous and demanding rather than straightforward. If the path was obvious, direct, and easily visible, it would have been travelled long ago.

8.10 Change Starts Within

In individuals and groups, fear creates resistance, inhibits worthwhile action, and slows forward momentum. We are all familiar with the uncertainty that can cause inactivity and doubt. In healthcare, fear over proposed organisational change or restructure also causes obstruction to progress. However, overcoming this resistance will lead to the profound leaps that are needed.

The answers to most of our personal problems lie within ourselves. The difficulty is finding the bravery and honesty to confront the truth. Admitting the truth often involves acknowledging a hidden and confronting personal agenda. It may require recognition of unhelpful attitudes and opinions. Whenever we can recognise and voice our fears about any issue, those concerns become less debilitating. And if it is possible in a group to respectfully discuss the anxieties that are held by some, the problems seem less scary and appear to have more easily discernible solutions.

The answers to any organisation's challenges in terms of culture and relationships lie within the group. The solutions are unlikely to come from an external program. Instead, they will become apparent when there is facilitation of open dialogue within the group. At this point, it is possible to shift focus from personal agendas and self-interest to what is required to begin collective forward motion. In his 1961 US presidential inauguration speech,[178] John F. Kennedy shared a similar view, "Ask not what your country can do for you – ask what you can do for your country".

Letting go of negative emotion allows innovation to emerge and relationships to develop. From a place of creativity and support, performance will rise. Amazing change – seemingly magical transformation – can then occur within a previously struggling organisation.

Through changes of focus and attitude, all organisations will improve. However, it is impossible to judge whether any given struggling organisation can elevate sufficiently to become an outstanding, exemplary, even a feted institution. The degree of improvement will vary according to circumstances, unified 'buy in', and leadership. No one can know for sure whether magical change is possible for a particular group, nor when it might happen. However, by examining personal resistance and exploring beliefs and attitudes, conditions are created that allow magic to more easily appear.

As Socrates said:[179]

> *"The secret of change is to focus all of your energy*
> *not on fighting the old, but on building the new."*

{mo·ti·vat·ing}

EACH OF US AT SOME POINT ESSENTIALLY DESIRES THE same things. When asked what we want from life, what we hope for, the answers are usually fairly uniform. The elements that give rise to the subjective experience of one's life relate to our health, longevity, professional success (however that is defined), accomplishments, relationships, and so on. These are the factors that lead to pleasure, contentment, and happiness. Considering that these are the 'big ticket items' in life, do we give enough thought to them and how we can increase these components of our lives? It may surprise some that how we choose to think, what we feel, and how we interact with others, all impact on the factors that we say we desire.

All of the hoped-for elements in life can be increased for any individual through the simple actions of improving the way we speak and listen; using different words with a more positive valence, allowing for different viewpoints of the same events, and promoting positive emotions such as gratitude. These are achievable actions that can create profound life benefits. To get such great rewards from seemingly simple interventions would appear – to borrow from business-speak – to be a wonderful return on investment.

9.1 What's in It for Me?

When proposing a need for change in healthcare or medical culture, some clinicians will not be convinced to alter their own habits and styles of behaviour based on arguments around a hospital's overall outcomes or financial viability. These will be seen as the role and concern of administrators or 'someone else'. Similarly, the issues of staff welfare, or experience and satisfaction of patients in other areas of the hospital, may seem a little removed from one's own domain. Many doctors will be unlikely to think beyond their own performance and life circumstances. They will focus on their own group of patients and their own 'patch'.

When encouraged to contemplate and assist a culture change initiative, these people will rightly ask, "What's in it for me?". This is an unsurprising response that reflects the individualistic attitudes of today's society. It may also indicate an understanding that change is not easy and that such ventures carry a high risk of failure with accompanying disappointment. Why be involved in a program that will have a cost in terms of the personal resources of time and emotional energy, when it has a poor chance of success? It is easier to contract the outlook to include only oneself and one's immediate concerns and needs.

When questioned about what they desire from life and what makes for a good life, people almost invariably discuss factors such as happiness, health, career satisfaction, a long life, good family relationships, and success.

When considering culture change in any setting, it is illuminating that all of these elements that are assessed as being components of an enjoyable and fulfilling personal life are increased by attention to an improved environment at work. An improved organisational culture will benefit each of us. More positive attitudes and generous communication leads to increased individual well-being. Through the measures of a slight change of attitude, listening, expressing gratitude, displaying positive regard for others, even simply saying hello, a happier, healthier, longer, more satisfying and successful life is produced.

While it may sound unrealistic and naïve, the evidence suggests that being a nicer person and a better friend and colleague leads to longevity, life enjoyment, and achievement.[180,181,182] So, when considering whether or not to buy into positive cultural change in organisations, the decision becomes about what each of us wants out of life for ourselves. That's what's in it for you.

9.2 The Power of Positive Emotion

The 'Nun Study'[183] shows how important positive emotion is in all our lives. Involving 678 Catholic nuns who were school sisters of the Notre-Dame congregation in the US, the study began as longitudinal research into aging and cognitive decline but developed into much more.

All sisters of the congregation who were born prior to 1917 were asked in 1986 to join the study with plans to perform ongoing cognitive and physical assessments on the group and with post-mortem examinations of their brains after death. All the nuns had lived in the same conditions with similar diets, exercise regimens, recreational activities, and access to medical care. The uniformity of the group's life experiences after joining the order became vital to the unexpected findings.

After the study was already in progress, it was discovered that all the women had been requested in 1930 by the order's Mother Superior to write a short autobiographical letter detailing their early life. Of the 678 responses that were found, 180 were deemed suitable for analysis of early language and cognitive ability.[184] Some of the early research found that cognitive impairment was not an inevitable consequence of aging and disease, and that low linguistic ability in early life,[185] and reduced educational achievement[186] during life, were associated with higher rates of Alzheimer's disease.

However, the most profound findings came later when it became apparent that the 'idea density' in the early letters was associated with longevity. Further assessment of the ideas, sentences, and words used in the letters revealed that expression of positive emotion was linked to longevity, irrespective of any other health indicators. After controlling for variables of early linguistic ability, education, and lifetime occupation, the most powerful finding was that the happiest nuns lived the longest.

This effect was noted in a stepwise fashion; the more positive emotion in the early letters, the greater the longevity. At the age of 85, more than 90% of the happiest nuns were still alive.

This correlation of positive emotion and longevity is supported by other longitudinal research,[187] including a study of 839 Mayo Clinic medical outpatient attendees who were followed over a 30-year period. At the initial self-referred visit for a medical complaint, the patients undertook a personality inventory. When the inventories were assessed 30 years later, a higher level of inherent optimism was significantly associated with reduced mortality and better health. A more optimistic explanatory style when evaluating life events correlated with a 50% decrease in mortality compared with a mixed or neutral explanatory style.[188] Other research has also shown that a pessimistic explanatory style of life's events may be linked to decreased longevity.[189]

Experiencing positive emotion, styles of expression, and interpretation of events is linked to better health and a longer, happier life. There are many factors related to longevity that are outside our control such as genetics. It is arguable whether individual personality is changeable. What we can try to optimise is the 'emotional environment' of our workplaces and within our teams.

9.3 Allowing Ourselves to Express Emotion

Allostasis is the body's adaptation to change while maintaining physiological systems and parameters within a normal range. Allostatic load refers to the physiological response to stress.

The experience of emotion is associated with autonomic nervous system arousal;[190] emotions such as fear and anger produce higher sympathetic nervous system arousal.[191] Of course, sympathetic arousal with 'fight-flight-freeze' response involving changes such as an increase in heart rate, stress hormone release, and diversion of blood to skeletal muscle is associated with an evolutionary survival benefit. An immediate response and appropriate changes in our physiology are desirable when confronted with the proverbial sabre-toothed tiger. Indeed, frequent emotional arousal seems beneficial to health,[192] as long as there is rapid resolution of emotion after the stressful situation has ended.

However, experiencing sustained negative emotion exerts adverse effects on our health.[193] Even worse than the experience of constant negative emotion may be trying to suppress the emotion. Not 'letting out' or allowing oneself to recognise negative states is associated with significant health risks and an ultimately reduced life span.[194] Suppression of any emotion, whether positive or negative, creates chronic activation of the sympathetic nervous system with a persistent stress response and chronic elevation of cortisol,[195, 196, 197] leading to increased allostatic load.

Imaging studies with functional MRI have shown that emotional suppression increases activity in the amygdala, an area of the brain involved with processing fearful, threatening, or negative stimuli.[198] Suppression of emotion also leads to dysregulation in the inflammatory and metabolic systems, and the hypothalamic-pituitary-adrenal axis,[199,200] thereby affecting stress levels and resulting in multiple unwanted physiological effects including poor sleep. Inflammation, stress, and poor sleep contribute to a worsening cascade that eventually manifests in decreased emotional control, poorer relationships, worsened memory, and an increase in depressive symptoms.[201]

All healthcare workers will experience frequent emotional situations in their professional lives. Doctors will have to deal with the stress of delivering awful news such as a diagnosis of cancer, and feel frustration and anger at poor outcomes or complications. To be an effective doctor requires constant emotional regulation, otherwise one's ability to perform will be compromised. Overly emotional responses from a doctor in response to certain situations could become a clinical liability. It has even been suggested that an ability to reduce empathy in certain situations could be a strength for those in clinical medicine.[202]

However, rather than reducing empathy, it appears that noticing and registering emotions is better for our health. Emotional regulation is a necessary skill, but it is not an instinctive ability. Emotional reappraisal is a technique that is associated with reduced allostatic load and better personal health outcomes.[203] Unfortunately, emotional regulation by reappraisal is infrequently taught in medical school. Instead, many doctors learn to suppress their emotions, with the cost being their own health.[204] Pointedly, at this time where burnout is of epidemic proportions in doctors, there is increasing evidence that regulating one's emotions through suppression techniques alone is associated with burnout in doctors.[205]

9.4 Managing Emotions

In 1964 at Yale University, Stanley Milgram performed a series of experiments that revealed the lengths that people will go to in order to follow the lead of an authority figure.[206] The controversial 'Milgram Experiments' involved study participants being instructed by a 'supervisor' dressed in a white lab coat to administer electric shocks to a 'learner' if the learner made an incorrect response on an educational task.

The study was described to the volunteers, largely college students, as an investigation into whether punishment with physical pain aided learning; but the study was really designed to explore the levels of obedience generated by figures of authority.

The supposed learners were actually actors, and no electrical shocks were delivered, however the actors performed as if the increasingly higher voltage shocks were transmitted. Through the course of the experiment, the participant, or 'teacher', was able to see the learner through a glass partition and hear their cries of apparent pain. If the participant expressed reluctance to continue, the supervisor would verbally encourage or prod the participant to provide ongoing shocks to the learner for a wrong answer. Most study participants continued to deliver the increasing shocks to a lethal dose, even when they felt that it was morally wrong. While the ethics of these experiments have been questioned, they do show the power of authority figures on subordinates, and the overwhelming desire that most people have to 'fit in' and comply with the prevailing system.

Even as medical students, there is pressure to suppress negative emotion in order to conform and "demonstrate worthiness for medicine".[207] As well as the subjective experience with medical training, there is objective evidence of emotional suppression in doctors. Studies with electro-encephalogram (EEG),[208] and functional MRI (fMRI)[209] have shown cohorts of doctors to have reduced or down-regulated emotional responses to images of pain producing techniques in other people. This lack of emotion, empathy, or care may not always be a strength and could, in fact, be implicated in the genesis of burnout.[210]

It has been suggested that burnout is a natural, even expected, coping mechanism to deal with excess stress.[211] When one 'ceases to care', the detachment becomes a mechanism for feeling less stress. This may free up cognitive resources to allow attention to be paid to other matters.

Unfortunately, this detachment and associated weakened relationships can lead to increased isolation and a downward spiral of worsening psychological distress. Overworked and emotionally less mature young doctors may find themselves suppressing emotions to cope with daily stresses and thus become prime candidates for burnout.

It is time to reinvent ingrained patterns of teaching, expectations, and our own responses. Rather than suppressing feelings and emotions, a different way of recognising what we are experiencing emotionally and then implementing coping strategies is overdue. After all, allowing ourselves to feel and express both positive and negative emotions may reduce our risk of burnout and also extend our lives.

9.5 The Benefits of Supportive Relationships

The Harvard study on adult development is another longitudinal study with important findings and implications for our well-being.[212] Initially named the 'Grant Study' after the first research director, the study commenced in 1938 using Harvard undergraduates to study the development of "normal people".[213] Note that this cohort of 268 "normal" people were all male (only men could attend Harvard at that time), white, well-educated, and privileged. Quite early in the study, 20 of the original cohort dropped out, but the other 248 have been followed throughout their lives. Most are deceased, with the survivors now in their 90s.

The study, now with its fourth long-serving director, has maintained health checks, psychological and social data, and regular interviews examining all facets of the men's lives. The focus of the research has altered slightly over time, reflecting societal changes and the different interests of each director. As the men have aged, instructive demographic data on impacts of certain life choices and circumstances has been obtained.

Occurring almost in parallel with the Harvard Study was the Sheldon Glueck study on inner-city youth in nearby Boston, commencing in 1939.[214] Glueck obtained funding to study 500 youths, 250 of whom had been in reform school and 250 had not. All had grown up in the low socioeconomic area of inner-city Boston with poverty and disadvantage. These youth, who were around 14 years of age at the time of entry to the study, had less schooling than their Harvard counterparts and were assessed to have slightly lower IQs on entry to the study. The Glueck males were restudied at 17, 25, and 32 years of age, with the last interviews conducted around 1961.

The third director of the Harvard Study, George Vaillant,[215] was granted permission in 1975 to re-contact the original inner-city youths of the Glueck study, now middle aged, and follow these individuals in conjunction with the Harvard study entrants from that point on, with the same biennial questionnaires and a five-yearly physical examination.

The 'inner-city' men had higher mortality when compared with the Harvard graduates. However, when controlled for smoking rates, alcohol intake, obesity levels, and education, there was no difference in mortality. The variables of income, IQ level, parental social class, and privilege did not influence mortality rates. As both groups aged, the most significant indicators of mortality risk were social supports, relationships, and the level of love experienced.

Men in both arms of the study who were more isolated than they would wish were found to be less happy, with earlier health decline in mid-life, earlier decline of brain function, and living shorter lives. Conversely, strong social supports led to less psychological distress and decreased mental and physical deterioration. Those more connected to family, friends, and community were happier and lived longer. The factors most strongly linked with life satisfaction and longevity were not genetics, but relationship quality.

Although many of the men were fortunate enough to have long-lasting, happy marriages, not all experienced this. Having a supportive marriage was beneficial in measures of health and well-being; however, it was the quality of all close relationships that mattered, not only marriage. Indeed, living with conflict in a marriage was worse for life satisfaction, health, and longevity than having no close relationships at all.

The important components contributing to a good life were the same for both groups. Life satisfaction and longevity were not influenced directly by income or privilege. Health, happiness, and length of life were most closely linked to the quality of one's relationships.

The things we often prioritise and aspire to in life, such as wealth, status, and symbols of financial success such as houses and cars, are not what creates well-being. Longer, healthier, happier lives relate to how we interact with those close to us.

9.6 The Effects of Stress

There is an accepted and growing realisation within medicine that much physical illness and disease has its origins in chronic inflammation.[216] Acute inflammation is a desirable occurrence in the presence of an insult such as infection or trauma. The inflammatory response begins the healing process through increased blood flow to the injured area, bringing appropriate immune cells to the area among other mediators of healing. Acute inflammation can last from minutes to days and is a critical response needed for survival.

However, systemic chronic inflammation refers to inflammatory processes that persist for extended periods, and well after the challenge has ended. This ongoing inflammation is associated with problems such as cardiovascular disease, diabetes, and autoimmune diseases such as arthritis. For example, underlying chronic inflammation within the body can promote the build-up of atherosclerotic plaque within coronary arteries, narrowing the vessel and thereby increasing risk of ischaemia and myocardial infarction. In layman's terms, the chronic inflammation that comes with psychological stress can cause an increase in chest pain due to reduced oxygen transport to the heart and subsequent increased risk of heart attack.

In addition to the well-recognised risk factors for chronic inflammation such as ageing, obesity, and smoking, there is also growing evidence to suggest that persistent psychological stress and negative emotional states can create chronic inflammation.[217,218] As we know, a sudden perception of threat, whether physical or psychological, will turn on an immediate 'fight-flight-freeze' response in our sympathetic nervous system. This induces physiological changes including the release of adrenaline and cortisol, mobilisation of glycogen stores, an increase in heart rate, and diversion of blood to skeletal muscle. After the threat has gone, the physiological changes dissipate, our pounding heart slows, and homeostasis resumes.

Chronic unremitting psychological stress can create a similar 'fight-flight-freeze' type response – but one that never settles. In this situation, there is continuous stimulation of the hypothalamic-pituitary-adrenal axis and overactivity of the sympathetic nervous system with unrelenting high levels of adrenaline, cortisol, and pro-inflammatory cytokines within the body.[219]

If chronic psychological stress causes chronic inflammation which can ultimately produce physical disease in an individual, it would seem that groups who collectively suffer significant chronic psychological distress should also exhibit an excess of physical disease. One such group is those who experience post-traumatic stress disorder (PTSD) with unremitting psychological distress. Indeed, within these groups, there is a strong link between poorer health outcomes over time and PTSD.[220]

In a large population registry in Denmark, those citizens (all non-veterans) who had suffered with PTSD had increased adverse cardiovascular events[221] compared with the rest of the population, even after accounting for confounding variables. PTSD sufferers also have increased rates of autoimmune disease,[222] endocrine dysfunction, and higher rates of diabetes,[223] pulmonary disorders, and cancer. Those exposed to childhood abuse suffer from ongoing life-long health conditions eroding health and "speeding up" biological ageing through a greater "dose" of stress early in life.[224]

In Australian hospitals, many healthcare workers have suffered significant psychological stress over recent years. With the high number of women who work in healthcare the results of the Nurses Health Study 2, which followed 49,978 female nurses for 20 years[225] are especially notable. Those nurses who endorsed four or more PTSD items on a seven-point scale had a 60% increased risk of cardiovascular disease. When considering young women, chronic stress and PTSD have also been found to have increased rates of endometriosis, pre-term birth, gestational diabetes, and pre-eclampsia.[226,227] Imaging studies in those suffering from chronic stress[228] have demonstrated reduction in size of the hippocampus (involved in memory and learning) and an increase in amygdalar volume (associated with the processing of fearful emotions and memory). These findings have been suggested to explain the changes in attention and executive function seen in stressful workplaces. Those experiencing chronic psychological distress reveal alterations in brain processing and connectivity on fMRI studies which may explain the impaired cognition seen in chronic stress states.[229]

If chronic low-grade inflammation impacts executive brain function, could it be that the increased professional errors found in hospitals with poor culture and in those suffering with burnout[230] have their origins in unrelenting workplace stress ultimately leading to chronic brain inflammation?

9.7 The Advantage of 'Undoing'

I was driving into the hospital at 4am one morning after being called by a midwife to come in for a patient who was having her second baby. The woman had presented in established labour and was progressing rapidly. While enroute, I received a second call from the same midwife to tell me that the fetal monitoring had become unsatisfactory with prolonged decelerations of the heart rate. The midwife had examined the woman and found her cervix to be fully dilated. She had encouraged the patient to begin pushing with contractions.

During fetal heart rate decelerations, the slowing of the heart can be associated with less oxygen being delivered to the baby's brain. However, it is not uncommon to see decelerations late in labour, and I was still expecting to come in for an uncomplicated delivery.

As I entered the dimly lit delivery room, the patient was screaming with pain. I noticed that the fetal heart rate was 60 beats per minute, less than half of what it should be, and the rate was not recovering at all between contractions. This situation could not continue due to the risk of hypoxic damage to the baby's brain. Quickly speaking to the woman, I told her that I would have to examine her and possibly assist delivery.

The internal examination, under duress due to the patient's discomfort with labour, revealed that she was indeed fully dilated. However, there was a problem. The baby's head was malpositioned; it was looking the wrong way and thus presenting as a larger object to pass through the pelvis than when in an optimal position. Also, the 'station' or level of the head in the pelvis was a little higher than ideal, and not far enough down to guarantee an uncomplicated delivery.

The unsatisfactory fetal monitoring mandated urgent delivery. The options were to try to rotate the baby's head with instruments in the labour ward to allow for delivery, or take her to the operating theatre for reassessment and possibly a caesarean section. Calling in theatre staff and an anaesthetist would take at least 30 minutes before the baby would be delivered at this time of night. I didn't think the situation could wait that long. On the other hand, trying to deliver the baby currently could be difficult. Rotation of the head with forceps, my preferred option as it gave a more reliable and quicker delivery, would be too painful for the mother without an epidural. A ventouse, or vacuum, delivery could be performed without an epidural but had a greater chance of failure than a forceps delivery did. I was also worried that if I tried to perform an instrumental delivery and was unsuccessful, I could have further worsened the status of an already compromised baby. There was no easy option. The labour ward at 4am can be a lonely place.

I decided to perform a vaginal delivery. It was the quickest way to deliver a baby that would need resuscitation. With the woman in lithotomy position and having instilled local anaesthetic to some-what numb the pelvic area, I applied a ventouse cup on the correct part of the baby's head. The baby's heart rate was still very low; mine was very high.

With a contraction, the mother pushing, and my traction on the ventouse, the baby's head descended well. Over a couple of minutes, the baby descended, head rotated, and was delivered. In the end, it was quite a straightforward birth. Initially quite stunned, the baby recovered with resuscitation. The baby, Olivia, was resting in her mother's arms soon after birth.

While waiting to deliver the placenta, I could feel my anxiety resolving. The midwives in the room also took a deep breath, as they had recognised the gravity of the situation. The new parents were blissfully unaware of the level of concern we had held.

Completing the birth, with a healthy crying baby and two joyful parents in the room, the principal midwife and I started to have some chat and banter. The type of warm, humorous exchange that often occurs in a well-functioning delivery suite. Minutes before I had been worried, but now I was feeling good, proud of the job I had done, and thrilled with the outcome for a lovely mother. I was left with a pleasant feeling.

Acute stress, both physical and psychological, is good for us when it dissipates quickly and completely. Our health is optimised when we experience a full range of emotions. Our physiological and psychological resources grow when we are exposed to stress along with the resolution of said stress. The 'undoing effect'[231] of positive emotions allows release of the 'fight-flight-freeze' sympathetic activation and contributes to our well-being.[232]

Just as we realise that impaired happiness can be both a consequence of and a contributor to physical ill-health,[233] cultivation of positive emotion can help prevent and be involved in the treatment of illness. Promotion of positive affect has been shown to be of value in the management of psychological conditions,[234] regulation of diabetes,[235] and reduction of pain disorders.[236] Clearly, positive interventions are not the sole treatment of illness and disease, however, they must increasingly become part of a complete plan of care.

Those who only experience negative thoughts and emotions are adjudged to have depression. Similarly, it would be unusual to only ever feel positive emotion. The balance is important. Within our hospitals, it is this balance that has become disordered. Our focus has come to rest solely on negative conditions, and our expression of emotion is overwhelmingly negative.

Facilitating the undoing effect with positive emotions may help long-term patients who have a small win in their otherwise frustrating recovery, or clinicians who can celebrate a good outcome within a seemingly never-ending workload. The undoing effect can be promoted through individual reflection or through interactions with team members. This aspect of a workplace can be fostered. This is an action that can contribute to individual well-being and improved outcomes.

9.8 The Quest for Individual Success

All people want to have a successful life. Of course, there are many different definitions of success. In our modern world, we are often motivated by objective success. The external trappings of success such as money, status, and possessions are big drivers in individualistic societies such as ours. These urges to attain visible markers of objective success are possibly reinforced through our upbringing, professional training, and societal expectations.

The evidence that promoting positive emotions and attitudes will lead to advantages with longevity, marital and relationship quality, and health benefits may seem like long-term esoteric goals to some. To many, short-term objective success will be more motivating. To a driven professional in their 30s, the desire for career advancement and financial enrichment may be a more pressing concern than the consideration of longer-term health and length of life.

These attitudes are not unreasonable. The concept of success relates to achievement of goals that are valued by one's society and culture. However, it is possible to view achievement of individual goals in a different way. It appears that cultivating positive mood states actually contributes to success in all of life's domains,[237] including professional advancement, wealth accumulation, and marital longevity.

Clearly, we cannot ascertain from a simple cross-section of the population whether success causes happiness or vice versa. Therefore, longitudinal assessments are needed. Examining the evidence reveals that positive affect leads to increased academic success,[238] and those with higher levels of positive disposition are more likely to get a 'better' job.[239] Employees with positive affect achieve higher ratings from superiors and are more likely to be assessed as leadership material,[240] and there is flow on to higher remuneration and achievement of leadership roles.[241,242]

In elite sport, mood and affect are similarly critical to success of both the performer and the team. The moods of all players affect team dynamics,[243] and the individual's mood has been shown to be a factor in subjective and objective assessment of their performance.[244] In top-flight cricket, regulation of negative mood states led to more subjective happiness for the player and the objective success of an increased individual batting average.[245]

9.9 The Importance of Workplaces

Work takes up a large proportion of our days. It is important in terms of allowing income production, generation of self-worth, facilitating purpose, and production of goods and services required and valued by society. Another crucial function of anyone's workplace is to allow human interaction and connection.

One motivating factor for embracing change in our hospitals should be the desire to facilitate relationships at work. In the presence of toxic culture or challenging times for a hospital, emotions such as anger and frustration are easy to identify. However, less obvious emotions such as sadness or loneliness can be hidden. Sometimes, it is hard to understand the magnitude of certain health risks,[246] especially with something like loneliness which is often silent and hidden, with insidious effects. Loneliness is endemic in our societies[247] and workplaces, including our hospitals and healthcare institutions.[248] The incidence of all types of disease are increased with loneliness.[249] Loneliness is dangerous for our health.

Although all causes of death are increased with loneliness,[250] it can be hard to intuitively understand the level of health risk that isolation at work exposes one to. In this setting, the concept of 'Microlives' can be valuable. Microlives are a mathematical construct that facilitate a more accessible understanding of risk and uncertainty. The concept of a microlife allows the effects of different habits and environments to be quantified in a 'real world' setting. The construct of a microlife revolves around one millionth of an adult life, which roughly equates to 30 minutes.[251]

Through this framework, we can assess our own behaviours and decisions, and the effects on the rest of our lives. For example, smoking two cigarettes is equal to removing one microlife from your life's total. Similarly, drinking an extra two alcoholic beverages or eating a hamburger is equal to removing one microlife. So, two cigarettes or two beers take 30 minutes off your lifespan.

Thus, we can appreciate how the effect of individual decisions repeated many times through the years impact the length of our lives. The good news is that a healthy diet adds four microlives per day, and 20 minutes of exercise each day gives us an extra two microlives.

The detrimental effect of loneliness on our health has been suggested to be equivalent with the risk from smoking. In terms of microlives, loneliness at work seems to be roughly equivalent to smoking 8 to 10 cigarettes per day. Smoking this many cigarettes has been estimated to reduce one's life by six and a half years on average.[252] By extrapolating these figures loneliness at work may shorten one's life by more than six years! Of course, loneliness may not be a permanent state. Different work practices and systems may alleviate isolation and loneliness. But while one is lonely, each day at work takes four to five microlives, or over two hours each day, from the end of one's life.

With the current rates of loneliness, it is likely that we, or someone close to us, will be isolated and lonely at work. By putting more effort into interpersonal interactions and relationships, we can improve the workplace and our own health, and maybe even prolong someone else's life. Perhaps those people who are not feeling lonely will be fortunate enough to generate extra microlives for themselves by expressing positive emotions each day. In this way, they can help those who are isolated while also benefitting their own life.

Energy science gives us a useful metaphor on the benefits of coming together. In nuclear fission, an atom is split apart to create enormous energy but great destruction. Nuclear fusion results from bringing together two positively charged atoms which results in no destruction, and production of even greater amounts of energy. This concept from the world of physics has an important parallel in human relationships. Division and separation can cause harm and trauma; coming together can produce positive effects for all.

9.10 Noticing Milestones

Our lives are so jam-packed and fast paced that time seems to pass in the blink of an eye. We all have a lot to mark, celebrate, and be grateful for, but we are often too busy to even notice. Surely our lives will be more enjoyable and happier when we reflect on the good that occurs every day.

After I had been an obstetrician for a number of years, I realised that the period of time immediately post-delivery with new parents seemed to have lost some significance for me. While there is clearly need for ongoing clinical care and vigilance, I felt that this interval had become a little cold, even perfunctory on occasion. In focusing too heavily on the medical side, I had perhaps lost sight of the emotional significance of the event. My usual practice was to complete the delivery, ensure there was no excessive bleeding or other complication for the mother, and give congratulations to the new parents after checking their baby over. I'd hang around in the delivery suite for a while to complete paperwork and perform another check of the mother before heading home or back to my consulting rooms.

It occurred to me that although my congratulations were genuine, it didn't feel enough – although I wasn't sure if the feeling of 'not enough' was for them or for me. In some way, I felt like my words were just part of the delivery process; expected and standard. I wondered whether the event – uplifting as every birth is – needed more marking. I further questioned what I could say that was of value to the new parents (especially if it was their first baby) and also for myself. What was this about, for me?

One realisation I had was that time was passing. I knew that many milestones had rushed past in my own life. Perhaps, like many young people, I hadn't stopped and reflected enough. Increasingly, I recognised the importance of what I did and how privileged I was to share in these important moments in others' lives. I started giving my congratulations in a different way after completing all my tasks. I tried to be more present and connected, rather than having my mind jump to the next upcoming job. I would say something like, "Congratulations. There are only a handful of really important days in anyone's life. This is one of the biggest – the birth of your first baby. You deserve to be proud. I'm so happy for you and I have loved being involved with your care."

My previous way of giving congratulations had also been sincere, however, with this style, which took less than a minute irrespective of how I worded my thoughts, it seemed that the parents took pause to reflect. It felt better. Maybe it didn't make any difference to the new and excited parents. Perhaps it was only important for me, to stop and reflect. But one thing was true – these were big and special days.

{e·volv·ing}

EVOLUTION IMPLIES INCREMENTAL CUMULATIVE CHANGE leading to modification and development. How any system evolves will depend on its situation and characteristics at origin, and the pressure and demands of the external environment. Under different conditions, two identical organisms or systems will evolve with varied trajectories. The change may be gradual and slow but still lead to dissimilar appearances. Sometimes, the outcomes may be vastly different.

A caterpillar will eat and eat until one day it creates an outer cocoon for itself. Within this casing, the caterpillar changes to emerge as a vastly different creature – a butterfly – with different behaviours, properties, and sources of nutrition. Most caterpillars do not successfully survive this transition. Fewer than 1 in 20 caterpillars transform into butterflies.

Similarly, healthcare institutions are constantly evolving. Unfortunately, most find significant improvement difficult to achieve. However, some organisations can successfully undergo radically transformative change, or metamorphosis, to emerge more wondrous and inspiring.

10.1 Standing on Shoulders

One hospital that I worked in as an obstetric registrar had a set up where each obstetric unit had three principal consultants. In one of these units, or teams, the head of unit was an older man with vast experience. His skills were legendary, and he was also a supportive and kind boss. He remains one of my heroes. The 'second in charge' was also an older obstetrician. Experienced, skilled, and friendly, but without the personal warmth exhibited by the head. The third consultant was younger, having relatively recently finished his specialty training. He was a driven, ambitious, clever doctor who was also good to work with. It was a great unit.

At our unit meetings after a ward round, we would discuss the patients. Occasionally, a rare condition would be discussed and the younger consultant often knew all the latest research and statistics. Sometimes, he would tell us the exact incidence of an extremely rare obstetric condition and what the recent peer-reviewed evidence and opinions were. The head of unit would listen to this and then tell us that he had personally looked after a handful of these cases and describe what happened to the patients. It was a fabulous combination, blending wisdom and experience with enthusiasm and the latest research.

Eventually, a few years later, the head of unit retired. The youngest consultant of the unit was appointed to the main role. He also became a good boss. Some of the old routines were retained, and new styles were also introduced. The unit continued to be a well-regarded rotation for registrars. Different, but still good, as the new replaced the old.

All systems change with time. Sometimes this is rapid, and in response to sudden challenges, and sometimes the change is so slow that it is hardly noticeable. However, like an old stately oak tree with an apparently unchanging daily appearance, there is movement.

Seasons pass, leaves age and decay to be replaced by new growth. Imperceptibly, the tree changes.

Our human systems are similar; decay of an old system leads to replacement by a new one. Although poor culture in hospitals often seems to be a static, ever-present condition, there is underlying change. Unfortunately, within these behaviourally problematic systems, the incremental changes can occur but then circle back to end up in a similar place. Conditions evolve, but the unhelpful cycle ends up rotating around to where it started.

Thankfully, changes in culture are not totally out of our control. The evolution of hospital systems can be directed and guided to move ever closer to the desired state. Small positive changes that are reinforced and repeated will create ripples that fan out to create change over time. The old ways can be allowed to decay at the same time as generating helpful interventions, affirming styles of behaviour, and people-friendly systems that allow green shoots of fresh growth.

10.2 Adversity Leading to Change

In 1959, the future US president John F Kennedy famously stated that the Chinese character for the word 'crisis' had two meanings – 'danger' and 'opportunity'.[253] While in a linguistic sense this may not be strictly true, it does illustrate the concept that uncertainty is associated with risk and potential for change.

Routine gives us safety and comfort and therefore we rarely embark on major changes without good reason. Recognition of the need for personal change will often only occur in the midst of a crisis in one's life. Difficult circumstances may lead to self-examination and an honest appraisal of the changes required. This intense self-reflection becomes the first step on the path leading to personal change in attitudes and behaviours. An ability and preparedness to honestly examine and question attitudes, biases, and assumptions is required.

In a similar way, all organisations will continue to operate in the same unchanging and 'comfortable' manner while conditions are productive and stable. Only the onset of disaster will upset the status quo and provoke deep exploration of systems and processes. Sometimes, a crisis is truly needed for an organisation to honestly examine its inner 'self'.

Hospitals and healthcare institutions have been significantly affected by the crisis of the Covid-19 pandemic, with ongoing unprecedented demand for services and a worsening of the burn-out epidemic. The systems that have worked for so long appear to be faltering. Small challenges that have been overlooked, denied, or resisted have aggregated. There is now a tsunami of problems. This wave of discontent and difficulty is crashing over our healthcare systems, and we are struggling to stay afloat. We are clinging to life rafts constructed around established systems. We are barely floating with our old methods and business-as-usual approach. We are hoping that the waters recede and allow a return to the solid land of happy routine.

However, deep down, most understand that this is a time of change. Conditions will never be the same again. There will be a 'new normal' at some point. Attempting to grasp desperately to our old ways will result in a state of perpetual almost-drowning. Not dead, but barely surviving.

10.3 Don't Waste a Crisis

This crisis is the point at which positive change can happen. The conditions necessary to allow sudden progress may only occur when everything is in turmoil. With the current climate of great uncertainty, we may be prepared for self-examination at both a personal and an organisational level. This could be the moment when we can honestly assess the reality of our processes and question previously held assumptions to inform the planning of where and how we would like our healthcare systems to be.

Of course, to propose major change in hospitals at this time of incredible demand may seem ridiculous. However, the process of change that I am proposing will not cause any disruption, as the initial changes are not about altering delivery of services. They will not immediately influence patient care systems. These changes revolve around interpersonal relationships and interactions. The biggest initial change relates to how people communicate with each other. Fostering positive communication styles allows all other issues to be raised and discussed rather than ignored and hidden.

In fact, through the seemingly-simple act of acknowledging and embracing the need for change, we begin to change. Through committing to a new way, incorporating an open, honest, and curious outlook, the journey begins. The mindset alters from feeling besieged and overwhelmed by current challenges, to become engaged with excitement and optimism relating to the future. The initial acceptance that change is needed is the necessary first step towards the destination.

Even in the midst of turmoil, some definitive movement is required. Otherwise, while we are trying to stay afloat, it seems that we are treading water. Working hard but not moving. We can't tread water forever – eventually we will go under.

10.4 Generation of Trust

In recent times, while leaders have continued with the same messages, styles, and belief in old systems, the situation in hospitals has grown worse. The attitude of continuing to do what has always worked and felt comfortable is unsurprising. We would all make the same choice. Everyone wants to hang onto routine unless forced to do otherwise. However, in this setting of continued challenges without clear direction forward, hospital staff have lost faith. They are overworked and feel undervalued, with little confidence in a leadership that appears to underestimate or deny the size and difficulties of the current work situation. Healthcare workers have toiled bravely and tirelessly in recent times. They deserve thanks and acknowledgement for what they have given. Hospital leaders owe these people a debt, and this debt must be paid with compassion and gratitude.

The faith and trust that has been lost will not be recovered easily; they must be earned through honesty and integrity. This starts with an admission from hospital management that no easy answers to the current situation are evident. Part of this honest message must be an assurance that all are valued, and that services will continue even while the hospital engages in an open process that seeks to enhance the organisation. Truthful and positive messaging, even when speaking about troubling issues, creates respect.

Leaders want staff to give them respect, faith, and trust. The staff want the same from the leaders. As US president Theodore Roosevelt said:[254]

> *"They won't care how much you know,*
> *until they know how much you care."*

10.5 Leadership in a Crisis

Leaders are not made for a crisis; they are created by a crisis. In difficult times, some individuals will find others following their lead. These individuals may not be designated leaders by title, yet they exert influence through connecting with others and by being able to exhibit positive qualities in the maelstrom of anxiety and uncertainty.

Indeed, when crisis occurs and interrupts life's comfortable humdrum existence, people are often more easily guided due to their desire to find stability and support. In this uncertain world, leaders can generate increased authority and their message becomes more poignant.

It is even more important in uncertain times to acknowledge emotions (one's own and those of others). This fosters human connection, with a joint understanding that we all share emotions and that experiencing fear and anxiety does not indicate weakness. The worst message may be to simply reassure or to convey a false sense of bravado. It is essential not to downplay real challenges and the resultant emotions.

The leader's messaging can always convey sentiments of trust in the ability of the team to rise to the challenge. A positive valence in all communication fosters confidence. It creates hope and belief. Hope is crucial in the darkest times. Fear, while acknowledged as being present, cannot be allowed to run through the organisation. Unexpected and unpredictable problems must be contained. Shared understanding and unity – built on communication – become paramount.

The leadership group must examine all information and data in a process that explores the disruption and its consequences and allows a joint understanding of the way forward. Rather than retreating into a 'leadership bunker' extolling advice, the leaders can choose to proceed in a human, caring way that involves people and cares for them. Organisational fear will not be dispelled through reinforcement of written protocols or emailed directives, rather from leaders who are prepared to stop, listen, and explain.

Personal uncertainty often causes us to resort to habits and routines that make us feel comfortable and safe. Even a simple disruption to one's own routine can create anxiety. The same applies to organisations. A change of routines disturbs the status quo. Therefore, in challenging times, existing rituals must be maintained and even promoted. While significant change is occurring, these practices that are part of the 'fabric' of the group must be cherished and saved. New rituals may come into existence during this period that also foster belonging. Doing familiar activities with trusted others helps with the understanding that the challenge is faced by many together, rather than by each person individually.

Leaders want their organisations to have attributes of interpersonal support, stability, honesty, and resilience. The best way to begin witnessing these behaviours is firstly by modelling them oneself. In this way, the organisation can be moulded and altered. As Gandhi said:[255]

> *"Be the change you want to see in the world."*

10.6 Healing and Recovering

After major disruptions, a hospital will eventually resume a state resembling 'normal'. It will recover from extraordinary demands and be able to resume a usual mix of work. Depending upon the healing process, the hospital may emerge a stronger and more resilient organisation, or it could be weakened from the insult and more vulnerable when future challenges occur. It will be critical to give attention to the nature of the crisis, how it was handled, and to ensure the full recovery of all staff. Without this conscious process of appraisal and 'taking stock', the hospital will move on quickly but perhaps feel as though there was unfinished business. Unless there is attention to 'closing the loop' and allowing healing, the hospital could become a more silent and damaged institution where future shocks may reverberate with even greater force.

The level of future resilience is influenced by the assessment made around the nature of the crisis and the current state of affairs. Again, sense-making[256] allows for development of shared beliefs and confidence that the organisation is strong and robust. Conversely, when events are poorly understood, anxiety about future challenges will fester.

The process of healing can lead to the creation and recognition of both internal and external resources. In-house resources may include new connections and deepening of interpersonal bonds. These relationships increase camaraderie and organisational strength. During the process of recovery, an awareness of improved external bonds with other institutions and hospitals may also become apparent.

Since disruptions and crises affect all staff in different ways, compassion must be a critical feature of the organisation. Compassion involves feeling, noticing, and responding to another person's emotional state. It requires an ability to become aware of and admit someone else's hurt, and a desire to follow up with actions that reflect this awareness. Compassion is essential for healing.

10.7 The Need for Hope

Proposed organisational change is an unsettling time for many. Organisational challenges or new directions can be threatening and scary events. All people interpret information and experiences in an affective, emotional manner, as well as cognitively. Data is processed through a filter of feelings and emotions, resulting in a mental formulation of the organisation's changes. Therefore, all understanding and cognition is made with an overlay of one's own emotions and the associated assumptions of the organisational culture.

Affection for leadership figures will allow unconscious sense-making to occur with trust in the organisation's decisions. This positive regard will allay some of the anxiety about the change and help individuals embrace the strategies and initiatives of the organisation. If there is mistrust of and lack of affection for leadership, a proposed change may result in negative behaviours with rumours, suspicion, and dissension.

The 18th century Scottish philosopher David Hume stated that human reason is "the slave of the passions".[257]

By passions, Hume meant feelings, not just overriding intense emotions such as anger. He was indicating that rational thought is not the deciding factor in our decision-making; rather, emotions and feelings drive our beliefs and cognitions. Sometimes, we may not act based on thoughts in the calculated way we believe we are capable of. Instead, our actions may be overwhelmingly influenced by emotion.

There can be a misunderstanding in our culture, and particularly within medical systems, that expressing love and affection indicates weakness. It does not. It shows power and confidence. Being able to express positive emotions removes limitations from us. It is an important characteristic when dealing with individuals as well as larger groups and systems. If those within an organisation can talk about the emotional state of the institution, they will be able to solve problems through more open cognitive processes that allow innovation and creativity.

Recent worldwide health challenges have eroded positive emotion within hospitals. Many cannot see the way forward. The situation has often seemed hopeless. When people don't feel good and have low individual well-being, it can be hard for them to commit to the collective ideals and live up to team and organisational goals. This is where leadership is crucial. Through authenticity, integrity, and kindness, leaders can build hope.[258,259] To have hope is to feel that there is a way forward despite the size of the challenge. It gives belief that one can make those initial steps. Trust in and love for the leadership allows for a generation of hope in the wider organisation.

The leaders must begin this process – to give love is to become loved. And by giving trust, one becomes trusted.

These ideas are not new. Two hundred years ago, Napoleon Bonaparte said:[260]

"A leader is a dealer in hope."

10.8 Slower Growth

Today, as every day, I looked in the mirror. The face that looked back at me was very different to the one I had seen 30 years before, when I'd just started working in hospitals. I haven't felt any different day to day, and I haven't noticed daily change – but there has been change, slow and definite. I am in many ways a different person to the one I was all those years ago.

Of course, this is the nature of life. This is evolution. Things are constantly changing. Sometimes quickly; often more slowly, with unnoticeable incremental alteration. With the slow change, other things build up or become ingrained. The result of many days of small changes. I have developed lines and wrinkles.

We can choose how to view the faces looking back at us from the mirror. We can see evidence of age, disrepair, and decay, or we can choose to see the evidence of experience, wisdom, and pride. The ingrained changes can be regarded as stress wrinkles, or laughter lines.

In hospital cultures, where it seems that things will never change, they are, in fact, changing constantly but slowly and in an unseen manner. Frustrations with lack of progress can lead to ingrained patterns of poor behaviour. Conversely, small positive actions and interactions can lead, over time, to embedding a culture of excellence.

There can be despair around management practices, obstruction to proposals, and difficult relationships where our opinions are not valued. However, in the two-way street that is any relationship, we often exhibit all the behaviours and attitudes that we accuse others of. We put up barriers, have pre-conceived expectations, and feel that we won't be listened to.

Evolution continues with never-ending change. Most of this is out of our control. However, looking at the mirror, I was seeing the first – and perhaps only – person I was able to change. When trying to achieve outcomes we think useful, first we must examine our own attitudes. Instead of concentrating on what we think is needed and what we can get, perhaps we should think about what we are prepared to give.

10.9 Guiding Change

It is understood that organisational culture change in hospitals is a long, complex, uncertain undertaking. To envisage a rapid journey from here to a well circumscribed 'there' is foolish and naïve. However, with the starting goal of creating the best environment for all, and honest appraisal of the path required, hospitals can move ever closer to where they would like to be. Progress may feel slow at times but then, after long periods of seeming inactivity, great advances can suddenly occur.

Each hospital has its own unique strengths, capabilities, and challenges. Therefore, no two change programs, and no two journeys, can be the same. Each individual hospital will evolve to a different place, with its own feel, culture, and practices. That is an appropriate, expected, and desirable outcome. Individual rich variation in hospitals, without problematic cultural aspects, should be an encouraged and treasured goal. However, the outcome that we hope for will not eventuate with detailed strategy and programmatic change; the result will come from fostering positive organic growth to guide evolution.

Traditional organisational change perspectives prioritise 'normal' accompanied by the desire for constant equilibrium. With this mindset, change is viewed as being linear and controllable. In this realm of strategic management theory, expertise and traditional practices are highly regarded. The goal is to continue with the present organisational structure and to restore balance whenever disruptions occur. With this thinking, anything that causes a gap between expectations and reality is considered a problem. As all unexpected events cause turbulence, the purpose of leaders and management revolves around problem identification and solving – trouble shooting. In this way, transactional leadership tries to control and reward those who engage in and achieve expected outcomes. However, uncertainty can be accepted and even embraced. Transformational leadership focuses on existing needs and operations while recognising that unpredictability may result in diversions leading to achievement of greater goals. These leaders allow the flexibility that is required to foster creativity and innovation.

Standard management styles lead to an organisation that becomes increasingly concentrated on the eradication of aberrant behaviour and any states analysed as being negative. Anything that deviates from the norm is viewed as a problem and a possible challenge to the organisation. This attitude results in leadership designed around control of people and behaviours, rather than leadership that focuses attention on learning from people and unexpected outcomes.

With traditional management styles, even 'positively deviant' practices, in which people or groups excel, can be seen as abnormal and a threat to current organisational structure. Processes become data-driven rather than data-informed. The leadership and the organisation become problem-centred, siloed, rigid, controlling, and reactive. Reactive versus creative: same letters, different outcomes.

10.10 Positive Evolution

Practices that guide positive change are essentially based around an ability to analyse the same events from different viewpoints to those which are usually employed. Instead of disruptions to normal operating conditions being feared and resisted, unexpected outcomes can be welcomed as natural challenges that may uncover new opportunities or lead to new learning.

Rather than just identifying problems to solve, positive change seeks out original thoughts and tries to disseminate improved practices. Positive organisations use enriching communication styles and collaboration. This allows them to build psychological assets and enlist relationship resources which can be utilised in future organisational challenges. For example, high-performing teams exhibit positivity ratios in their communication as high as 6:1.[261, 262] In less positive organisational cultures, where the primary focus is on identification and correction of problems, feelings of anger and anxiety can be magnified.[263] In these environments, with fear of reprimand for mistakes, organisational behaviour becomes silent and rigid with adherence to established patterns and protocols.

A positive organisational change process concentrates on identifying the best features of current practices and promotes these as part of the best possible future. This method compares with the standard practice of focusing on problems and eradicating these in an attempt to maintain the current reality.

Commencing positive evolution in healthcare begins with honesty and openness, and progresses to communication styles, ways of examining outcomes, and creating new filters for decision making. Honest, kind communication combined with the ability to forgive will begin to develop trust and break down walls. Dedication of time and resources to start the contemplation and discussion of what is valued and how we measure ourselves starts to build an improved organisational culture.

Consideration of these issues, such as production of a holistic index to guide decision making, is not costly in dollar terms yet indicates that sufficient commitment exists to re-imagine the current ways and processes. With this approach, communication styles and decisions are influenced more by organisational values than by financial pressures or the 'bottom-line'. Values, in addition to sound business sense, allow the most morally correct actions, rather than just the most financially expedient.

Positive change requires the courage to explore our own attitudes and assumptions without judgement, and then to apply these principles with our teams. Rather than telling people what to do, we can show them how to be. All communications and relationships involve at least two people, and these interactions are how leaders take others with them to build the teams and organisations they have dreamt of.

As the African proverb says:[264]

> *"If you want to go fast, go alone. If you want to go far, go with others."*

10.11 An Important Perspective

Einstellung is a German word that indicates the development of a mechanised and rigid state of mind that tries to do things in the same fashion time after time, even in different circumstances. It leads to an inability to imagine or implement new ways. There is a reaction to problems but no originality, flexibility, or innovation.

When considering the long-term operation of any large human system, such as a hospital, trying to resist unplanned change and expecting to maintain an unchanging path appears foolish, short-sighted, and doomed to fail. A more sensible attitude may be an acceptance that change occurs constantly, even if it's invisible. This attitudinal change could free up a new way of looking at processes in the hospital. Rather than the usual negative feeling over disruptions or unexpected events – with attempts to avoid adverse outcomes with rigidity and control – it may be more useful to consider the hospital a living and constantly-changing organic system. This may facilitate an understanding that we can guide system change rather than control it.

In any conversation about evolution, the words ascribed to Charles Darwin may be instructive:[265]

> *"It is not the most intellectual of the species that survives; it is not the strongest that survives; but the species [...] that is able to adapt and adjust to the changing environment in which it finds itself."*

Adhering to the same ways and trying to continue along the same path while resisting change is not helping to improve hospital culture. Times have changed and what is now needed is a willingness to embrace new methods and a desire to promote positive change. Evolution will always occur in unexpected ways. Acceptance of this fact may allow us to guide evolution in positive ways and adapt and adjust to our own rapidly changing healthcare environment.

{con·clud·ing}

OUR HEALTHCARE SYSTEMS NEED TO BE RECONSIDERED. What has worked well for past generations in our society is now failing, unable to meet demand, and damaging the people within the systems. We are running as fast as we can just to stay in the same place. Continued replication of the same practices and processes leads to the same outcomes. Even worse, ongoing replication and repetition will promote and exacerbate outdated, unexamined, second-rate systems.

We can take some solace from the fact that our systems have become so untenable. Without this realisation, we may have continued in the same vein for much longer. Understanding what bad looks like allows us to recognise good when it is achieved. We currently have an opportunity to re-invent and improve healthcare in Australia. This is a moment in time that must not be squandered.

The foundations of the required change are the very essence of what it is to be human. Our most unique and precious qualities. Through promoting the best of us as a species, those elements that have allowed human progress, we will be able to restore our systems and institutions to their rightful place. Successful change begins with collaboration and interaction. Positive emotion and communication styles facilitate the process of change. As humans, we have always achieved greatly when we have created cooperative and supportive groups and teams. These alliances function best when they aspire to operate with virtuous aims such as promoting trust, honesty, courage, openness, sharing, forgiveness, curiosity, respect, and integrity. The process operates optimally with acknowledgement and expression of positive emotions such as hope, happiness, joy, compassion, and gratitude.

With these united understandings and aspirations, we create a mission: to redesign and cultivate our systems to jointly produce something wonderful.

The Last Word

In many ways, an ending is only the beginning of something new. Hopefully, this book provokes some thought and discussion about our healthcare systems, maybe even some curiosity over what we could aspire to, and what could be created by viewing things differently.

The current difficulties in medical and hospital culture are not solely due to Covid. Problems were brewing long before the pandemic. However, the crisis may be the impetus needed to pursue a new future. Australian hospitals are wonderful institutions that have served us well. However, the systems that have been created to care for people have become overly mechanised and cold, and they are now starting to damage the people within them. It is time to examine our hospitals through a different lens.

As American anthropologist Margaret Mead said:[266]

> *"We are continually faced with great opportunities,*
> *brilliantly disguised as unsolvable problems."*

It is possible to imagine a new way, and it is possible to enact the changes required. We can guide the evolution of our systems to an ideal where the best of technological advances, modern practices, and wise business decisions are combined with human care and compassion.

Care is essential. We already care greatly for our patients and our institutions. Now it is time to reimagine and refocus on care and healing for ourselves as clinicians and for our team-mates. It's up to each of us.

My favourite, and perhaps the wisest, doctor – Dr Seuss – said it best:[267]

"Unless someone like you cares a whole awful lot.
Nothing is going to get better. It's not."

About the Author

Dr Simon Craig is a medical doctor who has specialised in Obstetrics and Gynaecology, working in both the public and private health systems. In addition to clinical roles, Dr Craig has been heavily involved with leadership and teaching. Guiding the development of junior staff and creating teams have been some of his greatest joys. With further study in conflict resolution and well-being science in the form of a Masters of Positive Psychology, Dr Craig's career and experience has turned to coaching and the optimisation of organisational culture.

His work can be accessed through www.posmed.com.au and he can be contacted through that site or at simon@simoncraig.com.au.

References

1   Shanafelt, T. D., Schein, E., Minor, L. B., Trockel, M., Schein, P., & Kirch, D. (2019). Healing the Professional Culture of Medicine. *Mayo Clinic Proceedings, 94*(8), 1556–1566

2   AMA Report on Health and Well-being of doctors, 2020

3   Tawfik, D. S., Profit, J., Morgenthaler, T. I., Satele, D. V., Sinsky, C. A., Dyrbye, L. N., Tutty, M. A., West, C. P., & Shanafelt, T. D. (2018). Physician Burnout, Well-being, and Work Unit Safety Grades in Relationship to Reported Medical Errors. *Mayo Clinic Proceedings, 93*(11), 1571–1580.

4   Brady, K. J. S., Sheldrick, R. C., Ni, P., Trockel, M. T., Shanafelt, T. D., Rowe, S. G., & Kazis, L. E. (2021). Examining the measurement equivalence of the Maslach Burnout Inventory across age, gender, and specialty groups in US physicians. *Journal of Patient-Reported Outcomes, 5*(1).

5   Vercio, C., Loo, L. K., Green, M., Kim, D. I., & Beck Dallaghan, G. L. (2021). Shifting Focus from Burnout and Wellness toward Individual and Organizational Resilience. *Teaching & Learning in Medicine, 33*(5), 568–576.

6   Barsade, S. G., Ramarajan, L., & Westen, D. (2009). Implicit affect in organizations. *Research in organizational behavior, 29*, 135-162.

7   Tawfik, D. S., Profit, J., Morgenthaler, T. I., Satele, D. V., Sinsky, C. A., Dyrbye, L. N., Tutty, M. A., West, C. P., & Shanafelt, T. D. (2018). Physician Burnout, Well-being, and Work Unit Safety Grades in Relationship to Reported Medical Errors. *Mayo Clinic Proceedings, 93*(11), 1571–1580.

8   Anderson, J. (2008, July 1). Physician suicide rates suggest lack of treatment: greater awareness of depression needed. *Clinical Psychiatry News, 36*(7), 1.

9   Ozcelik, H., & Barsade, S. G. (2018). No Employee an Island: Workplace Loneliness and Job Performance. *Academy of Management Journal, 61*(6), 2343–2366.

10   Ofei-Dodoo, S., Ebberwein, C., & Kellerman, R. (2020). Assessing loneliness and other types of emotional distress among practicing physicians. *Kansas Journal of Medicine, 13*, 1.

11   Holt-Lunstad, J., Smith, T. B., Baker, M., Harris, T., & Stephenson, D. (2015). Loneliness and social isolation as risk factors for mortality: a meta-analytic review. *Perspectives on psychological science, 10*(2), 227-237.

12   Jaremka, L. M., Fagundes, C. P., Peng, J., Bennett, J. M., Glaser, R., Malarkey, W. B., & Kiecolt-Glaser, J. K. (2013). Loneliness promotes inflammation during acute stress. *Psychological Science, 24*(7), 1089-1097.

13   Seppala, E., & King, M. (2017). Burnout at Work Isn't Just About Exhaustion. It's Also About Loneliness. *Harvard Business Review Digital Articles*, 2–4.

14   Jackson, E. R., Shanafelt, T. D., Hasan, O., Satele, D. V., & Dyrbye, L. N. (2016). Burnout and Alcohol Abuse/Dependence Among U.S. Medical Students. *Academic Medicine : Journal of the Association of American Medical Colleges, 91*(9), 1251–1256.

15   Creed, P. A., Rogers, M. E., Praskova, A., & Searle, J. (2014). Career calling as a personal resource moderator between environmental demands and burnout in Australian junior doctors. *Journal of Career Development, 41*(6), 547-561.

16   Henning, M., Hawken, S., & Hill, A. (2009). The quality of life of New Zealand doctors and medical students: what can be done to avoid burnout?.

17   Hope, V., & Henderson, M. (2014). Medical student depression, anxiety and distress outside North America: a systematic review. *Medical Education, 48*(10), 963–979.

18   Tawfik, D. S., Profit, J., Morgenthaler, T. I., Satele, D. V., Sinsky, C. A., Dyrbye, L. N., Tutty, M. A., West, C. P., & Shanafelt, T. D. (2018). Physician Burnout, Well-being, and Work Unit Safety Grades in Relationship to Reported Medical Errors. *Mayo Clinic Proceedings, 93*(11), 1571–1580.

19   Trzeciak, S., Roberts, B. W., & Mazzarelli, A. J. (2017). Compassionomics: Hypothesis and experimental approach. *Medical Hypotheses, 107*, 92–97.

20   Avey, J. B., Reichard, R. J., Luthans, F., & Mhatre, K. H. (2011). Meta-analysis of the impact of positive psychological capital on employee attitudes, behaviors, and performance. *Human resource development quarterly, 22*(2), 127-152.

21   Luthans, F., Avey, J. B., Avolio, B. J., & Peterson, S. J. (2010). The development and resulting performance impact of positive psychological capital. *Human Resource Development Quarterly, 21*(1), 41-67.

22   Work Health & Safety Act 2011, No 137, 2011. Compilation No 9, 31 July 2018. Australian Government.

23   Craiovan, P. M. (2014). Correlations between perfectionism, stress, psychopathological symptoms and burnout in the medical field. *Procedia-Social and Behavioral Sciences, 127*, 529-533.

24   Reivich, K. J., Seligman, M. E., & McBride, S. (2011). Master resilience training in the US Army. *American psychologist, 66*(1), 25.

25   Brown, B. (2010). *The gifts of imperfection: Let go of who you think you're supposed to be and embrace who you are.* Simon and Schuster.

26   Dyrbye, L., & Shanafelt, T. (2016). A narrative review on burnout experienced by medical students and residents. *Medical education, 50*(1), 132-149.

27   Smith, S. E., Tallentire, V. R., Pope, L. M., Laidlaw, A. H., & Morrison, J. (2018). Foundation Year 2 doctors' reasons for leaving UK medicine: an in-depth analysis of decision-making using semistructured interviews. *BMJ open, 8*(3), e019456.

28   Craiovan, P. M. (2014). Correlations between perfectionism, stress, psychopathological symptoms and burnout in the medical field. *Procedia-Social and Behavioral Sciences, 127,* 529-533.

29   Smith, S. E., Tallentire, V. R., Pope, L. M., Laidlaw, A. H., & Morrison, J. (2018). Foundation Year 2 doctors' reasons for leaving UK medicine: an in-depth analysis of decision-making using semistructured interviews. *BMJ open, 8*(3), e019456.

30   Hagqvist, E., Ekberg, K., Lidwall, U., Nyberg, A., Landstad, B. J., Wilczek, A., Bååthe, F., & Sjöström, M. (2022). The Swedish HealthPhys Study: Study Description and Prevalence of Clinical Burnout and Major Depression among Physicians. *Chronic Stress,* 1-8.

31   Frank, R. H. (2012). The Easterlin paradox revisited. *Emotion, 12*(6), 1188.

32   Clark, A. E., Frijters, P., & Shields, M. A. (2008). Relative income, happiness, and utility: An explanation for the Easterlin paradox and other puzzles. *Journal of Economic literature, 46*(1), 95-144.

33   Joshanloo, M. (2018). Income satisfaction is less predictive of life satisfaction in individuals who believe their lives have meaning or purpose: A 94-nation study. *Personality and Individual Differences, 129,* 92–94.

34   Smith, S. E., Tallentire, V. R., Pope, L. M., Laidlaw, A. H., & Morrison, J. (2018). Foundation Year 2 doctors' reasons for leaving UK medicine: an in-depth analysis of decision-making using semistructured interviews. *BMJ open, 8*(3), e019456.

35   Gawande, A. (2018). The Upgrade: A war between doctors and their computers. Why doctors hate their computers. The New Yorker, Nov 12.

36   Kulkarni, A. (2019). Navigating loneliness in the era of virtual care. *N Engl J Med, 380*(4), 307-309.

37 Sonnentag, S., Niessen, C., & Neff, A. (2012). Recovery: Nonwork experiences that promote positive states. *The Oxford handbook of positive organizational scholarship*, 867-881.

38 Shapiro, J., Zhang, B., & Warm, E. J. (2015). Residency as a social network: burnout, loneliness, and social network centrality. *Journal of Graduate Medical Education, 7*(4), 617-623.

39 Kulkarni, A. (2019). Navigating loneliness in the era of virtual care. *N Engl J Med, 380*(4), 307-309.

40 Baumeister, R. F., & Leary, M. R. (1995). The Need to Belong: Desire for Interpersonal Attachments as a Fundamental Human Motivation. *Psychological Bulletin, 117*(3), 497–529.

41 Slavin, S. J., Schindler, D. L., & Chibnall, J. T. (2014). Medical student mental health 3.0: improving student wellness through curricular changes. *Academic Medicine, 89*(4), 573.

42 Baumeister, R. F., & Leary, M. R. (1995). The Need to Belong: Desire for Interpersonal Attachments as a Fundamental Human Motivation. *Psychological Bulletin, 117*(3), 497–529.

43 Maslow, A. H. (1943). A theory of human motivation. *Psychological review, 50*(4), 370.

44 Mitra, B., & Cameron, P. A. (2012). Emergency department overcrowding and mortality after the introduction of the 4-hour rule in Western Australia. *The Medical Journal of Australia, 196*(8), 499.

45 Sithey, G., Thow, A. M., & Li, M. (2015). Gross national happiness and health: lessons from Bhutan. *Bulletin of the World Health Organization, 93*, 514-514.

46 Minkov, M., & Hofstede, G. (2012). Hofstede's fifth dimension: New evidence from the World Values Survey. *Journal of cross-cultural psychology, 43*(1), 3-14.

47 Sagar, A. D., & Najam, A. (1998). The human development index: a critical review. *Ecological economics, 25*(3), 249-264.

48 Abdallah, S., Thompson, S., Michaelson, J., Marks, N., & Steuer, N. (2009). The Happy Planet Index 2.0: Why good lives don't have to cost the Earth.

49 Grassl, W., & Habisch, A. (2011). Ethics and economics: Towards a new humanistic synthesis for business. *Journal of Business Ethics, 99*(1), 37-49.

50 Pavithra, A., Sunderland, N., Callen, J., & Westbrook, J. (2022). Unprofessional behaviours experienced by hospital staff: qualitative analysis of narrative comments in a longitudinal survey across seven hospitals in Australia. *BMC Health Services Research, 22*(1), 1-15.

51 Lindgreen, A., & Swaen, V. (2010). Corporate social responsibility. *International journal of management reviews, 12*(1), 1-7.

52 Chia, A., Kern, M.,Neville, B. (2020)CSR for Happiness: Corporate determinants of societal happiness as social responsibility. Business Ethics: A European Review. 29, 422-427.

53 Wallace, D. F. (2009). *This is water: Some thoughts, delivered on a significant occasion, about living a compassionate life.* Hachette UK.

54 Jones, D. (2011). *Cambridge English pronouncing dictionary.* Cambridge University Press.

55 Schein, E., & H. (1990). Organizational Culture: What it is and How to Change it. *Human resource management in international firms* (pp. 56–82). Palgrave Macmillan, London. ISBN: 0333515013.

56 Senge, Peter M. "The fifth discipline." *Measuring Business Excellence* (1997).

57 Marchetti, A. (2018). Glassdoor. com Data and Organizational Culture: A Methodology for Studying Acculturation Processes in Cross-Organization Interactions. *Academy of Management Global Proceedings,* (2018), 309

58 Sull, D., Sull, C., Cipolli, W., & Brighenti, C. (2022). Why Every Leader Needs to Worry About Toxic Culture. *MIT Sloan Management Review, 63*(3), 1-8.

59 Johns, G. (2011). Attendance dynamics at work: the antecedents and correlates of presenteeism, absenteeism, and productivity loss. *Journal of Occupational Health Psychology, 16*(4), 483.

60 Sull, D., Sull, C., & Zweig, B. (2022). Toxic culture is driving the great resignation. *MIT Sloan Management Review, 63*(2), 1-9.

61 Ward, S., & Outram, S. (2016). Medicine: in need of culture change. *Internal medicine journal, 46*(1), 112-116.

62 Emmons, R. S. (2019). Burnout No More: How to Push Back Against the Toxic Medical Workplace. *Journal of American Physicians and Surgeons, 24*(4).

63 Goh, J., Pfeffer, J., & Zenios, S. A. (2016). The relationship between workplace stressors and mortality and health costs in the United States. *Management Science, 62*(2), 608-628.

64 Braithwaite, J., Herkes, J., Ludlow, K., Testa, L., & Lamprell, G. (2017). Association between organisational and workplace cultures, and patient outcomes: systematic review. *BMJ open, 7*(11), e017708.

65 O'Meara, J., & Shaffer, T. L. (1964). Obscenity in the Supreme Court: A note on Jacobellis v. Ohio. Notre Dame Law., 40, 1.

66 Montgomery, A., Todorova, I., Baban, A., & Panagopoulou, E. (2013). Improving quality and safety in the hospital: The link between organizational culture, burnout, and quality of care. *British journal of health psychology*, *18*(3), 656-662.

67 Martinez, E. A., Beaulieu, N., Gibbons, R., Pronovost, P., & Wang, T. (2015). Organizational culture and performance. *American economic review*, *105*(5), 331-35.

68 Shanafelt, T. D., Schein, E., Minor, L. B., Trockel, M., Schein, P., & Kirch, D. (2019, August). Healing the professional culture of medicine. In *Mayo Clinic Proceedings* (Vol. 94, No. 8, pp. 1556-1566). Elsevier.

69 Shanafelt, T. D., Boone, S., Tan, L., Dyrbye, L. N., Sotile, W., Satele, D., ... & Oreskovich, M. R. (2012). Burnout and satisfaction with work-life balance among US physicians relative to the general US population. *Archives of internal medicine*, *172*(18), 1377-1385.

70 Han, S., Shanafelt, T. D., Sinsky, C. A., Awad, K. M., Dyrbye, L. N., Fiscus, L. C., ... & Goh, J. (2019). Estimating the attributable cost of physician burnout in the United States. *Annals of internal medicine*, *170*(11), 784-790.

71 Forbes, M. P., Iyengar, S., & Kay, M. (2019). Barriers to the psychological well-being of Australian junior doctors: a qualitative analysis. *BMJ open*, *9*(6), e027558.

72 Tough, A. M. (1968). Why Adults Learn; A Study of the Major Reasons for Beginning and Continuing a Learning Project.

73 McCall, M. W. (2010). Recasting leadership development. Industrial and Organizational Psychology, 3, 3-19.

74 Fredrickson, B. L. (2001). The role of positive emotions in positive psychology: The broaden-and-build theory of positive emotions. *American psychologist*, *56*(3), 218.

75 Samovar, L. A., Porter, R. E., McDaniel, E. R., & Roy, C. S. (2016). *Communication between cultures*. Cengage Learning

76 Drucker, P. F. (2020). *The essential drucker*. Routledge.

77 Kerr, J. (2013). *Legacy*. Hachette UK.

78 Steinbeck, J. (1989). Steinbeck: a life in letters. Penguin.

79 Novemsky, N., & Kahneman, D. (2005). The boundaries of loss aversion. *Journal of Marketing research*, *42*(2), 119-128.

80 Baumeister, R. F., Bratslavsky, E., Finkenauer, C., & Vohs, K. D. (2001). Bad is stronger than good. *Review of general psychology*, *5*(4), 323-370.

81 Spreitzer, G. M., & Sonenshein, S. (2004). Toward the construct definition of positive deviance. *American behavioral scientist*, *47*(6), 828-847.

82 Lawton, R., Taylor, N., Clay-Williams, R., & Braithwaite, J. (2014). Positive deviance: a different approach to achieving patient safety. *BMJ quality & safety*, *23*(11), 880-883.

83 Chamorro-Premuzic, T. (2019). Why do so many incompetent men become leaders?:(And how to fix it). Harvard Business Press.

84 Kelemen, T. K., Matthews, S. H., Matthews, M. J., & Henry, S. E. (2023). Humble leadership: A review and synthesis of leader expressed humility. *Journal of Organizational Behavior*, *44*(2), 202-224.

85 Truman, H. S. (1997). *Off the record: The private papers of Harry S. Truman* (Vol. 1). University of Missouri Press.

86 Good to Great. Jim Collins 2001. Harper Collins.

87 Rohsenow, J. S. (2001). *ABC dictionary of Chinese proverbs (Yanyu)*. University of Hawaii press.

88 Feltman, C. (2011). The thin book of trust: An essential primer for building trust at work. Thin Book Publishing.

89 Dirks, K. T., & Ferrin, D. L. (2002). Trust in leadership: Meta-analytic findings and implications for research and practice. *Journal of applied psychology*, *87*(4), 611.

90 Sarto, F., & Veronesi, G. (2016). Clinical leadership and hospital performance: assessing the evidence base. *BMC health services research*, *16*(2), 85-97.

91 Veronesi, G., Kirkpatrick, I., & Vallascas, F. (2013). Clinicians on the board: what difference does it make?. *Social science & medicine*, *77*, 147-155.

92 Clay-Williams, R., Ludlow, K., Testa, L., Li, Z., & Braithwaite, J. (2017). Medical leadership, a systematic narrative review: do hospitals and healthcare organisations perform better when led by doctors?. *BMJ open*, *7*(9), e014474.

93 Vainieri, M., Ferrè, F., Giacomelli, G., & Nuti, S. (2019). Explaining performance in health care: How and when top management competencies make the difference. *Health care management review*, *44*(4), 306.

94 Collins, J., & Hansen, M. T. (2011). *Great by Choice: Uncertainty, Chaos and Luck-Why some thrive despite them all*. Random House.

95 Covey, S.R. (1989). The Seven Habits of Highly Effective People. Simon and Schuster.

96 Sinek, S. (2014). *Leaders eat last: Why some teams pull together and others don't*. Penguin.

97 Sinek, S. (2009). *Start with why: How great leaders inspire everyone to take action*. Penguin.

98 Sandberg, S. (2013). *Lean In: Women, Work, and the Will to Lead.* Random House.

99 Marvel, M. K., Epstein, R. M., Flowers, K., & Beckman, H. B. (1999). Soliciting the patient's agenda: have we improved?. *Jama, 281*(3), 283-287.

100 Singh Ospina, N., Phillips, K. A., Rodriguez-Gutierrez, R., Castaneda-Guarderas, A., Gionfriddo, M. R., Branda, M. E., & Montori, V. M. (2019). Eliciting the patient's agenda-secondary analysis of recorded clinical encounters. *Journal of general internal medicine, 34*(1), 36-40.

101 Marvel, M. K., Epstein, R. M., Flowers, K., & Beckman, H. B. (1999). Soliciting the patient's agenda: have we improved?. *Jama, 281*(3), 283-287.

102 Zulman, D. M., Haverfield, M. C., Shaw, J. G., Brown-Johnson, C. G., Schwartz, R., Tierney, A. A., ... & Verghese, A. (2020). Practices to foster physician presence and connection with patients in the clinical encounter. *Jama, 323*(1), 70-81.

103 Wilmer, H. H., Sherman, L. E., & Chein, J. M. (2017). Smartphones and cognition: A review of research exploring the links between mobile technology habits and cognitive functioning. *Frontiers in psychology, 8*, 605.

104 Beckman, H. B., & Frankel, R. M. (1984). The effect of physician behavior on the collection of data. *Annals of Internal medicine, 101*(5), 692-696.

105 Grob, R., Darien, G., & Meyers, D. (2019). Why physicians should trust in patients. *Jama, 321*(14), 1347-1348.

106 Pearson, S. D., & Raeke, L. H. (2000). Patients' trust in physicians: many theories, few measures, and little data. *Journal of general internal medicine, 15*(7), 509-513.

107 Khullar, D. (2019). Building trust in health care—why, where, and how. *Jama, 322*(6), 507-509.

108 Birkhäuer, J., Gaab, J., Kossowsky, J., Hasler, S., Krummenacher, P., Werner, C., & Gerger, H. (2017). Trust in the health care professional and health outcome: A meta-analysis. *PloS one, 12*(2), e0170988.

109 Brown, R. E. (2015). *An introduction to the New Testament.* Yale University Press.

110 Innes, C. (Ed.). (1998). *The Cambridge Companion to George Bernard Shaw.* Cambridge University Press.

111 Ahmed N. (2005). 23 years of the discovery of Helicobacter pylori: is the debate over?. *Annals of clinical microbiology and antimicrobials, 4*, 17. https://doi.org/10.1186/1476-0711-4-17

112 Sweeney, J. (2004). lessons from the love lab. *Health (Time Inc. Health), 18*(8), 97–100.

113 Carrere, S., Buehlman, K. T., Gottman, J. M., Coan, J. A., & Ruckstuhl, L. (2000). Predicting marital stability and divorce in newlywed couples. *Journal of family psychology, 14*(1), 42.

114 Gottman, J. M. (1998). Psychology and the study of marital processes. *Annual review of psychology, 49*(1), 169-197.

115 Lox, C.L., (1994). Positive Coaching: Building Character and Self-esteem Through Sports. *Sport Psychologist,* 8(2),206-207.

116 Thompson, J. (1995). *Positive coaching: Building character and self-esteem through sports.* Balance Sports Pub.

117 Losada, M., & Heaphy, E. (2004). The role of positivity and connectivity in the performance of business teams: A nonlinear dynamics model. *American behavioral scientist, 47*(6), 740-765.

118 Jackson, P. (2012). *Sacred hoops: Spiritual lessons of a hardwood warrior.* Hachette UK.

119 Jackson, P., & Delehanty, H. (2014). *Eleven rings: The soul of success.* Penguin.

120 Baumeister, R. F., Bratslavsky, E., Finkenauer, C., & Vohs, K. D. (2001). Bad is stronger than good. *Review of general psychology, 5*(4), 323-370.

121 Weller, J., Boyd, M., & Cumin, D. (2014). Teams, tribes and patient safety: overcoming barriers to effective teamwork in healthcare. *Postgraduate medical journal, 90*(1061), 149-154.

122 Board, C. A. I. (2003). Columbia Accident Investigation Board: Report, Volume One. *Washington, DC: National Aeronautics and Space Administration and the Government Printing Office.*

123 Donaldson, M. S., Corrigan, J. M., & Kohn, L. T. (Eds.). (2000). To err is human: building a safer health system.

124 Maitlis, S., Vogus, T. J., & Lawrence, T. B. (2013). Sensemaking and emotion in organizations. *Organizational Psychology Review, 3*(3), 222-247.

125 Fredericks, B. A., Karen; Finlay, S. F., Gillian; Andy, S. B., Lyn; Briggs, L. H., & Robert. (2011). Engaging the practice of Indigenous yarning in action research. *Action Learning and Action Research, 17*(2), 12–24.

126 Senge, P. M., Scharmer, C. O., Jaworski, J., & Flowers, B. S. (2005). *Presence: An exploration of profound change in people, organizations, and society.* Currency.

127 Good to Great. Jim Collins 2001. Harper Collins.

128 Baum, G. (2022) 17th September. Football master class: How a Collingwood legend taught his sons the Daicos way. *The Age.* http://www.theage.com.au

129 Garland, E. L., Fredrickson, B., Kring, A. M., Johnson, D. P., Meyer, P. S., & Penn, D. L. (2010). Upward spirals of positive emotions counter downward spirals of negativity: Insights from the broaden-and-build theory and affective neuroscience on the treatment of emotion dysfunctions and deficits in psychopathology. *Clinical psychology review*, *30*(7), 849-864.

130 Agam, A., & Barkai, R. (2018). Elephant and mammoth hunting during the Paleolithic: a review of the relevant archaeological, ethnographic and ethno-historical records. Quaternary, 1(1), 3.

131 Nikolskiy, P., & Pitulko, V. (2013). Evidence from the Yana Palaeolithic site, Arctic Siberia, yields clues to the riddle of mammoth hunting. Journal of Archaeological Science, 40(12), 4189-4197.

132 Noonan Hadley, C., & Mortensen, M. Do we still need teams? Harvard Business Review, 26th April 2022.

133 Hajek, A. M. (2013). Breaking down clinical silos in healthcare. Frontiers of Health Services Management, 29(4), 45-50.

134 Alves, J., & Meneses, R. (2018, September). Silos Mentality In Healthcare Services. In 11th Annual Conference of the EuroMed Academy of Business (pp. 65-77).

135 Baumeister, R. F., & Leary, M. R. (2017). The need to belong: Desire for interpersonal attachments as a fundamental human motivation. Interpersonal development, 57-89.

136 Erzen, E., & Çikrikci, Ö. (2018). The effect of loneliness on depression: A meta-analysis. International Journal of Social Psychiatry, 64(5), 427-435.

137 Lam, L. W., & Lau, D. C. (2012). Feeling lonely at work: investigating the consequences of unsatisfactory workplace relationships. The International Journal of Human Resource Management, 23(20), 4265-4282.

138 Wright, S., & Silard, A. (2021). Unravelling the antecedents of loneliness in the workplace. Human Relations, 74(7), 1060-1081

139 Salas, E., Wilson, K. A., Murphy, C. E., King, H., & Salisbury, M. (2008). Communicating, coordinating, and cooperating when lives depend on it: tips for teamwork. The Joint Commission Journal on Quality and Patient Safety, 34(6), 333-341.

140 Mickan, S. M. (2005). Evaluating the effectiveness of health care teams. Australian Health Review, 29(2), 211-217.

141 Eastwood,O. (2021) Belonging – The Ancient Code of Togetherness.

142 Fiennes, R. (2014) Cold – Extreme Adventures at the lowest temperatures on Earth.

143 Kahneman, D. (2011) Thinking, fast and slow. Macmillan.

144 Crisp, R. (Ed.). (2014). *Aristotle: Nicomachean Ethics*. Cambridge University Press.

145 Noonan Hadley, C., & Mortensen, M. Do we still need teams? Harvard Business Review, 26th April 2022.

146 Havyer, R. D., Wingo, M. T., Comfere, N. I., Nelson, D. R., Halvorsen, A. J., McDonald, F. S., & Reed, D. A. (2014). Teamwork assessment in internal medicine: a systematic review of validity evidence and outcomes. Journal of general internal medicine, 29(6), 894-910.

147 Mazzocco, K., Petitti, D. B., Fong, K. T., Bonacum, D., Brookey, J., Graham, S., ... & Thomas, E. J. (2009). Surgical team behaviors and patient outcomes. The American Journal of Surgery, 197(5), 678-685.

148 Pavlich, M. Why Ross Lyon was the best coach I played under. The Age, 21st August, 2019

149 Four points: The questions De Goey should ask himself. The Age,19th June, 2022.

150 Hall, L. H., Johnson, J., Watt, I., Tsipa, A., & O'Connor, D. B. (2016). Healthcare staff wellbeing, burnout, and patient safety: a systematic review. PloS one, 11(7), e0159015.

151 Shanafelt, T. D., & Noseworthy, J.H. (2017). "Executive leadership and physician well-being: nine organizational strategies to promote engage-ment and reduce burnout." In Mayo Clinic Proceedings, vol. 92, no. 1, pp. 129-146. Elsevier.

152 Ryan, R. M., & Deci, E. L. (2000). Self-determination theory and the facilitation of intrinsic motivation, social development, and well-being. *American psychologist, 55*(1), 68.

153 Baumeister, R. F., & Leary, M. R. (2017). The need to belong: Desire for interpersonal attachments as a fundamental human motivation. *Interpersonal development*, 57-89.

154 Lambert, N. M., Stillman, T. F., Hicks, J. A., Kamble, S., Baumeister, R. F., & Fincham, F. D. (2013). To belong is to matter: Sense of belonging enhan-ces meaning in life. *Personality and Social Psychology Bulletin, 39*(11), 1418-1427.

155 Lambert, N. M., Stillman, T. F., Hicks, J. A., Kamble, S., Baumeister, R. F., & Fincham, F. D. (2013). To belong is to matter: Sense of belonging enhan-ces meaning in life. *Personality and Social Psychology Bulletin, 39*(11), 1418-1427.

156 Raj, K. S. (2016). Well-being in residency: a systematic review. *Journal of graduate medical education, 8*(5), 674-684.

157 Salles, A., Wright, R. C., Milam, L., Panni, R. Z., Liebert, C. A., Lau, J. N., ... & Mueller, C. M. (2019). Social belonging as a predictor of surgical resident well-being and attrition. *Journal of surgical education*, *76*(2), 370-377.

158 Buettner, D., & Skemp, S. (2016). Blue zones: lessons from the world's longest lived. *American journal of lifestyle medicine*, *10*(5), 318-321.

159 Jackson, P. (2012). *Sacred hoops: Spiritual lessons of a hardwood warrior*. Hachette UK.

160 'The Last Dance'. 2020. Netflix Docuseries.

161 Lewicka, M. (2011). Place attachment: How far have we come in the last 40 years?. *Journal of environmental psychology*, *31*(3), 207-230.

162 Younge, G. (2013). *The speech: the story behind Dr. Martin Luther King Jr.'s dream / Gary Younge*. Haymarket Books.

163 Stanaszek-Tomal, E. (2021). Anti-smog building and civil engineering structures. *Processes*, *9*(8), 1446.

164 Basner, M., Babisch, W., Davis, A., Brink, M., Clark, C., Janssen, S., & Stansfeld, S. (2014). Auditory and non-auditory effects of noise on health. *The lancet*, *383*(9925), 1325-1332.

165 Jiang, S. (2022). *Nature Through a Hospital Window: The Therapeutic Benefits of Landscape in Architectural Design*. Routledg

166 Münzel, T., Schmidt, F. P., Steven, S., Herzog, J., Daiber, A., & Sørensen, M. (2018). Environmental noise and the cardiovascular system. *Journal of the American College of Cardiology*, *71*(6), 688-697.

167 Chang, C. Y., & Chen, P. K. (2005). Human response to window views and indoor plants in the workplace. *Hort Science*, *40*(5), 1354-1359.

168 Ulrich, R. S., Simons, R. F., Losito, B. D., Fiorito, E., Miles, M. A., & Zelson, M. (1991). Stress recovery during exposure to natural and urban environments. *Journal of environmental psychology*, *11(3), 201-230.*

169 Wallace, W. E. (2011). *Michelangelo: The artist, the man and his times*. Cambridge University Press.

170 Alexander, C., & Hurley, F. (1998). *The endurance: Shackleton's legendary antarctic expedition*. New York: Knopf.

171 Butler,G. 2001. *The Endurance:Shackleton's legendary Antarctic Expedition [Movie]; White Mountain Films.*

172 Snyder, C. R. (2002). Hope theory: Rainbows in the mind. *Psychological inquiry*, *13*(4), 249-275.

173 Whitney, D., & Cooperrider, D. (2011). *Appreciative inquiry: A positive revolution in change*. ReadHowYouWant. Com.

174 Schmidt, A. M. (2019). Using Appreciative Inquiry Method to Help Retain Talented Female Officers in the US Army.

175 Richer, M. C., Ritchie, J., & Marchionni, C. (2010). Appreciative inquiry in health care. *British Journal of Healthcare Management, 16*(4), 164-172.

176 Hung, L., Phinney, A., Chaudhury, H., Rodney, P., Tabamo, J., & Bohl, D. (2018). Appreciative inquiry: Bridging research and practice in a hospital setting. *International Journal of Qualitative Methods, 17*(1), 1609406918769444.

177 Cooperrider, D. L., & Fry, R. (2020). Appreciative inquiry in a pandemic: An improbable pairing. *The Journal of Applied Behavioral Science, 56*(3), 266-271.

178 Kennedy, J.F;.Presidential Inaugural Address. 20th January 1961, Washington DC

179 Huffman, C. (2017). Aristoxenus' Life of Socrates. In *Aristoxenus of Tarentum* (pp. 251-281). Routledge

180 Wood, Alex M., Jeffrey J. Froh, and Adam WA Geraghty. "Gratitude and well-being: A review and theoretical integration." *Clinical psychology review* 30, no. 7 (2010): 890-905.

181 Fredrickson, B. L. (2006). Unpacking positive emotions: Investigating the seeds of human flourishing.

182 Jans-Beken, L., Jacobs, N., Janssens, M., Peeters, S., Reijnders, J., Lechner, L., & Lataster, J. (2020). Gratitude and health: An updated review. *The Journal of Positive Psychology, 15*(6), 743-782.

183 Danner, D. D., Snowdon, D. A., & Friesen, W. V. (2001). Positive emotions in early life and longevity: findings from the nun study. *Journal of personality and social psychology, 80*(5), 804.

184 Snowdon, D. A. (1997). Aging and Alzheimer's disease: Lessons from the Nun Study. *Gerontologist, 37*, 150-156

185 Riley, K. P., Snowdon, D. A., Desrosiers, M. F., & Markesbery, W. R. (2005). Early life linguistic ability, late life cognitive function, and neuropathology: findings from the Nun Study. *Neurobiology of aging, 26*(3), 341-347.

186 Mortimer, J. A., Snowdon, D. A., & Markesbery, W. R. (2013). Brain reserve and risk of dementia: findings from the Nun Study. In *Cognitive Reserve* (pp. 250-262). Psychology Press.

187 Peterson, C., Seligman, M. E. P., & Vaillant, G. E. (1988). Pessimistic explanatory style is a risk factor for physical illness: A thirty-five year longitudinal study. *Journal of Personality and Social Psychology, 55*, 23–27.

188 Maruta, T., Colligan, R. C., Malinchoc, M., & Offord, K. P. (2002, August). Optimism-pessimism assessed in the 1960s and self-reported health status 30 years later. In *Mayo Clinic Proceedings* (Vol. 77, No. 8, pp. 748-753). Elsevier.

189 Peterson, C., Seligman, M. E., Yurko, K. H., Martin, L. R., & Friedman, H. S. (1998). Catastrophizing and untimely death. *Psychological Science, 9*(2), 127-130.

190 Levenson, R. W. (2014). The autonomic nervous system and emotion. *Emotion review, 6*(2), 100-112.

191 Ekman, P., Levenson, R. W., & Friesen, W. V. (1983). Autonomic nervous system activity distinguishes among emotions. *Science, 221*, 1208–1210.

192 Krantz, D. S., & Manuck, S. B. (1984). Acute psychophysiologic reactivity and risk of cardiovascular disease: a review and methodologic critique. *Psychological bulletin, 96*(3), 435.

193 Goldin, P. R., McRae, K., Ramel, W., & Gross, J. J. (2008). The neural bases of emotion regulation: reappraisal and suppression of negative emotion. *Biological psychiatry, 63*(6), 577-586.

194 Gross, J. J., & Levenson, R. W. (1997). Hiding feelings: the acute effects of inhibiting negative and positive emotion. *Journal of abnormal psychology, 106*(1), 95.

195 Abelson, J. L., Liberzon, I., Young, E. A., & Khan, S. (2005). Cognitive modulation of the endocrine stress response to a pharmacological challenge in normal and panic disorder subjects. *Archives of General Psychiatry, 62*(6), 668-675.

196 Otto, L. R., Sin, N. L., Almeida, D. M., & Sloan, R. P. (2018). Trait emotion regulation strategies and diurnal cortisol profiles in healthy adults. *Health Psychology, 37*(3), 301.

197 Mikkelsen, M. B., Tramm, G., Zachariae, R., Gravholt, C. H., & O'Toole, M. S. (2021). A systematic review and meta-analysis of the effect of emotion regulation on cortisol. *Comprehensive Psychoneuroendocrinology, 5*, 100020.

198 Kim, M. J., Loucks, R. A., Palmer, A. L., Brown, A. C., Solomon, K. M., Marchante, A. N., & Whalen, P. J. (2011). The structural and functional connectivity of the amygdala: from normal emotion to pathological anxiety. *Behavioural brain research, 223*(2), 403-410.

199 Ellis, E. M., Prather, A. A., Grenen, E. G., & Ferrer, R. A. (2019). Direct and indirect associations of cognitive reappraisal and suppression with disease biomarkers. *Psychology & Health, 34*(3), 336-354.

200 Appleton, A. A., Buka, S. L., Loucks, E. B., Gilman, S. E., & Kubzansky, L. D. (2013). Divergent associations of adaptive and maladaptive emotion regulation strategies with inflammation. *Health Psychology, 32*(7), 748.

201 Gross, J. J., & John, O. P. (2003). Individual differences in two emotion regulation processes: implications for affect, relationships, and well-being. *Journal of personality and social psychology, 85*(2), 348.

202 Decety, J., Yang, C. Y., & Cheng, Y. (2010). Physicians down-regulate their pain empathy response: an event-related brain potential study. *Neuroimage, 50*(4), 1676-1682.

203 Ellis, E. M., Prather, A. A., Grenen, E. G., & Ferrer, R. A. (2019). Direct and indirect associations of cognitive reappraisal and suppression with disease biomarkers. *Psychology & Health, 34*(3), 336-354.

204 Lopez, R. B., Denny, B. T., & Fagundes, C. P. (2018). Neural mechanisms of emotion regulation and their role in endocrine and immune functioning: a review with implications for treatment of affective disorders. *Neuroscience & Biobehavioral Reviews, 95*, 508-514.

205 Jackson-Koku, G., & Grime, P. (2019). Emotion regulation and burnout in doctors: a systematic review. *Occupational Medicine, 69*(1), 9-21.

206 Milgram, S. (1963). Behavioral study of obedience. *The Journal of abnormal and social psychology, 67*(4), 371.

207 Crowe, S., Clarke, N., & Brugha, R. (2017). 'You do not cross them': Hierarchy and emotion in doctors' narratives of power relations in specialist training. *Social Science & Medicine, 186*, 70-77.

208 Cheng, Y., Lin, C. P., Liu, H. L., Hsu, Y. Y., Lim, K. E., Hung, D., & Decety, J. (2007). Expertise modulates the perception of pain in others. *Current Biology, 17*(19), 1708-1713.

209 Decety, J., Yang, C. Y., & Cheng, Y. (2010). Physicians down-regulate their pain empathy response: an event-related brain potential study. *Neuroimage, 50*(4), 1676-1682.

210 Jackson-Koku, G., & Grime, P. (2019). Emotion regulation and burnout in doctors: a systematic review. *Occupational Medicine, 69*(1), 9-21.

211 Dworkin, A. G. (2001). Perspectives on teacher burnout and school reform. *International Education Journal, 2*(2), 69-78.

212 Vaillant, G. E. (2012). Triumphs of experience. In *Triumphs of Experience*. Harvard University Press.

213 Heath, C. W. (1945). *What people are; a study of normal young men.* Harvard University Press.

214 Glueck, S., & Glueck, E. (1963). Potential juvenile delinquents can be identified: What next. *Brit. J. Criminology, 4*, 215.

215 Vaillant, G. E. (2012). Triumphs of experience. In *Triumphs of Experience.* Harvard University Press.

216 Furman, D., Campisi, J., Verdin, E., Carrera-Bastos, P., Targ, S., Franceschi, C., ... & Slavich, G. M. (2019). Chronic inflammation in the etiology of disease across the life span. *Nature medicine, 25*(12), 1822-1832.

217 Furman, D., Campisi, J., Verdin, E., Carrera-Bastos, P., Targ, S., Franceschi, C., ... & Slavich, G. M. (2019). Chronic inflammation in the etiology of disease across the life span. *Nature medicine, 25*(12), 1822-1832.

218 Miller, G. E., Cohen, S., & Ritchey, A. K. (2002). Chronic psychological stress and the regulation of pro-inflammatory cytokines: a glucocorticoid-resistance model. *Health psychology, 21*(6), 531.

219 Gill, J. M., Saligan, L., Woods, S., & Page, G. (2009). PTSD is associated with an excess of inflammatory immune activities. *Perspectives in psychiatric care, 45*(4), 262-277.

220 Bisson, J. I. (2019). Stress related disorders and physical health. *Bmj, 367.*

221 Gradus, J. L., Farkas, D. K., Svensson, E., Ehrenstein, V., Lash, T. L., Milstein, A., ... & Sørensen, H. T. (2015). Associations between stress disorders and cardiovascular disease events in the Danish population. *BMJ open, 5*(12), e009334.

222 Song, H., Fang, F., Tomasson, G., Arnberg, F. K., Mataix-Cols, D., de la Cruz, L. F., ... & Valdimarsdóttir, U. A. (2018). Association of stress-related disorders with subsequent autoimmune disease. *Jama, 319*(23), 2388-2400.

223 Ryder, A. L., Azcarate, P. M., & Cohen, B. E. (2018). PTSD and physical health. *Current psychiatry reports, 20*(12), 1-8.

224 Fitzgerald, M., & Notice, M. (2022). Childhood embedded: childhood abuse and chronic physical health conditions over a 10-year period. *Journal of Public Health.*

225 Sumner, J. A., Kubzansky, L. D., Elkind, M. S., Roberts, A. L., Agnew-Blais, J., Chen, Q., ... & Koenen, K. C. (2015). Trauma exposure and posttraumatic stress disorder symptoms predict onset of cardiovascular events in women. *Circulation, 132*(4), 251-259.

226 Shaw, J. G., Asch, S. M., Kimerling, R., Frayne, S. M., Shaw, K. A., & Phibbs, C. S. (2014). Posttraumatic stress disorder and risk of spontaneous preterm birth. *Obstetrics & Gynecology, 124*(6), 1111-1119.

227 Shaw, J. G., Asch, S. M., Katon, J. G., Shaw, K. A., Kimerling, R., Frayne, S. M., & Phibbs, C. S. (2017). Post-traumatic stress disorder and antepartum complications: a novel risk factor for gestational diabetes and preeclampsia. *Paediatric and Perinatal Epidemiology, 31*(3), 185-194.

228 O'Doherty, D. C., Chitty, K. M., Saddiqui, S., Bennett, M. R., & Lagopoulos, J. (2015). A systematic review and meta-analysis of magnetic resonance imaging measurement of structural volumes in posttraumatic stress disorder. *Psychiatry Research: Neuroimaging, 232*(1), 1-33.

229 Boccia, M., D'Amico, S., Bianchini, F., Marano, A., Giannini, A. M., & Piccardi, L. (2016). Different neural modifications underpin PTSD after different traumatic events: an fMRI meta-analytic study. *Brain imaging and behavior, 10*(1), 226-237.

230 Shanafelt, T. D. , Balch, C. M. , Bechamps, G. , Russell, T. , Dyrbye, L. , Satele, D. , Collicott, P. , Novotny, P. J. , Sloan, J. & Freischlag, J. (2010). Burnout and Medical Errors Among American Surgeons. *Annals of Surgery, 251* (6), 995-1000.

231 Fredrickson, B. L., Mancuso, R. A., Branigan, C., & Tugade, M. M. (2000). The undoing effect of positive emotions. *Motivation and emotion, 24*(4), 237-258.

232 Behnke, M., Pietruch, M., Chwiłkowska, P., Wessel, E., Kaczmarek, L. D., Assink, M., & Gross, J. J. (2022). The Undoing Effect of Positive Emotions: A Meta-Analytic Review. *Emotion Review*, 17540739221104457.

233 Steptoe, A. (2019). Happiness and health. *Annu Rev Public Health, 40*(1), 339-359.

234 Silton, R. L., Kahrilas, I. J., Skymba, H. V., Smith, J., Bryant, F. B., & Heller, W. (2020). Regulating positive emotions: Implications for promoting well-being in individuals with depression. *Emotion, 20*(1), 93.

235 Lopez, R. B., Denny, B. T., & Fagundes, C. P. (2018). Neural mechanisms of emotion regulation and their role in endocrine and immune functioning: a review with implications for treatment of affective disorders. *Neuroscience & Biobehavioral Reviews, 95*, 508-514.

236 Müller, R., Segerer, W., Ronca, E., Gemperli, A., Stirnimann, D., Scheel-Sailer, A., & Jensen, M. P. (2022). Inducing positive emotions to reduce chronic pain: a randomized controlled trial of positive psychology exercises. *Disability and Rehabilitation, 44*(12), 2691-2704.

237 Lyubomirsky, S., King, L., & Diener, E. (2005). The benefits of frequent positive affect: Does happiness lead to success?. *Psychological bulletin, 131*(6), 803.

238 Ge, X. (2021). Emotion matters for academic success. *Educational Technology Research and Development, 69*(1), 67-70.

239 Staw, B. M., Sutton, R. I., & Pelled, L. H. (1994). Employee positive emotion and favorable outcomes at the workplace. *Organization science, 5*(1), 51-71.

240 Staw, B. M., & Barsade, S. G. (1993). Affect and managerial performance: A test of the sadder-but-wiser vs. happier-and-smarter hypotheses. *Administrative science quarterly*, 304-331.

241 Walsh, L. C., Boehm, J. K., & Lyubomirsky, S. (2018). Does happiness promote career success? Revisiting the evidence. *Journal of Career Assessment*, *26*(2), 199-219.

242 Diener, E., Thapa, S., & Tay, L. (2020). Positive emotions at work. *Annual Review of Organizational Psychology and Organizational Behavior, 7*, 451-477.

243 van Kleef, G. A., Cheshin, A., Koning, L. F., & Wolf, S. A. (2019). Emotional games: How coaches' emotional expressions shape players' emotions, inferences, and team performance. *Psychology of Sport and Exercise, 41*, 1-11.

244 Totterdell, P. (1999). Mood scores: Mood and performance in professional cricketers. *British Journal of Psychology, 90*(3), 317-332.

245 Totterdell, P., & Leach, D. (2001). Negative mood regulation expectancies and sports performance: An investigation involving professional cricketers. *Psychology of sport and exercise, 2*(4), 249-265.

246 Davies, H. T. O., Crombie, I. K., & Tavakoli, M. (1998). When can odds ratios mislead? *Bmj, 316*(7136), 989-991.

247 Surkalim, D. L., Luo, M., Eres, R., Gebel, K., van Buskirk, J., Bauman, A., & Ding, D. (2022). The prevalence of loneliness across 113 countries: Systematic review and meta-analysis. *bmj, 376*.

248 Stubbs, J. M., & Achat, H. M. (2022). Are healthcare workers particularly vulnerable to loneliness? The role of social relationships and mental well-being during the COVID-19 pandemic. *Psychiatry research communications, 2*(2), 100050.

249 Holt-Lunstad, J., & Steptoe, A. (2022). Social isolation: An underappreciated determinant of physical health. *Current Opinion in Psychology, 43*, 232-237.

250 Holt-Lunstad, J., Smith, T. B., Baker, M., Harris, T., & Stephenson, D. (2015). Loneliness and social isolation as risk factors for mortality: a meta-analytic review. *Perspectives on psychological science, 10*(2), 227-237.

251 Spiegelhalter, D. (2012). Using speed of ageing and "microlives" to communicate the effects of lifetime habits and environment. *BMJ, 345*.

252 Shaw, M., Mitchell, R., & Dorling, D. (2000). Time for a smoke? One cigarette reduces your life by 11 minutes. *Bmj, 320*(7226), 53.

253 Remarks of Senator John F Kennedy. Indianapolis, Indiana, 12th April 1959. Presidenntial library and Museum.

254 Morris, E. (2010). *The Rise of Theodore Roosevelt*. Modern Library.

255 Easwaran, E. (2011). *Gandhi the man: How one man changed himself to change the world*. Nilgiri Press.

256 Maitlis, S., Vogus, T. J., & Lawrence, T. B. (2013). Sensemaking and emotion in organizations. *Organizational Psychology Review, 3*(3), 222-247.

257 Solomon, R. C. (1993). The philosophy of emotions. *M. Lewic & Haviland, The Handbook of emotions, 3*.

258 Helland, M. R., & Winston, B. E. (2005). Towards a deeper understanding of hope and leadership. *Journal of Leadership & Organizational Studies, 12*(2), 42-54.

259 Rego, A., Sousa, F., Marques, C., & e Cunha, M. P. (2014). Hope and positive affect mediating the authentic leadership and creativity relationship. *Journal of Business research, 67*(2), 200-210.

260 Iodice, E. F. (2022). Lessons from History: The Astonishing Rise to Leadership and Power of Napoleon Bonaparte. *The Journal of Values-Based Leadership, 15*(1), 13.

261 Fredrickson, B. L., & Losada, M. F. (2005). Positive affect and the complex dynamics of human flourishing. *American psychologist, 60*(7), 678.

262 Barsade, S. G. (2002). The ripple effect: Emotional contagion and its influence on group behavior. *Administrative science quarterly, 47*(4), 644-675.

263 Losada, M., & Heaphy, E. (2004). The role of positivity and connectivity in the performance of business teams: A nonlinear dynamics model. *American behavioral scientist, 47*(6), 740-765.

264 Etieyibo, E. (2022). African Proverbs. *African Ethics: A Guide to Key Ideas, 31*.

265 Darwin, C. (). *Charles Darwin's natural selection: being the second part of his big species book written from 1856 to 1858*. Cambridge University Press.

266 Bateson, M. C. (1980). Continuities in insight and innovation: Toward a biography of Margaret Mead. *American Anthropologist, 82*(2), 270-277.

267 Suess, Dr. (2017). *The Lorax*.

www.ingramcontent.com/pod-product-compliance
Lightning Source LLC
Chambersburg PA
CBHW030458210326
41597CB00013B/718